Perspectives on

The Origin of Indian Civilization

Perspectives on The Origin of Indian Civilization

Edited by

Angela Marcantonio
Girish Nath Jha

Center for Indic Studies
Dartmouth (USA)

DK PRINTWORLD
Publishers of Indian Traditions

Cataloging in Publication Data — DK
[Courtesy: D.K. Agencies (P) Ltd. <docinfo@dkagencies.com>]

Perspectives on the origin of Indian civilization / Angela Marcantonio, Girish Nath Jha.
p. cm.
Includes bibliographical references.
ISBN 13: 9788124606407

1. India — Civilization — History. I. Marcantonio, Angela. II. Jha, Girish Nath.

DDC 954 23

ISBN 13: 978-81-246-0640-7 ISBN 10: 81-246-0640-4
First published in India in 2013

Published by:
Center for Indic Studies
University of Massachusetts, Dartmouth
285, Old Westport Road
Dartmouth, MA - 02747 (USA)
Phone: 508-999 8588 *Fax*: 508 999-8451
e-mail: bsingh@umassd.edu
Website: www.umassd.edu/indic

and

D.K. Printworld (P) Ltd.
Regd. Office: 'Vedaśrī', F-395, Sudarshan Park
(Metro Station: Ramesh Nagar)
New Delhi – 110 015
Phones: (011) 2545 3975; 2546 6019 *Fax*: (011) 2546 5926
e-mail: indology@dkprintworld.com
Website: www.dkprintworld.com

Published by: D.K. Printworld (P.) Ltd., New Delhi

Preface

INDIAN Civilization, considered as the only living ancient civilization, has remained the fancy of scholars, travellers, businessmen, rulers and seekers of truth for millennia. This level of broad interest in people throughout the history has obviously attracted controversies of all kinds, including debate about the Indian Civilization's origin itself.

There are a variety of aspects which have been considered in the past by scholars to examine the origin and practice of Indian Civilization. These have included traditional fields of studies such as linguistics, archaeology, history, philosophy, and, of course, politics, but lately other more modern and scientific fields have begun to explore and compliment the information obtained from traditional fields. These fields have included natural history, genetics, physics and astronomy, mathematics, computer science, psychology and neuroscience.

In 2006, the Center for Indic Studies at University of Massachusetts, Dartmouth, organized a symposium on the Origin of Indian Civilization, inviting historians, philosophers, astronomers, archaeologists, geneticists, linguists and mathematicians. This was the first open meeting of this sort, and there were sparks of disagreements on usual fault lines of political entrenchment of disciplinary scholarship. However, progress was made to the extent that scholars from different fields were able to learn and appreciate perspectives of disciplines other than their own.

Proceedings of the 2006 Symposium is now published by

D.K. Printworld, a reputable publisher in Indology. The book has received very good reviews, and is being already used as a reference book by several institutions. I learned of a report from Johns Hopkins that the multiple authorship of volume is particularly attractive to instructors, as it obviously brings out several different perspectives. Such a response vindicates our strategy of utilizing multi-disciplinary approach to address an issue such as the origin of an ancient civilization. As is true for any other problem of science and technology, it is important to address a problem from all aspects of knowledge and expertise, and it needs to be done in an integrated way. This has remained generally a difficult issue in humanities and social sciences, where disciplines are more defined by individual opinions than reproducible objective data.

As the Director of the Center for Indic Studies at the University of Massachusetts, Dartmouth, I was confronted with the issue of facilitating the presentation of Indian Civilization in the most appropriate and academic way so that not only the Indian community living in the United States feels proper representation of their heritage but also the global community which should be informed of the most accurate information in today's world. Over 25 million strong Indian diaspora has its presence in virtually all the countries of the world. More and more people from across the world are moving to India for job and education. Many Indian businesses are acquiring corporations around the world. These developments make it more important to create a better understanding of the Indian Civilization.

It would only benefit all if most authentic, accurate and appropriate information is available on Indian Civilization. Its origin is critical because it is a continuing civilization, and its current practices are in many ways connected to its original practices.

The first symposium on the Origin of Indian Civilization

raised many issues, was contentious and left many issues unresolved. The most contentious issues were about the linguistic history of Indian Civilization. I had promised to revisit the issue again after five years, and continue to plan holding conferences on Indian Civilization every five years until the fundamental issues of its origin have been settled.

Much progress has taken place since 2006 on the question of the origin of the Indian Civilization, and there is room for expanding the list of scholars who have been working in various fields addressing this question. One of the goals of the Center for Indic Studies has been to foster dialogue (or multilogue) on this and many Indic subjects.

The 2011 conference on the Origins of Indian Civilization was fulfilment of the promise I made in 2006. There was a deliberate effort to pluralize the origin to invite various possibilities, allowing scholars to remain open to various perspectives and to the possibility that there may be more than one origin to a diverse civilization like that of India. We wanted to pay special attention to the linguistics, and were very fortunate to have Dr. Angela Marcantonio take a lead role in suggesting Indian linguistics scholars with varying perspectives. Dr. Nicholas Kazanas was very helpful to both Dr. Marcantonio and myself in contacting scholars. Not everyone we invited was able to join for a variety of reasons, we were pleased that five scholars (Clackson from Cambridge University, Jha from Jawaharlal Nehru University, Kazanas from Omilos Institute, Greece, Marcantonio from the University of Rome and Prasad from Stevens Institute of Technology) addressed the linguistic issues of Indian Civilization. In fact, Dr. M.G. Prasad was an impromptu addition after he commented on the oral traditions of Indian languages and their degree of preservation to date.

Although linguists dominated the discourse at 2011 symposium compared to 2006 conference where geneticists and physicists opened new ways to look at the origin and chronology of Indian Civilization, empirical scientific data was clearly presented in support of indigenous and continuing culture and traditions in India. Once popular pseudo-historical theories based on invasions by "Aryans" have given way to scientific methods based on art history (Rao of Soka University) archaeological (Schaffer from Case Western Reserve University) data, and astronomical calculations (Achar from University of Memphis) to set dates of events mentioned in Vedic and epic texts.

There is always a question in the minds of most people trying to learn about Indian Civilization — why and how the facts get distorted, even though many academic scholars are involved in such projects? Prof. R.P. Singh, a philosopher from Jawaharlal Nehru University, New Delhi, emphasized that a discourse on civilization involves the dialectics of Power and Civilization. A dominant civilization explains macro outcomes by aggregating a large set of civilizational concepts which are under domination. He felt that the corresponding institutions of cultural, linguistic, technological, economic, political or military-diplomatic knowledge are the key indicators in determining the extent of a civilization. To understand the origin of any civilization, its description cannot be divorced from prevailing power structure of the time.

Discussions at the conference were intense yet very civil and collaborative. This appeared a long journey from the 2006 symposium. The outcome was a better understanding and reconciliation of data and observations. There were Eastern and Western perspectives but in the spirit of creating a common understanding. There were indigenous and external perspectives but with the goal of reconciliation of data and frameworks. At least at this conference both Eastern and Western perspectives were discussed but a consensus emerged — through linguistics only the origin of Indian Civilization

1. Prof. Bal Ram Singh presenting his paper

can not be ascertained, opening the possibility that the Indian Civilization is largely indigenous. More work and a lot more discussions need to happen in years to come. More scholars with varying and even opposing views need to sit across the table. The Center for Indic Studies is committed to this discourse, and will continue to facilitate this multi-logue. It is hoped that Indian scholars themselves will engage in the comprehensive research to explore critical components of the consensus developing on the origins of the Indian Civilization.

However, it must be pointed out that, so far, India as a nation state has failed to provide a cohesive scholarly construction of its past, primarily due to its complex society which may have had varying narratives, but also due to lack of confidence and initiatives by its scholars. The idea of varying narratives is happening now in the rest of the world as the diversity takes root in the Western world as well. This would be right time to engage scholars from East and West to develop robust scholarly frameworks encompassing indigenous and universal features of all the civilizations.

I was pleased to read a recent article by a fellow scientist, Dr. T.R.S. Prasanna of Indian Institute of Technology, Mumbai, in *Current Science* (vol. 103(2), July 2012, pp. 216-21) in which he rejects the concept of Aryan Invasion Theory (AIT) as a basis of Indian Civilization. He proposes four questions to be addressed and concludes that based on those questions, AIT must be rejected. The questions he considered are:

1. Key astronomical references must be consistently interpreted to 800 BCE.
2. Justification for the use of four successive calendars from *Ṛgveda* — Vedāṅga Jyotiṣa (VJ) in a period of 800–1000 years.
3. Justification for interpreting *kṛṣṇa aya*s as smelted iron

even as Sanskrit scholars have differed for more than a century.

4. Justification for why "the first appearance of iron" should be used to date Vedic texts to 1000 BCE when an archaeologist has recently dated it to 1800 BCE and states: "The new finds and their dates suggest that a fresh review is needed." More significantly, scholars have implied that this entire approach is suspect.

While scientific approach and technology are being used throughout the world to verify traditional and historical knowledge, there is no other critically contentious issue as the origin of Indic civilization needing scientific analysis. It is heartening that scientists themselves are taking the trouble to examine traditional knowledge to question and provide misinterpreted and missing data for proper understanding.

In the same vein, a recent report appearing in *Science* journal (vol. 333, 20 July 2012, p. 288) describes how modern science can help discover civilizational continuity of India at least for the past 4,000 years. According to this report, using the analysis of phytoliths, "Anthropologists Arunima Kashyap and Steve Weber of Washington State University, Vancouver, analysed starch grains from human teeth from the ancient town of Farmana, west of Delhi, and found remains of cooked ginger and turmeric. They also found those ingredients inside a cooking pot." It is notable that these and other spices are not just foods but are commonly used as medicines as well.

Scholars still are debating whether such items were wild or cultivated. However, the report from the discussion at the meeting of European Association for South Asian Archaeology and Art (Paris, France, for 2-6 July 2012) published in *Science* suggests that

> Indus farmers also grew a surprisingly wide array of grains and beans. Many archaeologists once thought that the

> society depended primarily on crops such as wheat and barley, which were planted in winter. But new data from rural villages challenge that idea.

Researchers found that "villages practised summer and winter cropping". The findings, dated between 2200–2500 BCE, suggest that the spices in Indus region were not only found in human consumption but also in cow teeth as well.

Researchers make a connection between the past and the present and in a way reaffirm a long-held view of people in India that their civilization is a continuing civilization unlike many others which were its contemporaries (Egypt, Iran, Mesopotamia, Rome, etc.) which have been largely lost or transformed. The *Science* report quotes Steve Weber of Washington State University as "It's like India today." "Cattle wander around eating trash, including the remains of cooked meals." Report mentions that "in some Indian regions such as the western province of Gujarat, some families still leave food remains outside the house as a ritual offering to cattle". Thus, the traditional practices of at least villages appear to link Indian Civilization's present and past.

The conclusions at the European Association for South Asian Archaeology and Art meeting certainly provide support to the continuing practices of the Indian Civilization, which may in fact be interesting for its scholarly value, and also for the factual verification of the history and anthropological knowledge. However, one must note a lack of indigenous perspective in these conclusions, and also demeaning attitude of researchers towards the target culture of study. To throw in comments such as "cattle wander around eating trash like in India today" is to negate the continuing practices of ancient India which may reflect a sophisticated society for its medicinal foods, diverse agricultural practices, environmental preservation and ecological understanding. Of course, the report is only a summary of the meeting. It is quite possible and hoped that the scholarly articles when published will include a more balanced account of the past even as it relates to the present practices.

It is true that cattle are fed the food remaining after the meal, but only people from villages (who generally do not have any voices in the foreign and even Indian scholarship) can explain the traditional practices of taking out food for animals (cattle, especially cow, birds, etc.) before beginning their meals. This is different from "food remains" outlined in the report. Also, it is a common practice with farmers in the village to keep leftover foods in a clay vessel to mix with the fodder. I come from a farming family and have seen this practice everyday. It is called *sānī* or mixer. It is also common to feed bread and *khalī* (mustard cake after extracting of its oil). It is also a common practice to prepare a mixture of turmeric and dried ginger (locally known as *soṇṭha*) with buttermilk for warding off diseases. These practices are folk medicines passed on from generation to generation, without much involvement of modern medicine.

The idea of embracing perspectives is important and we at the Center for Indic Studies, University of Massachusetts, Dartmouth, are very fortunate to have advanced the issue of multidisciplinary approach to examine any topic of research, be it a science, humanity, or social science related subject. In case of civilizational topics, indigenous perspectives are critically important for scholarly understanding of the subject and for its academic discussion. In the case of phytoliths and archaeology, scholars would only be enriched if the local perspectives are included.

In case of the origin of Indian Civilization, we believe we are reaping the wonderful fruits of the collaboration of the scholars with Eastern and Western perspectives. We are very grateful to Dr. Angela Marcantonio and Dr. Girish Nath Jha, who took all the trouble to edit the volume. These two scholars are most passionate about bringing the truth to the fore. Their dedication has brought this book out within one year of the conference. This compares with four years I had taken to get the proceedings of the 2006 symposium published. Contributions of all the authors are highly appreciated. It was and honour for us to host them at our campus. They exhibited true spirit of academicians in discussing their differences and in presenting their research work.

The Center for Indic Studies appreciates the financial support provided by the Uberoi Foundation and the Advaita Academy that made this conference possible. We also acknowledge the support extended by the 3 R Foundation in hosting delegates and in supporting the conference.

The Center's staff, Maureen Jennings, Sonia Balli and Shivi Chandra worked tirelessly in organization and smooth operations of the conference, including linking up with those scholars who had to make remote presentations via internet. We also would like to express our appreciation to Ms. Koyel Ghosal for her musical performance, and help from Anne-Marie Bryant and Mario Oliveira for photography and other aspects of the conference, including transportation.

Finally, we are extremely grateful to DK Printworld, particularly Susheel Mittal, for their utmost patience, meticulous work in designing, formatting and copy-editing the chapters.

The proceedings is a piece of marvel, showing incremental advancement that is capable of turning a major historical page in the origin of Indian Civilization. We hope the readers will agree and respond accordingly.

Dartmouth, July 2012 **Bal Ram Singh**

Contents

2. Dr Angela Marcantonio presenting her paper

Introduction

Angela Marcantonio
Girish Nath Jha

1. The Main Thrust and Novelty of the Volume

1.0. The reader who takes this volume in his hands might ask: Why another symposium (after several already, as reported in the "Preface"), and another book on the issue of the origin of Indian[1] Civilization, given that this is now a long-standing, intense debate, going on at least since the time of the English colonization of India? Furthermore, this academic debate has recently been extensively summarized in the volume by Bryant (2001) and Bryant & Patton (eds. 2005), as well as on the pages of several issues of the *Journal of Indo-European Studies* [see for example vol. 30, 2002 and vol. 31 (1 & 2), 2003], volumes that have brought into the fore, through the so-called "Aryan Debate", the two most popular theses regarding the origin of

1. We have chosen to use the name 'Indian' to refer to the languages (and civilizations) of India traditionally referred to as 'Indic', particularly within the Western tradition (see for example the article by J. Clackson, who consistently uses 'Indic'). The reason for this is twofold. First, to maintain continuity with previous publications by the publisher DK Printworld, that uses indeed the definition 'Indian'. Second, to use a neutral term with regard to the debated issue of whether or not the Indo-Aryan languages form a language family distinct from the other language families of India, such as, for example, Draviḍian.

the Indian Civilization, polarized into: "intrusive *vs* indigenous".

Thus, what does this volume, with its contributions, add to the overall debate on the origin of Indian Civilization? We believe that the main thrust of the volume, and its novelty, is "to reconcile" the various perspectives, the various theses put forward thus far on this issue. This means, in practice, an attempt to reconcile Eastern and Western perspectives. However much odd this may look at first, this is indeed the case, as the reader will realize going through the contributions of the volume, whose main claims and results are summarized in the four points listed below. More specifically, the claims reported in point (1) to (3) further confirm and reinforce the results of previous linguistic and archaeological research, whilst the claims reported in point (4), to our knowledge, represent fresh views on important methodological aspects regarding the search for the origin of pre-historical languages and civilization in general, and Sanskrit and the Indian Civilization in particular.

1.1. Let us then have a look at the results achieved by the present volume.

First (point (1)): *The absence of archaeological evidence in support of the Invasion/Migration Theory* (the corollary of the Indo-European (IE) linguistic theory), that is, the thesis that the bearers of the Sanskrit language and civilization originated outside the Asian subcontinent, somewhere in the West, and then moved into it later on (as emerges from the article by J. Shaffer & D. Lichtenstein and K. Elst; see also the contribution by N. Rao).

Second (point (2)): *The unbroken nature, the continuity of the early Vedic language and culture from old (however much un-definable) times well into the Haṛappan culture, down to more recent times*. As a matter of fact, reading the contribution of those scholars that point this out, independently but unanimously (the contribution by R.P. Singh, N. Rao, N. Achar and M.G. Prasad), it looks like the question: "is the Indian Civilization indigenous or not?" does not even arise, or, at least, not explicitly: only the concept of "continuity" is highlighted and dealt with. There is one exception: the contribution by G.N. Jha.

Third (point (3)): *The existence of a South Asian "linguistic area" / Sprachbund, involving the various, numerous languages/ language families of India,* as first pointed out by Emeneau (1956), and reaffirmed by subsequent research by several scholars, in particular by Masica (1976 & 1991). This in practice means that Sanskrit and the other Indo-Aryan languages share so many features (at any level of language) and in such an intricate way, with the non-Indo-Aryan languages of India that it is mostly difficult to trace back the precise origin (or rather, origins) of these features, and therefore to draw a clear-cut path of descendant for them — contrary to received wisdom. Actually, the situation is even more complex than this, because of the existence of what Masica calls the "persistent anachronism of the Indo-Aryan literary languages", as clearly illustrated by the following statements (Masica 1991: 53-54):

> "Indo-Aryan" historical linguistics is complicated, despite the documentation of various early stages, by the fact that the languages recorded at successive stages are often *not in direct historical relationship with one another* [. . .]. It was often a different dialect or dialect mixture that formed the basis of the literary language at each stage [. . .] e.g., Classical Sanskrit, Pāli, Saurasenī Prākr̥t, Literary Apabhraṁśa, and various forms of Western Hindi [. . .] all do represent in a general way the language of the midland at various stages.

Thus, it is an anachronism that, for example (Masica 1991:55),

> Classical Sanskrit, fixed by Pāṇini's grammar in probably the fourth century BCE on the basis of a class dialect (and

> preceding grammatical tradition) of probably the seventh century BCE, had its greatest literary flowering in the first millennium CE and even later, much of it therefore a full thousand years after the stage of the language it ostensibly represents.

Masica (1991: 56) also warns the reader that: "Anachronism is not the only source of *artificiality in the data for the older stages of Indo-Aryan*". In fact, with regard to the highly stylized, so-called Dramatic or Literary Prākṛts, Masica observes (ibidem) that

> Although among themselves they represent somewhat different stages of linguistic evolution (as well as ostensibly different areas), not only were they in literary use together (*often in the same composition*), but also *simultaneously with Sanskrit* and partly Apabhraṁśa. — italics added

In other words, the reality is that Sanskrit and the other Indo-Aryan languages are coexistent (regional and/or stylistic and /or social) varieties of the same contemporary dialectal *continuum*, rather than Sanskrit being the "mother" of the later Middle and Modern Indo-Aryan languages (at least in terms of their actual use), as pointed out in the contribution by G. Jha. Thus, the language of the Vedas may certainly be very old, but that does not mean that other languages/dialects did not exist in parallel to it. In fact, the Indian tradition is very clear on this, since it mentions at least two dialectal varieties: *vaidika* (belonging to the Vedas), the variety used indeed to compose the Vedas, and *laukika* (belonging to the people (*loka*)), the variety used by ordinary people, the latter variety being the Prākṛts. This being the case, it is erroneous to claim that one language/variety "descended" from the other. That this is indeed the case appears to be confirmed also by the fact that the oldest Sanskrit inscription dates only from CE 150, and the habit of making inscriptions in Sanskrit is a rather late one, gradually ousting the existing habit of making them in Prākr̥t — as pointed out again by Masica (1991: 55). These linguistic "facts" are by now well known, and the related *Sprachbund* model of explanation is also well established; nevertheless, the traditional family-tree model, clearly at odds with the evidence, is still widely used in textbooks and also in specialized literature. It may be worth mentioning at this point that this situation is not unique to the South Asian linguistic area, and that the family tree model is still widely used to represent other linguistic areas — despite the available evidence (and documentation) contradict it. For example, it is typically written in textbooks that (spoken) Latin has developed into the Romance languages (now known by the names of French, Italian, Spanish, Portuguese, etc.), according to the simple, clear-cut family-tree diagram. However, this description, for a non-linguist audience, or even for linguists who are not specialists of Romance languages, can be misleading, since it suggests the following "wrong" facts: (a) the areas where the Romance languages were formed were empty of population and languages, apart from Latin; (b) Latin gradually and by its own accord divided itself in a binary way, and more or less regularly and systematically, into various dialects; (c) these dialects carried on developing and "diverging" from one another so as to eventually form the modern Romance languages. Contrary to what purported by this "top-down", "divergence" model, the available linguistic data, the archaeological data and the documentation (including epigraphical documentation), tell us a totally different story. Let us take the example of the Italian territory — and what has now become the Italian language. In this territory, well before the Christian Era, there was a complex *continuum* of languages/dialects (whether genetically related or not) that co-existed with Latin, or even pre-existed it, at the point that several linguists have coined the expression: *lega linguistica italica*, that is: "*Italic* linguistic area (/*Sprachbund*)" to define this linguistic situation; see for example Pisani (1978). These languages/dialects interacted and "converged", that is, exchanged and shared features through contact and became (more) similar to one another even before the expansion of Rome and its own dialect, Latin. Of course, the prestige of Latin and the power of the Roman empire and culture later on reinforced this process of convergence, also becoming its main propulsive force and component. Eventually, the various, modern Italian dialects/dialectal groups were formed, and, in turn, they "converged" into what we consider now as "standard Italian" — this being a relatively recent process, accomplished only last century. As is self-evident from what has been stated above (and well documented), these early Italian dialects/ dialectal groups were not formed as the outcome of a simple, orderly and mechanical process of divergence from (just) Latin. They represent instead the variegated outcome of a complex process of interaction between (the various, socially differentiated levels of) Latin and the other coexisting, collateral — so to say — *Italic* languages, although the latter languages typically played a subordinate, a "*sub-stratum*" role. That this is indeed the real scenario is also confirmed by the well-documented fact that the modern Italian dialects have often preserved and/or internally developed numerous, original, pre-Latin/*Italic* linguistic features, in this way (completely) bypassing the influence of Latin at this regard [see for example Alinei (1996), Zamboni (2002), Varvaro (2001), etc.]. The same applies, of course, to the other Romance languages, that are equally the result of the complex interaction of Latin and the local, *sub-stratum* languages. Thus, despite its popularity (for whatever reason; see discussion in A. Marcantonio's contribution), the family tree model has been proven to be inaccurate, to say the least, in several cases, including the case of the Indian and Romance languages.

Fourth (point (4)): *A basic consensus on behalf of the contributing* *linguists regarding the "artificial" nature of the linguistic reconstructions* — the linguistic elements at the heart of the thesis of the IE origin of Sanskrit. In other words, reconstructions are theoretical constructs, an artefact of the method of analysis (the comparative method), and they are not to be confused with the real words, real sounds, real grammatical elements, etc. of a real language (although there are divergences of views on other aspects of this issue within this broad consensus, as discussed below). The same applies to the concept of "reconstructed proto-language" in general, and the "reconstructed IE proto-language" in particular: it is not a real language that has been spoken in a definite space and time in prehistorical past, but a theoretical construct that does not have a transparent relation (or, according to some more radical views), no relation at all, with the real world and its assumed speech community this construct is supposed to represent. This emerges from the contribution by J. Clackson, N. Kazanas, A. Marcantonio and G. Jha. This basic interpretation of the concept of "proto-language" appears to be endorsed also in the contribution by K. Elst. It is true that words such as "distortion", "artefact" or "theoretical construct" do not feature in his article, but the extreme "flexibility in interpreting the linguistic data", with all its obvious implications, is amply demonstrated by the author.

1.2. Thus, one can conclude from the claims and arguments listed in points (2) to (4) above that linguists, archaeologists and anthropologists could easily be misled if they place too much faith in reconstructions and proto-languages, in order to go "*In search of the Indo-Europeans*" (see Mallory 1989), or in their quest for the origin of Sanskrit (even more so because these linguistic findings are in agreement with the "absence of evidence" in favour of the Aryan Migration Theory). This "conventionalist" interpretation of reconstructions and proto-languages is not in itself a novelty. Several linguists, in fact, have since long pointed out that historical linguistics cannot be considered "a branch of prehistory" (see for example Harrison 2003: 231), or, in any case, it cannot be considered as a safe, "scientific" branch of prehistory. What is new instead, and most relevant for the issues under discussion, is the fact that the claim of the artificial nature of reconstructions and proto-languages is made here not just as a consideration of general character, but with precise reference to the traditional IE reconstructions and the IE proto-language. As J. Clackson puts it in the concluding remarks of his contribution:

> The Indo-European model, as a model of language relationships and of linguistic descent, tells us nothing certain about the origin of the Indic civilization.

At this point it could be objected that the rejection of the IE model does not *ipso facto* prove the indigenous origin of Sanskrit and the Indian Civilization. Neither could the indigenist hypothesis be demonstrated through the adoption of the "linguistic area/*Sprachbund*" model, despite the fact that the latter is more adequate than the family tree model to describe the correlations among the languages of India. This is certainly correct. As a matter of fact, from the linguistic data alone, without taking into account the evidence from archaeology, palaeo-anthropology, or early texts, it is not possible to draw definite conclusions about the (prehistorical) origin of languages in general, and Sanskrit in this case. However, it is this very "state of the art" of the debate that represents the first step toward a possible process of reconciliation of the Eastern and Western perspectives: the thesis of the indigenous character and continuity of the Sanskrit language and culture, although not directly "demonstrable", does nevertheless acquire new light within this context, and stands up as a good, plausible alternative to the IE/Migration Theory — actually, the only plausible alternative given the state of our knowledge, unless, of course, new (linguistic and/ or extra-linguistic) evidence comes up that suggests otherwise.

It goes without saying that the plausibility of the indigenist hypothesis appears to be supported by the results of archaeological, palaeo-anthropological and, in more recent times, genetic research. These results consistently show that, thus far, no relevant trace of intrusion into the South Asian Continent during the time frame presupposed by the Aryan Migration Theory has been found (see the contribution by J. Shaffer & D. Lichtenstein, N. Kazanas and N. Rao).

Thus, the state of the debate as proposed in this volume, in our opinion, represents a good starting point for a new, "joint" approach in the quest for the origin of Sanskrit and the Indian Civilization, and this is, we believe, the main thrust and novelty of the volume.

2. Presentation of the Contributions

2. 1. WESTERN PERSPECTIVES

For two centuries, scholars have assumed an IE/Aryan migration/invasion from the north-west into South Asia to explain the formation of historic Indian Civilization (although there are exceptions; see a criticism of this assumption in the article by Clackson). In contrast, the South Asian archaeological data reviewed in the contribution by Jim Shaffer & Diane Lichtenstein, titled "South Asian Archaeology: Late Prehistoric Cultural Continuity or Discontinuity", does not support (any version of the) migration/invasion hypothesis — this being the latest in a long series of research and essays that have already shown this to be the case. More precisely, in the authors' words: "There is **no** evidence of a population movement from the north-west regions outside South Asia into the Indus Valley at this time (**nor** is there evidence of a migration westwards from South Asia)." The authors' research shows how at the beginning, in the third millennium BCE, there was a population shift eastward from the Indus Valley, the "Haṛappan Diaspora", this being "the only major population displacement documented for the mid-second millennium BCE, the "traditionally accepted date" of the Indo-Aryan migration into South Asia". In other words, "The population movement indicated in the Vedas is essentially the Haṛappan Diaspora". As is clear, the archaeologists' data and arguments are in strong contrast not only with the assumption of the invasion/migration paradigm, but also, implicitly, with the "realist", as against "conventionalist" interpretation of the concept of "(IE) proto-language" (see discussion in section **1.2.**)

James Clackson, in his article "The Origin of the Indic Languages: The Indo-European Model", argues that the faith placed in the linguistic reconstructions as a means to unequivocally attain and therefore safely reconstruct the culture of the speakers of IE, is actually "misplaced". Indeed, the relationship between the reconstructed proto-language itself and the actual spoken parent language is not straightforward; it is instead complex and can even be "distorted", although this in itself — the author argues — is not sufficient to dismiss the theory of the ancestor of a biological family. The nature of this "distortion" can be easily understood through a metaphor, the metaphor of the constellation, as proposed by the author himself: "we see the constellations as two-dimensional, dot-to-dot pictures on a curved plane. But in fact, the stars are not all equidistant from the earth; some lie much further away than others. Constellations are an illusion and have no existence in reality". In the same way, linguists could have some confidence that: a reconstructed form such as *b^hereti* ('he brings, carries') corresponds not to a real word, but to a *potential* formation of spoken IE". In a word, Clackson believes that there must have been some sort of reality, a common IE mother language, beyond the theoretical, reconstructed one, although its real nature and structure may be beyond our reach, because it cannot be directly observed and compared against the evidence. This being the case, Clackson concludes that: "The IE model, as a model of language relationships and of linguistic descent, tells us nothing certain about the origin of the Indic civilization".

Angela Marcantonio, in her article "The Origin of Indian Civilization: Critical Analysis of the Contribution of Linguistics", agrees with the basic claim put forward by Clackson that reconstructions and proto-languages are a "product" of the methods of analysis. Actually, she goes further than that since she considers them as "artefacts" of the method, according to the meaning of "artefact" as understood within science: "something observed in a scientific investigation or experiment that is not naturally present but occurs as a result of the preparative or investigative procedure" (*Oxford English Dictionary* on-line). In simpler words, an error in a scientific apparatus and/or investigation. In her contribution the author justifies this claim through two main arguments: (a) applying simple statistical calculation, it turns out that most of the identified similarities among the various IE languages (and therefore between Sanskrit and the other IE languages) are not genuine similarities, because they lack statistical significance; they are therefore "artificial" similarities; (b) the principle that underpins the application of the comparative method, the famous principle of the (basic) "regularity of sound change" is not supported by the linguistic evidence in general, and the IE linguistic evidence in particular. Marcantonio concludes that there is no reason to uphold the thesis of the (Indo-)European origin of the Indian Civilization, and that this issue needs revisiting, and not just through the means of linguistic analysis, but also through the contribution of other disciplines involved in the investigation of prehistorical past.

Yet slightly different conclusions from those reached by Clackson and Marcantonio are attained by Nicholas Kazanas, who, in his article titled "R̥gvedic all-inclusiveness", basically claims that: (a) a IE proto-language must have existed, as proven by the numerous "similarities" (as against "correspondences") existing among the various IE languages — not to talk of the extensive, deep cultural similarities; (b) nevertheless, contrary to wide belief, a IE proto-language is not at all "reconstructable" (according to the parameters of the traditional comparative method), mainly because of the fallacy of the "regularity principle"; (c) Sanskrit does belong to this assumed family, again because of the linguistic similarities as well as the deep cultural commonalities that, in a "self-evident" manner, tie Sanskrit to the other IE languages (actually Sanskrit would have preserved many more common elements from proto-IE than any other IE language); (d) the linguistic evidence from Sanskrit, in terms of the nature and structure of its correlations with the other IE languages, particularly the nearby, closely related Iranian languages, also suggests that the rise of the Vedic culture is indigenous, and not the result of an Aryan/IE invasion, or migration — although nothing more precise than this can be stated on this issue. The suggested thesis of the indigenous character of Sanskrit language and culture accords with the thesis of its "continuity", put forward by the Indian scholars.

Koenraad Elst, in his article titled "Some Unlikely Tentacles of Early Indo-European", surveys a rich and varied amount of linguistic and non-linguistic data, and argues that:

> The scientific status of historical disciplines is inevitably precarious, mainly because their object cannot be subjected to repeatable experiment. Worse, it isn't even really there and can only be inferred secondarily from an uneven set of data, such as fossils for dinosaurs. In the case of historical linguistics, the same problem exists, just as no fossil researcher has ever seen a dinosaur, no linguist has ever heard a single native speaker utter a sentence of proto-IE, proto-Sino-Tibetan, proto-Draviḍian or any other reconstructed language deemed to be the common origin of a whole family of existing languages.

This precarious status of reconstructions is clearly reflected in the extremely flexible and often highly contradictory results that can be achieved by analysing the same linguistic data, and through the adoption (supposedly) of the very same methods of analysis, that is, the methods of historical linguistics, including linguistic palaeontology (methods underpinned by the assumed neo-grammarian principle of the "regularity of sound change"). Thus, for example, several IE homelands, located in regions often very far apart within Eurasia (and related population movements), as well as several estimates of the "antiquity" of Sanskrit have been proposed thus far. Similarly, the IE proto-language has been claimed to show correlations, whether through contact or genetic inheritance (or both), with all sorts of other, more or less distant and "exotic" language families, such as Caucasian, Finno-Ugric and even Chinese. The author concludes that "purely linguistic evidence is a fairly soft type of evidence", and that, therefore, great caution has to be exercised when claiming to "prove" anything.

2 2. EASTERN PERSPECTIVES

Let us now introduce the contributions by the Indian scholars, starting with the article by Girish Nath Jha, who takes into account both the Western and Eastern approach in the quest for the origin of Indian Civilization.

In his contribution "Some Remarks on the Origin and Development of Indian Languages and Linguistic Area", G. Jha first presents an overview of the variegated socio/politico-linguistic scenario of India, with particular attention, of course, to the (Old and Middle/Modern) Indo-Aryan languages. Second, the author compares the traditional Western methods of historical linguistics with the traditional, Eastern, "internal" approach to the analysis of the Indian languages, discussing strengths and weaknesses of both methods. Third, the author highlights the fact that:

> Ancient Indian texts are full of references that Prākr̥t and "Sanskrit" (the name given to the standardized variety of one of the Prākr̥ts) co-existed. This fact, which is well known to Indian scholars of Sanskrit and ancient religions and philosophies, was grossly missed by the Western Indologists, who were too eager to accept the "common source" theory and devised linguistic comparisons to derive European and Indian "descendants" from the common "mother" language.

Thus, Sanskrit literature uses both Sanskrit and Pāli/Prākr̥t in the same text, as already discussed above (see the quotes by Masica). In turn, this means that: (a) the method of analysis adopted for claiming that the Middle Indo-Aryan languages are offshoots from Sanskrit are not well founded; (b) the reconstruction of proto-IE backwards from Sanskrit, adopting the same methods of analysis, is also flawed. Jha concludes that all the Indian languages form indeed a "common linguistic zone". Not only referring to the Aryan/Draviḍian controversy, the author claims that a common origin (possibly Proto-Indic) could be suggested for these two language families, traditionally assumed to be distinct. To support this claim, he gives evidence from the "language technology industry, that derives clear benefits from the common features and a shared heritage of the Indian languages".

The history of civilizations has typically been dominated by discussion on race, superiority and what R.P. Singh, in his contribution titled "Dialectics of Power and Civilization", terms "centrisms", such as: Euro-centrism, Indo-centrism, Afro-centrism, etc. The author discusses the predilection of the modern world on tracing civilizations to one or the other pole, instead of looking for possible simultaneous origins and impact. In fact, usually, people, resources, ideas, consciousness and, above all, civilizations, move (and often quite fast) from one place to another, so that the question to be asked is not the polarized question typically posed within the Western cultural context and investigation: "is the Indian Civilization indigenous or not?" Rather, the correct question to be asked should be the following (using Singh's own words): "What exactly is that basic feature of Indian Civilization through which it can be identified, even after so many upheavals and transformations?" The answer, according to Singh, is: "Continuity and Plurality". In other words, the author defines the Indian Civilization as knowledge based, as well as a "colossal *continuum* of power in terms of contact, conflict and confluence" (the theme of "continuity" being a central theme also in the articles reported below). Therefore, the author argues, one should look beyond all kinds of centrisms, focusing on essential traits of Indian Civilization, its emergence and evolution. In addition to this, the author presents a balanced review and critique of the "Proceedings" of the previous symposium dealing with Indian civilization, titled: *Origin of Civilizations,* ed. Bal Ram Singh (2010).

The dating of Indian texts has been a known problem for long time, and for various reasons, an insufficient knowledge of Sanskrit and an insensitive attitude toward the Indian culture being the most prominent ones. B.N. Narahari Achar, in his contribution "R̥gveda: Its Chronology on the Basis of Astronomical References", tries to establish the chronology of the Vedas on the basis of the astronomical references present in them, specifically, in the earliest known (Vedic) texts of astronomy. The author argues that it is now time to dismiss some long-standing misconceptions and misrepresentations associated with the astronomical events referred to in the Vedas, as well as in the epic *Mahābhārata*. In fact, these events and references can now be tested and verified, or otherwise, using astronomical methods and simulations through the aid of Planetarium Software (that can project the view of the sky at any time and at any place), this being exactly what the author has done. Thus, these new measurements appear to confirm the correctness of the astronomical knowledge present in the Vedas, as well as a high degree of "internal" consistency in the dating of the various events and of the texts themselves, such as, for example, the dating of the Vedas with respect to the dating of the Mahābhārata war. The accuracy of this re-investigation — only recently made possible by Planetarium Software technology — is increased by the fact that astronomy has always played a vital role in Indian culture (for establishing the appropriate timing of the performing of rituals, for example), so that there is plenty of astronomical events to rely upon in carrying out the investigation. The results of the research suggest that a high chronology for the origin of Sanskrit, and the Indian Civilization has to be postulated, certainly much higher than the conventional 1,500 BCE proposed by the supporters of the IE theory, and related Aryan Migration Theory.

The Indus Valley Civilization (IVC) has been a topic of intense debate ever since its "discovery" in the 1920s. The questions of Aryan *vs* Draviḍian linkages with the Vedic culture, the un-decipherability of the IVC script and, most, importantly, the strong "isms" associated with the whole issue have prohibited any meaningful conclusions. Nalini Rao, in her contribution titled "An Analysis of the Concept of Sacredness in Indus Valley Art", has taken the IVC iconography to eke out possible conclusions. Though a difficult area of research, the author has nicely juxtaposed animal figurines from various IVC sites and nearby provincial regions, and has found some pattern within so much diversity. The IVC may have attributed high status to its women, considering their role in family and society. According to earlier interpretations of female figurines in IVC sites, the reason for attributing high status to women is not only their reproductive capacity (naked representations, tree emanating from womb, etc.), but also their general motherly, caring attitude. This is certainly in tune with general Indian concepts even today. Another aspect highlighted by the author is the impeccable cleanliness of the houses in the IVC sites; this would indicate not only a high level, well-organized lifestyle, but also the fact that destructive invasions — of the kind suggested by the Aryan Migration Theory — did not take place at all. Once again, the main result of the research carried out by this contributing scholar is the unbroken nature of the Indian Civilization.

The last article in this section, by M.G. Prasad, with the title "Oral Tradition in Indian Civilization", stresses, once again, the concept of "continuity". The content of the article at first might appear not to be directly related with the theme of the volume. However, this is not the case, since "oral tradition plays a significant role in the search of the origins of Indian Civilization", as underlined by the author himself. In fact, the Vedic oral tradition has existed in India from Vedic times to present times, and its continuous use, together with the cultural and social life associated with it, "represent the Indian Civilization from its origins to nowadays". It is therefore vital to understand how this tradition has been passed on, orally, from one generation to the other, from *gurus* to disciples, in order to correctly interpret the Vedic texts. To achieve this, in turn, a deep knowledge and correct pronunciation of the sounds and metres used is required, in addition to a deep knowledge of the grammar and all the other aspects proper of a refined, literary language. So pressing was the emphasis on the correctness of sounds and utterances that well four out of six ancillary texts considered to be critical for understanding the Vedas deal with the science of language: Śikṣā (phonetics), Chanda (metre), Vyākaraṇa (grammar), Nirukta (etymology). Prasad, in this article, deals with phonetics and metrics, describing and explaining some of the well-known metres and pronunciation techniques. The author finally observes that the phonetic tradition, the Śikṣā tradition is huge, with at least 100 texts, although the most notable and translated text is *Pāṇinīya Śikṣā* (the phonetic guidelines by Pāṇini). With regard to the metrics (Chanda) tradition, *Chandoma-jar'* is considered to be a standard text.

References

Alinei, M., 1996, *Origini delle Lingue d'Europa. I: La Teoria della Continuità*, Bologna: Il Mulino.

Bryant, E.F., 2001, *The Quest for the Origins of the Vedic Culture: The Indo-Aryan Migration debate*. Oxford University Press.

Bryant, E.F. & Patton L.L. (eds.), 2005, *The Indo-Aryan Controversy: Evidence and Inference in Indian History*, London/New York: Routledge.

Emeneau, M.B., 1956, "India as a Linguistic Area", *Language* 32: 3-16.

Harrison, S.P., 2003, "On the Limits of the Comparative Method", in B.D. Joseph & R.D. Janda (eds), *The Handbook of Historical Linguistics*, Oxford: Blackwell, 213-43.

Mallory, J.P., 1989, *In Search of the Indo-Europeans: Language, Archaeology and Myth.*, London: Thumes & Hudson.

Masica, C.P., 1976, *Defining a Linguistic Area: South Asia*, Chicago University Press.

———, 1991, *The Indo-Aryan Languages*, Cambridge University Press.

Pisani, V., 1978, Le lingue pre-romane d'Italia: origini e fortune", In A. L. Prosdocimi (ed.), *Popoli e Civiltà dell'Italia Antica. VI: Lingue e Dialetti dell'Italia Antica*. Roma: Biblioteca di Storia Patria. 15-78.

Singh, B.R. (ed.) 2010, *Origin of Indian Civilizations*. Proceedings of the Symposium on "Origin of Indian Civilizations" held at University of Massachusetts, Dartmouth, USA, published by Delhi: D.K. Printworld.

Varvaro, A., 2001, *Linguistica Romanza: Corso Introduttivo*, Napoli: Liguori.

Zamboni, A., 2002, "Tipologie dialettali e classificazione", in S.C. Trovato (ed.), *Linguistica Storica e Dialettologia*, Biblioteca della Società Italiana di Glottologia 27: 11-91.

1

Some Remarks on the Origin and Development of Indian Languages and Linguistic Area

Girish Nath Jha

Abstract

The paper, while presenting the linguistic scene in India and the well-known theories in Indian languages, language families, genealogies and linguistic area, points out the inconsistencies in the existing models. To prove a point, the author considers selected data from two cotemporary languages Hindi and Bangla and proves that one is a parent language of the other by using the argument of language change used by the classical comparative philologists. The section "Languages of India" talks about the Indian languages and language families in general, their constitutional position and the status of Sanskrit. The next section "Genealogy in Historical Linguistics" discusses some of the well known arguments and pitfalls in the comparative historical methods. This section uses illustrations to show some of the sound change laws which the historical linguists have used to prove a point. The next section "Language Change from Old Indo-Aryan to Middle and Modern Indo-Aryan" presents phonological and lexico-morphological changes from Sanskrit to Pāli, Prākṛta, Apabhraṁśa and modern Indo-Aryan languages and points out problems in the well-known positions. In a subsection of this section, the author presents data from Bangla and Hindi, the two contemporary modern Indo-Aryan languages and presents some conclusions which can be derived (on the lines of conclusions derived earlier by the historical reconstruction linguists. The next section argues for a common linguistic area, presents several views and argues for a practical approach towards settling the questions related to the origin of Indian languages. In this context, the paper presents the current language technology scene in India and the benefits to be derived if a common origin for Indian languages is proposed.

1. Languages of India

INDIA is a linguistic ocean in terms of the sheer number of languages spoken and diversity that these languages display. With more than a billion people, 2,000 castes, 43,000 sub-castes, five language families — Indo-Aryan, Draviḍian, Austro-Asiatic, Tibeto-Burmese and Andamanese — more than 1,600 languages spoken in 25 states, there is no place as diverse as a single country in the world than India. Among all the spoken/ documented languages, the Indian constitution has so far recognized 22 as national languages with 12 scripts as shown below:

Most of these languages are also the official languages of the states they are spoken in. The last ten-yearly census was done in 2011. Since the linguistic data for this census is

Language	**Script**
Hindi	Devanāgarī
Sanskrit	Devanāgarī
Marathi	Devanāgarī
Konkani	Devanāgarī
Nepali	Devanāgarī
Maithili	Devanāgarī

Sindhi	Devanāgarī
Bodo	Devanāgarī
Dogri	Devanāgarī
Santhali	Devanāgarī, Ol Chiki
Bengali	Bengali
Assamese	Bengali
Manipuri	Bengali, Meithei
Gujarati	Gujarati
Kannada	Kannaḍa
Malayalam	Malayalam
Oriya	Oriya
Punjabi	Gurmukhī
Tamil	Tamil
Telugu	Telugu
Urdu	Perso-Arabic
Kashmiri	Perso-Arabic Devanāgarī

still to trickle down, the previous (2001) census reports as many as 100 mother tongues and 1,000 documented languages and dialects with Hindi (constitutional status as *National Official Language*) topping the list with about 45-50 per cent plus speakers. English serves as the *Associate Official Language* (AOL) with approximately 6 per cent speakers. An overwhelming majority of Indians (97.6 per cent) speak Indo-Aryan and Draviḍian family of languages as shown below —

CONSTITUTIONAL PROVISIONS

Indian constitution has been very sensitive to protection of languages and language policies in the union. The Constitution

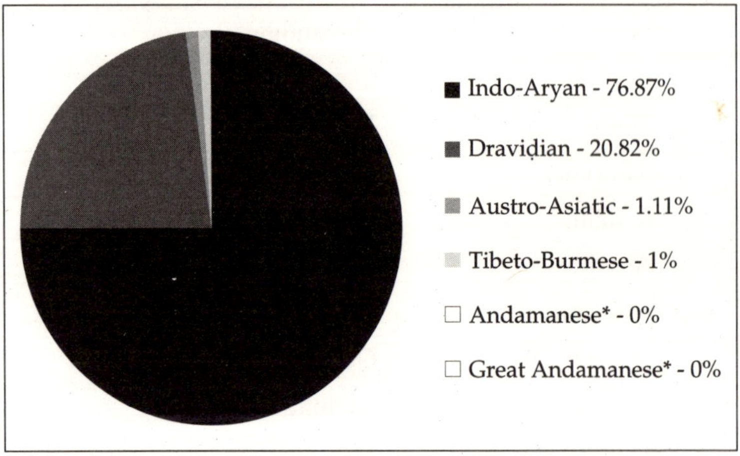

came into effect in 1950 and had given official status to fourteen major languages in its XVIIIth Schedule. In total, the Constitution has 448 Articles and 12 Schedules. The following Articles guarantee linguistic freedom and protection to minority languages (Baldrige 1996) —

- Part III — Fundamental rights
- Part IV — Directive Principles of State Policy
- Part IV A — Fundamental duties
- Part XVII — Official Language, Regional Languages, Language of the Supreme Court and the High Courts

There are designated government bodies and ministries to look after the language development tasks — Ministry of Human Resource Development, Ministry of Communications & Information Technology and Ministry of Culture among many other bodies which are involved in supporting the development of Indian languages.

2. Sanskrit: The Old Indo-Aryan

Sanskrit is a national language of India with negligible speakers (as per Indian government census data). Only one of the 25

Indian states (Uttarakhand) officially claims it as its official language. Usage wise, it is used in some electronic and print media, and significantly in digital media. It is the official language for religious rites, rituals and also a powerful medium to express India's traditional sciences, philosophy, history and culture. Genealogically, it is considered the mother of most of the Indian languages, their vocabulary and grammatical systems. It is also considered as (a) common repository for India's intellectual, religious and spiritual heritage, (b) common source for much of Indian literature, art and culture, and (c) major intellectual medium for Hinduism, Buddhism and Jainism.

EVOLUTION OF SANSKRIT

Sanskrit evolved into a powerful intellectual medium through the following distinct phases:

- Old Sanskrit (Vedic)
- Middle Sanskrit (pre-classical Sanskrit)
- Classical Sanskrit (the Sanskrit we know)

The Old (Vedic) Sanskrit was the sole language of the four Vedas (the Saṁhitās) . The Middle Sanskrit or the pre-classical Sanskrit was the language of the ancillary and exegetical texts and other texts explaining the Vedas in general, their philosophy and language such as:

- Brāhmaṇas (commentaries on each of the Vedas, description of rituals, etc.)
- Āraṇyakas (similar to Brāhmaṇa texts, describe rituals which have to be learnt in forests)
- Upaniṣads (fundamental texts of Hindu philosophy — Vedānta)
- Kalpasūtras (guidelines for rituals, social events, etc.)
- Vedāṅga (ancillary disciplines for Vedic study)

- Pariśiṣṭa (appendices explaining *sūtras*)
- Anukramaṇī (order of verses)

The Classical Sanskrit is the language of the epics (*Rāmāyaṇa, Mahābhārata*), Purāṇas and most of the Sanskrit literature dating as far back as Aśvaghoṣa.

LANGUAGE CHANGE FROM VEDIC TO CLASSICAL SANSKRIT

The Vedic language had spread to a large area in (the then) India and the West. The change in the language in terms of phonological and lexico-morphological systems was eminent. The linguists (Burrow, 1965) have explained the change as follows —

SOUND

- *ḷ ḷh* → *ḍ ḍh*
- *-iy / -uw* → *y/w*

MORPHOLOGICAL

- Variety of forms → fewer forms
- *-yu* → ceases in classical Sanskrit, except only for very few words like *manyu, dasyu,* etc.
- Some compounds got extinct

LEXICAL

- Disuse of many words — *atka* (garment), *apas* (work), *andhas* (juice), *āma* (strength), *iṣira* (vigorous, strong), *titau* (sieve), *gnā* (wife of god), *tvakṣ-* (to be active)
- Homonym pairs → one of them loses currency
  - a) *asura* (possessed), *asura* (demon) → only the latter sense stays
  - b) *ari* (devoted, trustworthy), *ari* (enemy) → latter stays
- change of meaning

3. Dr Girish Nath Jha presenting his paper

i) *vahni* (carrier) → fire

ii) *dasyu* (non-Aryan) → robber

iii) *dāsa* (name of a tribe) → slave

iv) *śūdra* (name of a tribe) → fourth *varṇa*

v) change in meaning due to misunderstanding of meaning in the Vedic texts

vi) *kratu* (wisdom, insight) → *kratu* (sacrifice)

vii) *mātariśvan* (divine being who discovered fire by rubbing two sticks) → *mātariśvan* (wind)

viii) false etymologies led to change in meaning

ix) *a* was considered a negative particle in *asura* (demon) *asita* (black) → *sura* (god), *sita* (white)

x) need for fixing the meaning of words led to compilation of glossaries like *Nighaṇṭu–Nirukta* (the glossary of words with ethmological explanation authored by Yāska. Much later, the *Bhāṣya* of Śāyana was a more mature and elaborate compilation.

PĀLI, PRĀKṚTA AND APABHRAṀŚAS, BUDDHIST HYBRID SANSKRIT (THE MIDDLE INDO-ARYAN LANGUAGES)

Unlike Sanskrit which is still a spoken language, these languages are not spoken any more and can be mostly seen in canonical literature of heterodox sects like Buddhism and Jainism. In ancient India, these were promoted by Magadhan and Mauryan empires. Later on, Sanskrit regained its supremacy and many north Indian Buddhist writers also adopted Sanskrit. A brief note on the extent of literature in these languages can be seen below (Winternitz 1927):

Pāli (literary Prākṛta)

- Jātaka literature
- Three Piṭakas (Tripiṭaka)

- Gāndhārī Dhammapada
- Aśokan inscriptions
- Theravāda Buddhism

Prākṛta

It was the vernacular spoken in many varieties. Mahārāṣṭrī was considered the best variety. The famous works in this variety are *Rāvaṇavaha* (c. sixth century) and *Karpūramañjarī* (Rājaśekhara, c. ninth century) → completely in Prākṛta. Śaurasenī was the language used by characters other than kings/captains. Māgadhī was used by lower characters in the plays. Ardhamāgadhī is found in early Jaina canons. Jaina Mahārāṣṭrī (non-canonical works) is seen in Vimala Sūri's *Paumacariu* (c. third century). Paiśācī (or Bhūta-Bhāṣā, both meaning "Language of Demons") was the language of the original *Bṛhatkathā* of Gunāḍhya. It was also the source of the Sanskrit book of stories *Kathā-saritsāgara*.

Buddhist Hybrid Sanskrit

Some Buddhist works were written using a mixed language. Among these works is the *Mahāvastu*, the core of which is thought to date from the second century BCE.

Apabhraṁśa

Some of the earliest references to this variety can be dated to third-fourth century CE in the 4th Act of Kālidāsa's drama *Vikramorvaśīya* which has Apabhraṁśa verses. Subsequently, in the sixth century CE, it is found in the inscriptions of King Dharasena II of Valabhi, in which the king praises his father as being adept in Sanskrit, Prākṛta, and Apabhraṁśa compositions. Among the known Jaina literature, *Paumacariu* of Svayambhū (eighth-ninth century), *Harivaṁśa Purāṇa* of Puṣpadanta (tenth century) and *Sanatkumāra-cariu* of Haribhadra (twelfth century) may be cited as texts of Apabhraṁśa.

3. Modern Indian languages

The two major families as shown earlier in the diagram are the Indo-Aryan and the Draviḍian. The former is considered to have descended from Sanskrit via the middle Indo-Aryan languages, and the latter is considered to have descended from some proto-Draviḍian family.

MODERN INDO-ARYAN

The modern Indo-Aryan (MoIA) languages are spoken from Pakistan to Bangladesh, and from Nepal to Sri Lanka. The linguistic features of MIA (Abbi 2001) can be summarized as follows —

The phonological system in MoIA is very diverse. Masica (1991) reports a range from 6 vowel system in Oriya to 14 in Konkani. The lexical system has words directly borrowed from Sanskrit (categorized as *tatsama*), of Sanskrit origin (*tadbhava*), of native origin (*deśaja*) or of foreign origin (*videśaja*). The *tadbhava* category shows a marked simplification of complexities of Sanskrit morphology and phonology. The verbs carry the number gender features. Two gender system is common and the number system is also the regular two except in Konkani which has dual also. The syntax shows a flexible SOV pattern with reasonable scrambling across phrasal constituents.

The Draviḍian languages are mostly found in southern India and northern Sri Lanka. Besides these, Brahui, a western Pakistani language and Kurux and Malto, spoken in the state of Jharkhand, are also of Draviḍian origin. The Draviḍian family displays a basic five vowel system. The consonants have richer points of articulation (Abbi 2001). Toda and Malayalam have six-way contrast in point of articulation (*/p t′, t, ṭ, c, k/*). Nasal stops also have six points as */m, n′, n, ṇ, ñ, ṅ/*. Tamil and Malayalam do not have aspirated sounds. Telugu and Kannada have voiced and voiceless aspirates, which many claim as being borrowed from Sanskrit. Retroflex sounds are very common in all Draviḍian languages. The north Draviḍian (Kurux, Malto) languages have velar fricative /x/ and glottal stop /?/.

Lexical/morphological system of the Draviḍian languages shows a preponderance of Sanskrit *tatsama* words. These languages are considered agglutinative (morphemes are segmentable with clean boundaries) and suffixial in nature. Words/morphemes are strung together linearly as lexical root + (*der* suffix) + *infl* suffix. Primarily, nouns and verbs are major categories. Negation is conveyed through morpho-syntax of verbs which have two tenses (past/non-past), two propositions (affirmative and negative). Like the MIA, these languages also use post-positions to express syntactico-semantic relations. The gender system is human (mas/fem) *vs* non-human and the word order is the SOV with verb carrying the agreement features.

4. Origin of Indian Languages

The MoIA languages have been clubbed as part of the IE family, and the languages in southern India are considered descendants of the proto-Draviḍian family. This division has been questioned by many as having been inspired by the colonial rulers of India. The historical comparative method used to determine genealogy looked for similarities in basic vocabulary (numerals, kinship, domestic animals, everyday activities) and similarities in grammar, for example, the initial *d-* in Sanskrit, Greek, Latin, Slavic (Sk. *daśam,* Av. *dasa,* Gk. *deka,* Lat. *decem*) and the third person singular *–ti* (e.g. Lithuanian *eiti* → he goes). The name *IE* was given by Thomas Young in 1914. This was immediately flashed as the most important language family in terms of the then geo-politics, economy and colonialism. Other labels for this family are *Indo-Germanic* and *Aryan.*

Courtesy Halvor Eifring & Rolf Theil (2005): *Linguistics for Students of Asian and African Languages.*

The methodology followed by the Indo-Europeanists were generally the following:

LATIN			ITALIAN		
ORTH.	PRONUN	MEANING	ORTHO.	PRONUN	MEANING
habere	/ha'be:re	to have	*avere*	/a've:re/	to have
herbam	/'herbã/	grass	*erba*	/'ɛrba/	grass
hora	/'ho:ra/	time, hour	*ora*	/'o:ra/	time, hour
homo	/'homo/	man	*uomo*	/'wɔmo/	man

- Study of language change between a pair of languages to establish their genealogical relationship
- If the changes were regular, then the older language was considered "parent" and others "children"

Example of Latin >> Italian

PROBLEMS IN THE HISTORICAL COMPARATIVE METHOD

1. It considers only those features among languages that are believed to be genealogically inherited, and assumes that a parent language gave birth to the daughter languages. This method is fraught with many unscientific assumptions. One of them is that there are speakers of "superior" or prestige languages which colonize and implant their language on the speakers of seemingly "inferior" languages, and in the process, the speakers of "inferior" languages completely give up their native language and adopt the "superior" language. Thus a "descendant" of the "superior" language emerges, creating a family tree. The argument for the so called Aryan Invasion Theory (AIT) stems from this assumption. Another assumption can be that there are communities with no language and are waiting to be invaded and colonized and thus "get" a language.

Ancient Indian texts are full of references that Prākr̥ta and "Sanskrit" (the name given to the standardized variety of one of the Prākr̥tas) co-existed. This fact, which is well known to Indian scholars of Sanskrit and ancient religions and philosophies, was grossly missed by the Western Indologists who were too eager to accept the "common source" theory and devised linguistic comparisons to derive European and Indian "descendants" from the common "mother" language. There were several kinds of languages before the standardization of Sanskrit — *Vaidikī* (the compositional variety in which the Vedas or spiritual texts were composed) and *laukikī* (the ordinary spoken variety), as one would have in any culture. By the time of Pāṇini, these languages had changed significantly and there was a need for etymological, phonetic and grammatical texts so that ancient scriptures could be still explained. The fact that there were ten great grammarians before Pāṇini and four out of basic disciplines necessary to understand Vedas dealt with linguistics is a clear indication of this. The grammar of Pāṇini targeted the dominant local variety (Pāṇini's mother tongue) called Bhāṣā (means "language" in modern Indian languages). Much after Pāṇini, this variety of language became so standardized that the name "Sanskrit" (meaning "standard", "refined", "cultured" etc.) gained currency for this variety. Since India has always been linguistically diverse, the scholars of the time needed a standard language to communicate with the scholarly community all over the length and breadth of India, Sanskrit became a logical choice.

2. It ignores the sharerd areal features which are predominant in the Indian subcontinent due to the fact

that the speakers of the languages have been interacting constantly for over 5,000 years.

Let us discuss (1). Traditionally, Sanskrit or Old Indo-Aryan (OIA) is considered the mother of Middle Indo-Aryan (MIA) languages like Pāli, Prākṛta, Apabhraṁśa and other Modern Indo-Aryan (MoIA) languages of northern India. This assumes the following rationale:

(a) that Sanskrit is older than all the MIA languages, and

(b) that the laws of sound change should proceed regularly and systematically, in the evolution of phonology, lexicon, etc. from the OIA to MIA. Let us look at the following examples:

- Simplification of Sk *ṛ/ḷr* to into MIA —

  ṛkṣa → *accha* (bear)

  ṛṇa → *ina*

  ṛju → *uju* (straight)

  pṛcchati → *pucchati*

  maitrī → *metti*

- Simplification of diphthongs /*ai*/ and /*au*/ to vowels /*e*/ and /*o*/

  aurasa → *orasa* (breast-born, legitimate)

- Simplification of /*aya*/ and /*ava*/ to / *e*/ and / *o*-/

  jayati → *jeti* (conquers)

  avadhi → *odhi* (duration)

- Deletion/re-syllabification of final consonants

  Final consonants were generally not liked and were either deleted (*sarpis* → *sappi*) or re-syllabified with an /*a*/ as in *śarad* ("autumn") → *śarada* and *sarita* ("stream") → *sarita*

- Clusters were simplified

  kṣetra → *khetta*

  dakṣiṇa → *dakkhina*

  agni → *aggi*

  pūrṇa → *punna*

  oṣṭha → *oṭṭha*

- Conjuncts were simplified by vowel insertion

  bhāryā → *bhāriyā*

PROBLEM WITH 1 (a)

Sanskrit literature uses both Sanskrit and Pāli/Prākr̥ta in the same text — the former for educated and the latter for the uneducated. Sanskrit literary texts are well known for maintaining this linguistic distinction all the way through. Almost all of Kālidāsa's plays (*Śākuntalam, Vikramorvaśīyam,* etc.). all of Bhāsa's plays and all subsequent writers have used this technique. Since these plays were staged before erudite gatherings, it was expected that it would portray the society's use of language accurately; thus the linguistic distinction that has been an everyday fact in a diverse country like India had to be portrayed. This compares with the linguistic situation in India today, where parallel vocabularies exist among the standard variety of a language and all its dialects. Hindi, with 47 listed varieties, is a good example of this, whereby these varieties are connected to one another through (more or less regular) sound changes (as it can be seen in the dialect dictionary of Hindi, under preparation by the Central Institute of Hindi in Agra) but may not have necessarily evolved from Hindi. For example *baccā* (Hindi) >> *butrū* (Bhojpurī) can be said to be genealogically related in a sense that they are maintaining the initial /b/. However, this should not lead to a conclusion that Bhojpurī is a descendant of Hindi.

PROBLEM WITH 1 (b)

It is a generally understood that reduction in the complexities of Sanskrit sounds led to simpler combinations in the MIA words. Looking at the data above, and following the inherent assumptions of the comparative method, we can safely conclude that:

Conclusion 1: *Sanskrit is the mother of MIA languages Pāli, Prākṛta and Apabhraṁśa*

Let us consider some examples from MoIA pair Hindi and Bangla

FINAL CONSONANTS ARE NOT LIKED IN BANGLA

Since the final cosonants are not preferred in Bangla, the following equation can be proposed:

Hindi *rām* >> Bangla *rāmo*

Hindi *śarad* >> Bangla *śarado*

Based on the data above and conclusion (1), we can safely conclude that:

Conclusion 2: *Bangla has evolved from Hindi* (sic)

ARGUMENT AGAINST (CONCLUSION 1 AND 2)

Hindi is not the mother of Bangla. Therefore if the arguments in Conclusion (2) are false, then by the same argument conclusion (1) will also be proved to be false. There is another argument against Conclusion 1 in the fact that both Sanskrit and Prākṛta co-exist in many Sanskrit texts and therefore Sanskrit cannot be older than (and hence parent of) Prākṛta.

Based on the above arguments, it can be argued that methods adopted for establishing MIA as an offshoot of Sanskrit was not logical or empirical. Therefore, the reconstruction of PIE backwards from Sanskrit adopting similar methods is also not either logical or based on empirical data.

ARGUMENTS FOR A COMMON LINGUISTIC AREA

M.B. Emenou (1956) in his well-argued paper "India as a Linguistic Area" gave the argument that Indian languages appear as belonging to a common linguistic zone. This, he argues, was due to thousands of years of contact and mutual give and take. Though this cannot be taken as an argument against the linguistic genealogy of Indo-European, it certainly points to the fact that Indian languages have drawn sounds, words, morpho-syntactic, conceptual and stylistic features from one another freely over an unusually long period of time, which may make it difficult to draw conclusions from genealogical relations alone on the basis of the identified similarities/correspondences among words, sounds, grammatical elements, etc.

As noted above, there are more features shared between the two dominant families of India, Indo-Aryan and Draviḍian, than between Indo-Aryan and the western members of the Indo-European family. The sound systems of all Indian languages across families show remarkable similarity in terms of vowel and consonant systems, syllable structure and the *sandhi* phenomenon. The lexical and morphological system show more cohesiveness, either post-positional (where free morphemes like *ko, me, par* (Hindi) etc. are used to express case relations) or inflectional (where bound morphemes are used to express the same (as more common in Bangla, Maithilī etc.). Similarities in verb root based primary derivation processes, as well as productive secondary derivation processes and compounding and similar syntactic frames point to a common heritage. The common vocabulary store of the Indian languages on both sides of the Vindhyās (the mountain ranges that divide north and south India and hence Indo Aryan and Draviḍian families) is in excess of 50 per cent, Malayalam, the newest Draviḍian language, has as much as 75 per cent Sanskrit vocabulary when used in the literary domain. Tamil has 48 per cent or more. The rich morphological system of the Indian languages gets extended into an equally cohesive syntactico-semantic system (*kāraka*). The linguistic common ground of the Indian languages extends to literature and culture, where the commonality increases phenomenally.

Thus, on a closer comparison of the Indo-Aryan and Draviḍian languages, one may find surprising similarities. The areal and typological similarities among Indian languages (across so-called genealogical boundaries) are so great that one may even fancy a common origin for them. This has support from the genetic studies as well. The genetic relationship among Indians (north and south) is far closer than between the north Indians and the Europeans. The genealogists should have taken into account the areal and typological features of the Indian languages into consideration. It is, therefore, not surprising that more and more scholars are now finding fault with the comparative method which created an imaginary PIE family (Marcantonio 2011/2012).

CONTROVERSY OVER ĀRYA *vs* DRAVIḌA

The controversy on the MoIA and Draviḍian languages extends to the controversy between the words Ārya and Draviḍa. The former derived as Ārya >> *ṛ* (speed, profession, knowledge) + *ṇyat* has many meanings but none suggest a race in the sense the Western world understands. Similarly, the *Draviḍa* >> dru (sense of water, prosperity, strength, integrity) does not connote any racial sense. The earliest reference of *dravida* can be found in *Mahābhārata* (*Mbh*) as follows:

पाण्ड्यांश्चद्रविडांश्चैव सहितांश्चोड्रकेरलैः। अन्ध्रांस्तलवनांश्चैव कलिङ्गानोष्ट्रकर्णिकान्।।

(सभापर्व>दिग्विजयपर्व>अष्टाविशोंऽध्याय: (28)>श्लोक 48)

(Courtesy: Mahābhārata Indexing system at JNU Sanskrit server http://sanskrit.jnu.ac.in/mb/ibasic.jsp)

Based on these textual and other references, Jha (2012) argues that the word *tamil* originates from *draviḍa* through the following sound laws: Sanskrit-Prākr̥ta sound change rules as follows — *draviḍa* > *daviḍa* > *damila* > *tamiḷa* (r>ϕ). *kārya* > *kāyya* > *kāj*. Śaṅkarācārya also uses the word *draviḍa*. Daṇḍī (*Avantīsundarīkathā* — tenth century CE) refers to *damila*. B. Krishnamurthy (2003, *Draviḍian Languages*) reverses the derivation process when he says *draviḍa* came from *damila* which is referred in a Cylonese chronicle the *Mahāvaṁśa* of pre-Christian era. Earlier Caldwel (1856) and Zvelebill (1990) also gave the same argument.

In fact, many of the properties of this word (if we relate it to the base *drav*) like "prosperity", "strength", etc. can be found to be in agreement with various meanings assigned to the word *ārya*.

5. Advantages of Common Heritage and Linguistic Area

Further evidences of a single system for Indian languages can be obtained from the language technology community in India which is progressively inclined to the idea that one linguistic system can explain all Indian languages. The fact that all Indian scripts have evolved from a common source has helped the Centre for Development of Advanced Computing (CDAC) develop the common script interchange programme for all Indian language scripts. Ancient grammarians have tried Pāṇini grammar on Tamil and other Indian languages. Earlier efforts by the Anusāraka group at IIIT Kanpur and then at IIT Hyderabad in leading efforts for Indian language technologies based on Pāṇini's grammar point to the fact that Indian languages are explained better by an Indian language grammar model like that of Pāṇini. Efforts by Microsoft Research India (Baskaran et al. 2008) and then by the Bureau of Indian Standards (BIS) for evolving a common annotation scheme for all Indian languages and then funding by the Technology

Development for Indian Languages (TDIL) programme of the Government of India to prepare a national corpora based on common national standard for all Indian languages indicates the fact that there is a lot to derive from the commonness of Indian languages than to hark upon the much-hyped differences among them.

6. Conclusion

The paper, while presenting the well-known problems with the comparative historical methods in the Indian context, argues that carefully selected data can be used to prove any point. In this context, the author has highlighted the fact that the whole argument of genealogical relationships in the Indo-European family be re-examined taking insights from the areal and typological features of the Indian languages. The paper ends with some related arguments on the Āryan/Draviḍian controversy and suggests a common origin (Proto Indic > Indic) for these two language families (so far assumed distinct from each other). To emphasize this point, the author has given evidence from the language technology industry which has clear benefits from the common features and a shared heritage.

References

Abbi, A., 2005, *A Handbook of Field Linguistics*, Mouton.

———, 1991 (ed.), "India as a Linguistic Area Revisited", Special issue of *Language Sciences* 13.2.

Burrow, T., 1965, *Sanskrit Language*.

Caldwel, 1856, *A Comparative Study of Draviḍian Languages*.

Eifring, Halvor & Rolf Theil., 2005 (ms), *Linguistics for Students of Asian and African Languages*.

Emeneau, M.B., 1956, "India as a Linguistic Area", *Language* 32: 3-16.

Hock, H.H., 1991, *Principles of Historical Linguistics*, Berlin: Mouton de Gruyter.

Jason Baldridge, "Reconciling Linguistic Diversity: The History and the Future of Language Policy in India," University of Toledo Honors Thesis, 1996.

Jha, Girish N., 2012, "Arya vs Dravida and the Linguistic Foundations of Indian Languages", International WAVES Conference, University of Massachusetts, USA, 2012.

Kashyap et al., 2010, "Aryan Gene Pool in Indian Populations: Myth or Reality — Genetic Evidences from the Subcontinent", in *Origin of Indian Civilizations*, Bal Ram Singh (ed.), Delhi: DK Printworld, 2010.

Marcantonio, Angela., 2011, *The Origin of Indian Civilization: Critical Analysis of the Contribution of Linguistics*, presented at an International seminar on "Origin of Indian Civilizations", Dartmouth: University of Massachusetts.

Winternitz, M., *A History of Indian Literature* (tr. into English by Subhadra Jha).

Underhill, P., 2010, "Patterns of Y Chromosome Diversity in the Contemporary South Asian Gene Pool," in *Origin of Indian Civilizations*, Bal Ram Singh (ed.), Delhi: DK Printworld, 2010.

2

Ṛgvedic All-inclusiveness

N. Kazanas

Abstract

The *Ṛgveda* contains and seems to preserve more common elements from the Proto-Indo-European Culture than any other branch of the family. This essay examines various points of language, poetry and philosophy but it focuses mainly on grammatical elements, lexical and syntactical, and on aspects of (fine) poetry. This is one aspect showing that Vedic and its culture is much closer to the PIE language and culture than any other branch in that family. Moreover, it shows that it is most unlikely that Vedic moved across thousands of miles over difficult terrains to come to rest in what is today north-west India and Pakistan, in Saptasindhu or the Land of the Seven Rivers. Certain other aspects show that Iranian moved away from Vedic and Saptasindhu and most probably the other branches did the same at a very distant but undetermined period. Finally, monotheism is also a notable feature in the *ṚV* despite its pronounced polytheism.

1. Max Müller Wrote Early On

[A]s in his language and in his grammar [the Indian] has preserved something of what seems peculiar to each of the northern [Indo-European] dialects singly, as he agrees with the Greek and the German where the Greek and the German

> seem to differ from all the rest . . . *no other language has carried off so large a share of the common Aryan heirloom* — whether roots, grammar, words, myths or legends.
>
> — 1859:14 square brackets and italics added

In other words, the Vedic culture preserves more elements of the IE (=Indo-European) heritage than any other extant IE branch.

Let us start with some common IE names of deities.

2. Theonyms: Names of Deities in the R̥V and Other Branches

There are more than 20 such theonyms in the *R̥V* alone (Kazanas 2009: ch. 3). Here we shall look at 6 of them only: Agní, Aryamā́n, Dyàus, (Apā́ṁ-)Nā́pāt, Sū́rya, Uṣás.

Agní : Hit. *Agnis;* Sl. *Ogon/Ogun*. Lat. *ignis,* Lith. *ugnis*, Lett. *uguns* — all 'fire'. Iranians had as demons Indra, Saurva but, despite their fire worship, preserved only in proper name *Daśt-ayni*. For "fire" Ht. has *paḫḫur,* Gk. *pur-* and Gmc. *fyr-* and variants; so it would have been more natural for Hittite to have a fire-god whose name was related to *paḫḫur*! (**Note**: Av = Avestan = Old Iranian; Lithuanian & Lettish = Baltic; Sl. = Slavic, i.e. Old Bulgarian, Russian, etc.)

Aryamā́n : Av. *Airyaman;* Myc. *Areimene* (Gk. *Are-s*?); Celt. *Ariomanus* (Gaul), *Eramon* (Ireland); Germanic *Irmin*. The stem *ar-/or-* "move, rise" in most IE branches: Gk. *or-numi* "rise", Lat. *orior,* Gmc. *rinn-* "run"; Arm. *y-ar-ne* "rise"; etc .

Dyàus : Hit. *D-Siu-s;* Gk. *Zeus/DiFa-;* Lat. *Ju[s]-pitar/Iov-;* Gmc. *Tīwaz;* Rus. *Divu*(?); *A ú* .

Apā́ṁ-Nā́pāt : Av. *Apām-Napā;* Lat. *Nept-unus;* Irish *Necht*|*-an* (*-p-*changes to other RAI 2 consonants).

4. Dr Girish Nath Jha comments as Prof. Nicholas Kazanas look on

5. Audience active in question-answer session

Sûrya : Kassites *Surias*; Gk. *Heli(F)os*; Lat. *Sol*; Gmc *savil/sol*; Welsh *saul*; Sl. *slunice/solnce*: all "sun".

Uṣás : Gk. *Eos*; Lat. *Au[s]-rora*; Gmc. *Eos-tre*. Av. *uśah-*; Lith. *auśra*, Lett. *auśma*; Celtic. *gwaur*, etc.

Vedic 6; Greek 4; Latin 4; Germanic 3; Hittite 2; Slavic 2; Celtic (Irish, Welsh, Gallic) 2.

(**Note**: The *ṚV* is considerably smaller than the Greek corpus consisting of Homer, Hesiod, Aeschulos, Pindar and so on.)

But, moreover, the stem for the natural phenomenon "fire" does exist in some of them, like *ignis* in Latin, *uguns/ugnis* in Baltic; or the "sun" in Gmc. *savil/sol*, Celtic *saul*, Sl. *solnce*; and so on. Clearly, the other branches lost the theonyms. And no two branches have a theonym in common to the exclusion of the *ṚV*! Note also an additional feature connected with the Sun-god. In Greek *Helios* is masculine and has retained the gender to modern times. In Germanic the sun acquired the feminine gender and is now *die Sonne*. Vedic had both: *Sūrya* was the male Sun-God and *Sūryā* the divine Sunmaiden who accompanied the twin Aśvins, the Horse-gods of the twilight.

3. Poetic Art.

Germanic had alliterative poetry. For example in Modern English *Roll on, roll on you restless waves* where the *r* repeats; or *Do not go gentle into the good night* where the *g* repeats. *If all would lead their lives in love like me* where the *l* repeats.

Greek had strict metrical structure. Homer's heroic hexameter in his epics and others with variants of iambic, dactylic, trochaic metre, etc. — but not alliteration.

pā́ntas gar phi lé es ken ho dōí épi oi kí a naí ōn

– –| – ⏑ ⏑| – ⏑ ⏑| – ⏑⏑ | – ⏑ ⏑ | – –

"he entertained all living in a house on the high road":

Homer: *Iliad* 6, 15 (no alliteration).

hós min xei non eón ta ka té ktane hoi e ni oí koi

– –| – ⏑ ⏑| – ⏑ ⏑| – ⏑ ⏑| – ⏑⏑| – –

"he killed him who was a guest in his house"

Odyssey 21.27 (same as above) strict metre only.

In Germanic poetry we find the opposite: alliterative verses but no strict metre. Take an example from *The Seafarer* 44-45, an Old English poem:

*Ne biþ **him** to **h**earpan **h**yge ne to **h**ringþege,*

*ne to **w**ife **w**yn ne to **w**orulde hyht...*

'His thought is not for the harp nor the receiving

of rings, nor joy in a woman nor pleasure in the world'.

Modern English verse has metre and alliteration:

If all would lead their lives in love like me :

⏑ x | ⏑ x | ⏑ x | ⏑ x | ⏑ x |

This is the Iambic pentameter with stress, which substitutes the length of vowels.

Vedic has both alliteration and fairly strict metre: e.g. from *Ṛ̥V* 6.47.29, with Triṣṭubh structure, i.e. eleven syllables and strict cadence

sá ***dundubhe*** sajū́r *índreṇa* ***devaír***

⏑ – ⏑ – ⏑ – – – ⏑ – –

dūrā́d dáviyo *ápa sedha śatrū́n*

– – ⏑ – – ⏑ ⏑ – ⏑ – –

O drum, along with Indra and the gods, do
drive our foes to farthest distance.

It has both alliteration and the fairly strict metre of .tubh with 11 syllables in each quarter of the stanza and also assonance (u, u, ū, e, e, e; ā, a, a, a, a, a.)

Riddles are found in all traditions, all nations. Here are two from *R̥V* 8.29.5,7:

tigmám éko bibharti hásta áyudha.
śúcir ugró jálāṣabheṣajaḥ:

One, bright [and] fierce, with cooling remedies,
carries in his hand a sharp weapon. (*jálāṣabheṣaja*.)

trī́ṇy-éka urugáyo vícakrame
yátra devā́so madanti:

One, far-going has made three strides
to where the gods rejoice. (*urugáyaḥ*)

The two clues signal Rudra and Viṣṇu respectively.

I close this section with the words of Calvert Watkins: "the language of India from its earliest documentation in the *R̥gveda* has raised the art of the poetic figure to what many would consider its highest form" (2001: 109).

One of many splendid stanzas: 3.54.8

vísvéd eté jánimā sáṃvivikto
mahōdevā́n bíbhratī ná vyathete;
éjad dhruváṁ. patyate viśvam ékaṁ
cárat patatṛ́ víṣuṇaṁ víjātám.

'The two truly encompass (*saṁ*) and sift all births/beings, bearing the mighty *devas*, yet do not stagger. Moving yet fixed, the One governs the whole, what walks and flies — the manifold manifest creation.'

Apart from alliteration and rich assonance with *vi* especially, note that the neuter gender affords multiple interpretations (*víśvam ékam*). Or take 4.40.5:

> *haṁsáḥ śuciṣád vásur antarikṣasád dhótā vediṣád átithir duroṇasát;*
> *nṛṣád varasád ṛtasád vyomasád abjā́ gojā́ ṛtajā́ adrijā́ ṛtám.*

> The swan in the clear brightness, the Vasu in midsky, the summoner at the altar, the guest in the house; what is in men, what is in excellence, what is in Natural Order, what is in heaven; what are born of Waters, of light, of Cosmic Order, of the Unbreakable — that is the Law.

Here the art is based on the repetition of *-ṣaḍ* "being, dwelling, sitting in" and *-já* "born of". In the first two *padas* we see a descent from the brightness of the sky down to a house; then in each of the other two we see an ascent. Of course, *go* commonly means "cow" but often denotes "light" and this must be the sense here; similarly *ádri-* usually means "rock, stone, mountain" even "cloud, lightning" but the basic sense is "unbreakable" (probably from a form of Ö*dṛ* "breaking (through, piercing" and the negative *á-*). Natural Law shapes and runs through all phenomena and this alone has permanence — it is implied — whereas all else is like a passing guest.

There are many other passages I can cite, like 2.21.1 where we find the repetition of *-jite* or 10.67.13 with repetition of *svasti*, etc. We find also all figures of speech that form fine poetry from *atiśayokti* "hyperbole" (e.g. 3.55.7, etc. and *upamā* "comparison simile" (with *iva*, *na*, etc.) to *yamaka* "assonance, paronomasia" (4.1.2, etc. and *śleṣa* "harmony, pun" (6.75.17, etc. but discussing them would lengthen this essay unnecessarily. The words of Watkins should suffice.

4. Grammar

Sanskrit, according to Burrow is "more readily analysable,

and its roots [=*dhātu*] more easily separable from accretionary elements than is the case with any other IE language" (1973: 289). Indeed, consider how from simple *dātus*, that are also nominal stems, arise nouns and adjectives and verbs in tenses and moods. Or as Elizarenkova put it, "the verb-root is basic to both inflexion and derivation . . . it is irrelevant that for some roots such nouns are not attested" (1995: 50) — except that simple "seed form" would be better translations for *dātu.*

(A) DHĀTU OR ROOT-FORM AND DERIVATIVES

√*cit* "perceiving, being conscious of" > *cit* adj "one cognizant, perceiving" or (f) "awareness, cognizance, perception"; *cití* "understanding", *citrá* "bright, excellent, variegated", *cétas* "splendour, intelligence" *caitanya* "consciousness"; verb forms – *cétati, cittá, cikéta, ácait*, etc. etc., where the principal or vowel gradation (*i*>*e*>*ai*) unfolds in regular order. We could take also √*ad* "eating", √*īś* "ruling", √*ṛc* "praising, reciting", √*krudh* "anger", √*jñā* "knowing", etc., etc. But compare S *hu* and Greek *cheo.*

S √*hu* "sacrificing, pouring into fire" > verb and noun forms *jú-hu-ati, hutá, hótum, hótṛ, hóma, áhauṣit* — etc., etc., where the principle of vowel gradation (*u*>*o*/*au*) unfolds regularly and beautifully. Now compare this with the chaos in —

> Greek *ché-o* "I pour" : *che-u ma* "flow, stream"; *chu-ma* "fluid";
>
> *cho-ē* "libation, pouring"; *chou-s* "earth, soil":
>
> root ? *che-, cho-, chū* - (–S *hu* > *juhóti*)?

Or compare another probable pair of cognations: –

> Sanskrit : *dhṛ dhariṣyáte, dadhré, dhṛtvā, dhṛtí, dhara, dhartṛ, dharṇaṣí, dhárma-, dhāra, dhāraṇa*, etc.
>
> Greek : *thranío* "stool", *thrónos* "throne", with vowels *a, o* but no root or verb.

(B) NEGATION & PROHIBITION

Some IE branches have *na/ne/no* for "do/must not" (e.g. Latin, Celtic, Slavic, Germanic.

Some have *mā/mi/me* (e.g. Tocharian, Armenian, Greek).

Sanskrit and Avestan have both *na* and *mā*.

(C) THE AUGMENT IN PAST TENSES.

Armenian had it (with initial consonant in monosyllabic stems only) and Greek had it: e.g. Arm *e-likh* "left", Gk *é-lipe* "left". On the other hand, Hittite (*dais* "he set"), Gothic and Old English (*band* "one bound") and others did not have it.

Vedic has both forms : *ábhet/bhét* "one feared", *ádur/dúr* "they gave", etc. However, it should be mentioned that Homeric Greek has some unaugmented forms (e.g. *philéesken* in §3 above) and so does the older Mycenaean language.

(D) PERFECT

Some branches did not have one (Toch, Arm).

(a) Reduplicated perf: Av. *ta-taś-a* "has fashioned"; Gk. *dé-dork-a* "I have seen"; Gmc. *hait-hait* "has been named".

(b) Simple perf: Av. *vaeδa*, Gmc. *wait* "has known"; Lat. *gnov-it* "has learnt, knows" (=S *jñā-*), etc.

(c) Periphrastic perf: (fem. form of) main verb + auxiliary verb –as in Engl. "*have*" aux + "*gone*" main. Ht: *markan* (main) + *harteni* (aux "cut you have").

Vedic and Avestan have all three perfect forms.

(E) SIGNIFICANT DIFFERENCE BETWEEN

VEDIC AND AVESTAN

Vedic redupl. : *ta-takṣa* "has fashioned", *da-darśa* "has seen"; Av. *tataśa*;

simple : *veda* "has known, knows"; Av. *vaeδda;*

periphr : *gamayā́ṁ cakāra* "has caused someone to go" (*AV* 18.27.2);

mantrayām sa (*Brāhmaṇas,* etc. "has advised": i.e. main verb, fem. acc sing + auxiliary *k* - "do", *as-* "be". BU in this form —

Av. has only with *ah-* (=S *as-* "be": *stara yeintīm* + *ah-* "must have corrupted".

Since Av. has only verb + aux *ah-*, this indicates that Av. separated from Vedic after Vedic developed *as-* as auxiliary. Otherwise Vedic would have aux *as-* first! Let us see.

Mainstream doctrine teaches that original homeland of IEs is the Pontic (South Russian) Steppe, just above the Black Sea. But the direction of movement should be reversed.

According to the mainstream Doctrine (the Aryan Invasion/Immigration Theory, actually), the Indo-Iranians formed one unified people then and moved to Iran passing from the Urals. Then the Indo-Aryans left the common Iranian homeland and moved into Saptasindhu *c.* 1500 BCE. (For a detailed discussion, see Bryant 2001.) But if this is true, then they should have had developed first the periphrastic perfect with auxiliary verb *as-* "to be" like the Iranians, and afterwards the aux *kr̥-*. This evidence shows that first they developed main verb + auxiliary *kṛ-* in *Atharvaveda* and long afterwards main verb + aux *as-* in the Brāhmaṇas. Since the Vedics and Iranians are supposed to have been together and since they certainly appear to share so many features in common, this means that they, the Iranians, left the common fold, not the IAs (Indo-Aryans)!

Avestan & Sanskrit Common Features

	Avestan	Sanskrit	
prohibitive	*mā*	*mā*	"must not";
perfect	*ta-taśa*	*ta-takṣa*	"has fashioned";
	vaδa	*veda*	"has known, knows";
noun	*haoma*	*soma*	"sacrificial drink";
	ahura	*asura*	"lord" (later S "demon");
country	*Haptahəndu*	*Sptasindhu*	"land of 7 rivers"

Now consider *-həndu* and *-sindhu.*

In Sanskrit the word *sindhu* has several related words: e.g. compounds *sindu-kṣit sindhu-ja, sindhu-pati*, etc. and derivatives like *saindhava,* and so on. It is thought to derive from the root *syand* "flowing" or *sidh* "reaching, having success". In Avestan *-həndu* stands isolated, and the word for river is commonly *θrāotah* (=S *srotas*) and *raodah.* This again is indicative of the Iranians moving away from the IAs and taking with them the memory that they had lived in a region with Seven Rivers. This was spotted even as early as Max Müller:

"Zoroastrians were a colony from northern India . . . [who] migrated westward to Arachosia and Persia" (1875: 248).[1]

I discuss this issue very extensively with much more evidence in "Vedic and Avestan" (Kazanas 2012).

5. There is Additional Evidence to Support the Movement Out of India

First, archaeologists like B. & R. Allchin (1997), Chakrabarti (1999), Kennedy (1995), M. Kenoyer (1998), Lal (2009 & 1984), Gupta (1984), Schaffer (1995 & 1999) and Lichtenstein (1999), McIntosh (2002), G. Possehl (2003) and all other experts in that area, find no evidence at all of any entry and certainly no invasion (Dales 1966! and many others thereafter) into Saptasindhu. The culture they unearthed there known as the Indus-Sarasvatī (or Indus Valley or Haṛappan), is a native one with unbroken continuity from the seventh millennium down to 600 BCE. Then, geneticists (e.g. Sahoo et al., 2006) now find that the genes spread out of India both to the north-west and south-east.

Second, there is the literary evidence of the Indic texts: — *ṚV* 4.1.3 & 7.76.4 say that

"We and our ancestors have always been here [in Saptasindhu]" — the Aṅgiras and Vasiṣṭha families.

Also *ṚV* 5.10.6 says:

"Our sages should pervade all regions (*víśvā ā́sās tariṣáni* " and "Aryan laws be diffused over the earth" in 10.65.11.

---

1. Müller did make several blunders, of course, in having the Aryans invade India and in assigning the *ṚV c.* 1200 — something which he repudiated later giving dates as early as 3000 and even 5000 BCE.

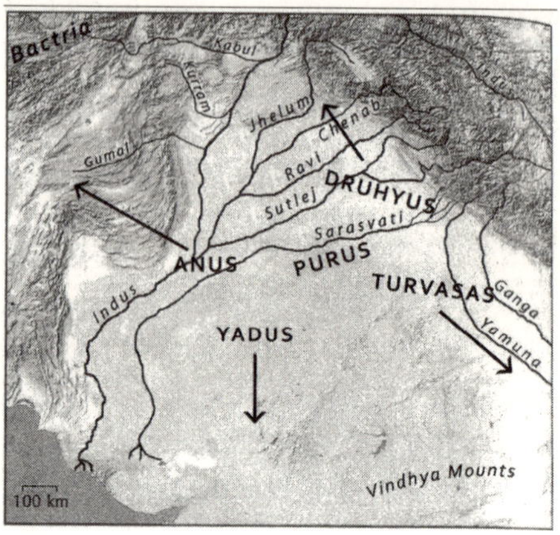

Thus they spread in all directions.

6.61.9, 12 says that Sarasvatī has spread us all (ie. the five tribes, Anus etc) beyond the Seven sister-rivers.

Baudhāyana's *Śrauta-Sūtra* 18.14 mentions two migrations: one eastward, the Āyava; one westward, the Āmāvasa

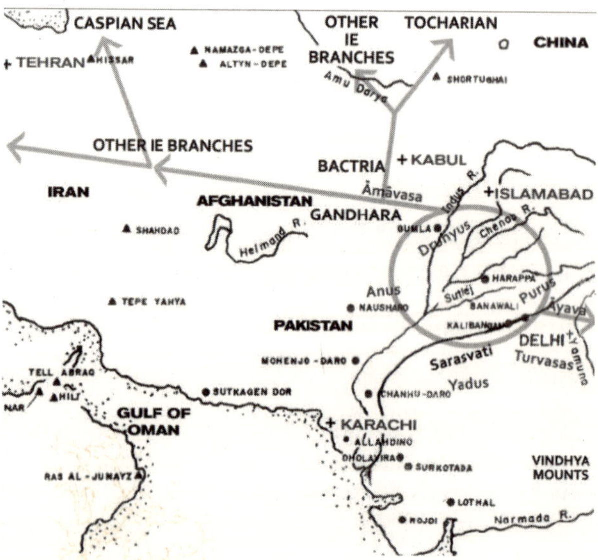

producing the Gāndhārīs, Parśus (=Persians) and Arāttas (=of Urartu and/or Ararat on the Caucausus).

Back in 1997 Johanna Nichols calculated on linguistic grounds that the area of dispersal of IE branches was Bactria.

As we saw this was part of the greater Saptasindhu after the Aryan tribes, mainly Anus and Druhyus, spread Westward. Now, back to the Ṛgvedic all-inclusiveness.

6. Eight Words of Closest Human Relations.

1. brother : S. *bhrā́tr̥*, Av. *brātār-*; Toch. *pracar;* Arm. *elbayr;* Gk. *phratēr;* It. *frātēr;* Celt. *brathir;* Gmc. *broðdar;* Sl. *bratrδ;* Lith. *broter-;* **Not Hit.** (**Note**: It. = Italic, mostly Latin.)
2. daughter : S. *duhitŕ̥;* Av. *dugδdar-/duδdar-*; Toch. *ckācar;* Arm. *dustr;* G. *thugáter;* It. *futir;* Gmc. *daúhtar;* Lith. *dukte* Sl. *d-ū́ti.* **Not Hit., Celt.**
3. father : S. *pitŕ̥* ; Av. *pitar/(p)tar-;* Toch. *pācar;* Arm. *hair;* Gk. *patēr* ; It. *pater;* Celt. *athir* ; Gmc. *fadar.* **Not Baltic (=Lith. or Lett.), Sl., Ht.**
4. husband, lord **:** S. *páti;* Av. *pa tiś;* Toch. *pats;* Gk. *posis;* It. *potis (*=capable); Gmc. *–fal̠(s);* Lith. *pats/patis;* Sl. –*podδ.* **Not Arm., Celt., Hit. (but Hit. *pat* -"just").**
5. mother : S. *mātŕ̥* ; Av. *mātār-;* Toch. *mācar;* Arm. *mair;* G. *mētēr;* It. *māter;* Celt. *māthir;* Gmc. *modor;* Sl. *mati.,* **Not Hit.; Lith. *mote* "wife".**
6. sister : S. *svásr̥* Av. *xvanhar;* Toch. *sar;* Arm. *k'oir;* It *soror;* Celt. *siur;* Gmc. *swister;* Lith. *sesuo;* Sl. *sestra.* **Not Hit.; Gk. *eór* "daughter".**
7. son : S. *sūnú;* Av. *hunuś;* Gmc. *sunus;* Lith. *sūnus* ; Sl. *synδ;* **Not Toch., Ht., Arm., G. (*hui-óζ?*), It., Celt.**
8. wife/mistress : S. *pátnī* ; Av. *paθnī;* G. *potnia;* Lith. -*patni* **Not Toch., Arm., Hit., It., Celt., Gmc., Sl.**

Only S. & Av. have them all. Hit. has none! Yet comparativists persist in calling Hittite the most archaic IE tongue! How is it possible not to have even one of these nouns for the most common of human relations yet be the most archaic IE tongue? Why would all the others innovate suddenly? (One Anatolian language does have a cognate for "sister". This is not of help to Hittite.)

7. Philosophy: One and Many

For last, but certainly not least, I have left a philosophical subject. There are many more issues: cosmogony and anthropogony, reincarnation, ethics and the like. But consideration of all these issues would take much much longer. So let us look at only one more aspect. There are many cosmogonies in the *ṚV* but underlying them all is the idea of One from which arise the Many. Obviously there is polytheism with many gods; also henotheism, as one clan or family *gotra* worships a particular deity and ascribes to him (or her, in the case of Aditi or Jñāna/Vāc) the emergence of the creation. But there are also several references to the One from which all deities arise: so there is also monotheism or the one Absolute.

SUMMARY

Polytheism : many deities as in all other IE branches.

Henotheism: one clan worships a particular deity and this is said to be the best (and creator).

Monotheism: all deities, all worlds, all creatures come from One, which remains unmanifest.

Deities have divinity only by partaking of the power of the One.

> *mahád devā́nām asuratvám ékam* 3.55: "single and great is the high-lord-power of the gods" (in which they partake to be gods or *asuras*).

1.164.6: *ékam sád víprā bahudhá vadanti* (also 10.114.5): "it is One but the sages call it by many expressions."

10.90 : everything is produced from Puruṣa's parts.

10.129 *Nāsadīya: ā́nid avātám svadháyā* ***tád ékam*** : "that One breathed without air of its own".

8.58.2 *ékam vāidáṃ víbabhuva sárvam.* "Being One it became all". 3.54.8 *éjad dhruváṁ patyate ékam víśvam, cárat patatṛ́ vīṣuṇaṃ víjātám.* "Moving yet unmoving the One rules the whole, what walks and flies, all this manifests multiplicity".

8. Obviously, when the IE speakers that emerge from the mists of pre-historic Europe and come to be known as Greeks, Germans, Celts, etc., they are barbarians, fond of war, pillage and conquest. The *R̥V* also speaks frequently of war and battles. Here the weapon of victory is more often than not *Brāhman*, the mystic power inherent in ritual and prayer, an inner force of the spirit or "silent meditation" as Puhvel calls it (1989: 153 in referring to Sage Atri's rehabilitation of the sun (*R̥V* 5, 40, 6). This is the power used by the Sage Vasiṣṭha when helping King Sudās defeat his numerous enemies (*R̥V* 7,33) and, of course, by the R̥bhus when accomplishing the wondrous deeds that earned them godhood. And hymn 6, 75, 19 says "My closest/inner armour is *Brahman*" (=this same mystic power). This very word *Brahman* becomes, not without good reason, the name of the Absolute in post-R̥gvedic literature, mainly the Upaniṣads. Yet, the Absolute is not entirely absent from the *R̥V*, as Keith observed: ". . . India developed the conception of a power common to the various gods . . . just as the unity of the gods even by the time of certain R̥gvedic hymns" (1925: 446).

Hymn R̥V 10, 90, shows how creatures and world-elements are produced from different parts of the Puruṣa, the primordial Man: thus multiplicity comes from unity. More so, the Nāsadīya hymn 10, 129, describes the evolution of the whole creation including the gods from the One *ekam*. Taking cosmogonic myths from Iran, Greece, Rome and/or North Europe, some scholars rightly state that the creation arises from two primordial elements, "the action of heat on water", and that this "reflects a multi-layered dualism that pervades Indo-European myth and religion" (Stone 1997, ch. 5; see also Puhvel 1989: 277. But in the *R̥V Creation Hymn* 10,129, it is out of the One alone, breathing without air, of Its own power (*ā́nid av táṃ svadháyā tád ékam*), that arose all else; only in the third stanza appears *salilám* (water?) and *tápas* (heat?)[2] within *támas* "darkness", within *tuchyá* "void"; and then follows one existence, desire and so on. Here at least it is the Unity that is the basic primordial substratum. This is no different from the Absolute of the Upaniṣads. And this we meet in other hymns also. R̥V 8, 58, 2 says *ékam vā idáṃ ví babhūva sárvam* "It being One has variously (*vī*) become this All (and Everything)'. Hymns 1,164,6 and 10,114,5, say that the wise poets speak of It, being One, in many ways/forms — naming it Agni, Yama, Indra, etc. Thus the different divinities are the manifestations of that One. This is reinforced by the acknowledgement that the gods are gods by virtue of a single godhood or god-power, as the refrain in 3,55, states plainly: *mahád devā́nām asuratvám ékam* "Single is the great god-power (*asuratva* of the gods". Utilizing different material in the *R̥gveda*, K. Werner makes the same point (1989).

2. I put question-marks because I feel certain, against the received notions, that *salila* here does not mean "water" but "flux of energy" generally and *tapas* "power of transformation" — as I argue in my 2009 (pp. 86-87 and note 1; or ch. 2, §11). I repeat here that there is still nothing material in this third stanza within "darkness" *tamas* and "void" *tuchyā*.

This notion of a Single One, of which all divine and mundane phenomena are manifestations, is absent from all other IE branches. Thus the Vedic Aryas, far from being bloodthirsty or primitive barbarians deifying out of fear natural phenomena like the storm or the fire, would seem to belong among the most highly cultured people on earth with a culture that consisted not so much of material artefacts as of inner spiritual power.

9. Conclusion

I have not spoken explicitly of the origins of Indian Civilization. It should be obvious, however, that I regard the rise of the Vedic Culture as indigenous and not the result of an (Aryan or proto-Indo-European) invasion or immigration.

I cannot speak of the origin of this civilization because I do not know it. And I don't think anybody else does. Of course, as is usual, there are many theories and many publications. Archaeologists and anthropologists tell us of an unbroken continuity in the remains excavated in Saptasindhu. This seems to start at the beginning of the seventh millennium BCE. But these are the grossest indications in stone, wood, mud and bricks. They certainly bespeak of a civilizations but do not tell us very much. To my mind a civilization is a condition of society and an inner state of man which promotes civility, consideration for others, honesty, justice, liberality, unity with the creation and the Creator and a general nobility as close to absolute goodness as possible. (For a discussion of different views on civilization see Kazanas & Klostermaier 2012.) These qualities of civilizations are found, I believe, in the *Ṛgveda* and are spelled out explicitly and repeatedly in the various post-Ṛgvedic texts. Some of the motifs of the *RV* have been described adequately in this paper.

No, I do not know much about the origin of Indic civilization because, having its start in remote prehistory, it is not so evident. But one literary jewel of the Vedic culture, the *Bhagavad-Gītā*, says *ṛdhvam lam adhas kham* (15.1): creation has its roots high in heaven and its boughs and leaves here below. I would think the same applies to the Indic civilization.

References

Allchin, B.R., 1997, *Origins of Civilization*, Delhi: Viking Penguins.

Bryant, E., 2001, *The Quest for the Origins of Vedic Culture*, Oxford: Oxford University Press.

Chakrabarti, D., 1999, *India: An Archaeological History*, Cambridge (U.K.): Cambridge Uiversity Press.

Dales, G., 1966, "The ecline of the Harappans", *Scientific American*, vol. 241(92-9).

Elizarenkova, T., 1995, *Language & Style of the Vedic Ṛṣis* (tr. Wendy Doniger), NY: SUNY Press.

Kazanas, N., 2009, *Indo-Aryan Origins and Other Vedic Issues*, Delhi: Aditya Prakashan.

———, 2012, "Vedic and Avestan" in *Vedic Venues* 1 (Delhi).

Kazanas, N. & K. Klostermaier, 2012, "Vedic Civilization and its Spread" in *Vedic Venues* 1 (Delhi).

Keith, A.B., 1925, *The Religion and Philosophy of the Veda & Upaniṣads*, 2 vols, Delhi: Motilal Banarsidass (1989 rpt. of Harvard Oriental Series).

Kennedy, K., 1995, "Have Aryans been Identified in the Prehestoric Skeletal Record from South Asia?" in G. Erdosy, *The Indo-Aryans of Ancient South Asia* Berlin: De Guyter.

Kenoyer, M., 1998, *Ancient Cities of the Indus Valley Civilization* Karachi/Oxford: Oxford University Press.

Lal, B.B., 2009, *How Deep are the Roots of India Civilization?*, Delhi: Books International.

Lal, B.B. & S.P. Gupta (eds.), 1984, *Frontiers of the Indus Civilization* Delhi: Indian Archaeological Society.

McIntosh, J.R., 2001, *A Peaceful Realm* Boulder (Colorado), Westview.

Müller, F. Max, 1859, *The History of Ancient Sanskrit Literature*, London, Williams & Norgate.

———, 1875, *The Science of Language* New York: Scribner.

Nichols, Johana, 1997 (-1998), "The Epicentre of the IE Linguistic

Spread' in Blench & M. Spriggs, *Archaeology & Language* NY/ London: Routledge, vol. 1 (122-48).

Possehl, G., 2003, *The Indus Civilization*, Roman & Littlefield (Non NBN); Delhi: Vistaar.

Puhvel, J., 1989 (1987), *Comparative Mythology*, Baltimore: John Hopkins University Press.

Sahoo et al., 2006, "A Prehistory of Indian Y-chromosomes", *Proceedings of the National Academy of Sciences (USA)*, vol. 103, no. 4, pp. 843-48.

Shaffer J., 1995, "The Cultural Tradition and Palaeoethincity in South Asian archaeology", in G. Erdosy (ed.), *The Indo-Aryans of Ancient South Asia* Berlin/NY: de Gruyter.

Shaffer J. & Lichtenstein D. 1999, "Migration, Philology and South Asian Archaeology", in J. Bronkhorst and M. Deshpande (eds) *Aryan and Non-Aryan in South Asia* Cambridge (Mass.), H.O.S. (pp. 1-18).

Stone, A., 1997, *Ymir's Flesh*, Loughborough (U.K.): Heart of Albion Press.

Watkins, C., 2001, *How to Kill a Dragon* (1995), Oxford: Oxford University Press.

Werner, K., 1989, "From Polytheism to Monism . . ." *Cosmos*, vol. 5, *Polytheistic Systems*, ed. G. Davies, Edinburg University Press (12-27).

3

Some Unlikely Tentacles of Early Indo-European

Koenraad Elst

Abstract

Contacts of Indo-European languages and of their putative ancestor Proto-Indo-European with other languages have been posited and studied for almost two centuries, chiefly those with the Semitic and Uralic families. Here, we look into the *status quaestionis* of such research concerning other language families, where a historic contact with Indo-European is less likely. We find some "Western"-looking languages to be seriously anchored far to the east of the Euro-Asian border, a fact probably rich in implications for the Homeland question. Conversely, we discover some indications for east-to-west and south-to-north movements. Given the complexity and large scale of the history of Indo-European expansion, we must none the less-caution against drawing facile or sweeping conclusions from these findings.

1. Introduction

1.1. THE HOMELAND QUESTION

In the old search for the *Urheimat* or Homeland of the Indo-European (IE) language[1] family, where the putative ancestral

1. Note on transcription: For reconstructed forms, in principle we reproduce whatever form a quoted author has used,

→

language Proto-Indo-European (PIE) was spoken, the dominant paradigms locating it either to the North or to the West of the Caucasus mountains, in the Pontic steppe *casu quo* in Anatolia, have recently been challenged by a revival of the oldest contender, the Out-of-India Theory (OIT). Indeed, even before the birth of IE linguistics, French sceptical philosopher Voltaire (1777, letter of 15 December 1775) mused that the origin of European civilization lay in India: "I am convinced that everything has come down to us from the banks of the Ganges, astronomy, astrology, metempsychosis, etc." Among the first Indo-Europeanist scholars, Friedrich Schlegel (1808) considered India as the Homeland of the European languages and culture.

In the course of the nineteenth century, India fell out of favour, and the Homeland was shifted westward, to Bactria at least (Friedrich Max Müller's preference), to the Pontic steppes (V. Gordon Childe, Marija Gimbutas, James Mallory and now most Western experts), South Caucasus (Thomas Gamkrelidze and Vyacheslav Ivanov), Anatolia (Colin Renfrew) or even North-Central Europe (lately still upheld by Lothar Kilian). From the Indian viewpoint, these scenarios all imply that the Indo-Aryan branch of the IE family was brought in from outside by "Aryan invaders". Therefore, among Indians and India-watchers, the different versions of European or West-Asian Homeland hypotheses are jointly called the Aryan Invasion Theory (AIT).

The Indian answer to the AIT has been called the OIT, a term which to our knowledge was coined by US scholar Edwin Bryant *c.* 1996, when he was writing his PhD dissertation on

→ otherwise we follow the system used in Mallory & Adams (2006). But we are aware that different systems are in competition, in keeping with rivalling theories; and that these reconstructions can never be more than approximative. Surely scholars of historical and comparative linguistics can always guess which form is meant.

this dispute. He assumed the kinship and (at least partial) common origin of the IE languages as a given, with the implication that either its non-Indian branches originated in (and expanded or emigrated from) a Homeland in India or the Indian branch(es) moved into India from a non-Indian Homeland; so denying the AIT automatically implied positing the OIT. But this describes the position of only a section, or rather two sections, of Indian anti-AIT opinion.

On the one hand, a non-academic group of Hindu nationalists, starring the late P.N. Oak, assert that more or less everything of value in the world was brought or created by ancient emigrants from India. Thus, England really is the Hindu colony *Angulisthāna*, the Vatican was founded as *Veda-Vāṭikā*, and Dutch is the language of the *daitya*s. We need not discuss that school of thought in any more detail here. On the other hand, a very small handful of scholars, especially Misra (2005) and Talageri (2000, 2009), have tried in right earnest to build a case for a scenario in which emigration from an Indian Homeland explains the presence of IE languages outside India.

However, most Indian scholars who oppose the AIT, both professional and amateur, including hundreds of archaeologists, confine their effort to refuting the Aryan invasion of India. Their horizon stops at the Khyber Pass, questions about the IE languages outside the subcontinent simply are not an issue for them. This neither-immigration-nor-emigration position is definitely the most popular answer to the AIT among Indians (e.g. Lal 2008, Kalyanaraman 2010). When pressed for an explanation for the commonalities between Indo-Aryan and the European languages, they tend to insist that mutual borrowing between otherwise unrelated languages can take care of the unmistakable similarities (e.g. Waradpande 1989). Whoever has studied the linguistic data and method more closely than they have, cannot follow them down that road.

1.2. STATUS OF PROTO-INDO-EUROPEAN

In the debate for and against the AIT, the science of historical and comparative linguistics itself has been questioned. N.S. Rajaram dismisses comparative and historical linguistics, which generated the AIT, as "a scholarly discipline that had none of the checks and balances of a real science" (1995: 144), in which "a conjecture is turned into a hypothesis to be later treated as a fact in support of a new theory" (1995: 217).

The scientific status of historical disciplines is inevitably precarious, mainly because their object cannot be subjected to repeatable experiment. Worse, it isn't even really there and can only be inferred secondarily from an uneven set of data, such as fossils for dinosaurs. In the case of historical linguistics, the same problem exists: just as no fossil researcher has ever seen a dinosaur, no linguist has ever heard a single native speaker utter a sentence of PIE, proto-Sino-Tibetan, proto-Draviḍian or any other reconstructed language deemed to be the common origin of a whole family of existing languages. IE linguists work on the assumption that Sanskrit *pitā*, Latin *pater* and English *father* have all developed from a common PIE Ur-form **pater* or **ph²ter*, but the asterisk represents an honest admission that this is an unattested, purely reconstructed form, rather less than a scientific fact.

Today, IE reconstruction is under attack from different sides, and its uncertain scientific status is a popular target for its critics. These include eccentric linguistic alternatives such as the Palaeolithic Continuity Theory taught by Alinei (1996) *cum suis*, which holds that the IE languages have evolved extremely slowly and been established more or less in their present habitats since before the Ice Age; and, in India, those in the anti-AIT camp who reason that since the AIT is both wrong and based on IE reconstruction, the latter must be wrong, either wrong on specifics or flawed as a project. This Indian school also likes to cite the Western authors who reject the reconstruction of an ancestral PIE language by way of belated reaction to the political misuse of the notion of "Indo-Europeans", thus denying implicitly or explicitly that such a community speaking the same language ever existed, e.g. Lincoln (1999) and Arvidsson (2006). But in fact, the modern political use allegedly made of a previously developed historical-linguistic theory has no impact whatsoever on the rightness or otherwise of the theory. Further, there is nothing particularly right-wing about the mere notion of a PIE speech community, as shown by its expert treatment under the hands of left-wing authors like Martinet (1986) and Sergent (1995).

Indeed, originally the theory of a common ancestral prehistory between Europe's languages and those of "the so-called Niggers of India" gave, according to F. Max Müller (1883: 28), "a shock to prejudices most deeply ingrained in the mind of every educated man". The common ancestry of the Indians (or "Aryans" as Rudyard Kipling called them), and Europeans, while soon used by the British colonizer as a justification for the Empire, was also welcomed by many in the Indian freedom movement as a basis for equality and hence decolonization. It is Eurocentric to confine the political dimension of the IE discovery to colonialism and Nazism; and it is unscholarly to let the truth of a theory depend on its ulterior political use and abuse. So, while taking note of these criticisms of our discipline and its masterpiece, IE reconstruction, we intend to stay on course and work within the framework of comparative-historical linguistics.

1.3. LINGUISTIC PALAEONTOLOGY

One of the reasons for the nineteenth-century philologists to exclude India as a candidate for Homeland status, for which it had been the first favourite, was the findings of a fledgling new method called *linguistic palaeontology*. The idea was that from the reconstructed vocabulary, one could deduce which flora, fauna and artefacts were familiar to the speakers of the proto-language, hence also their geographical area of habitation. The presence in the common vocabulary of words denoting northern animals like the bear, wolf, elk, otter and beaver seemed to indicate a northern Homeland; likewise, the absence of terms for the lion or elephant seemed to exclude subtropical countries like India. A West/Central-European Homeland was also famously deduced from the existence of the IE-looking word *beech* (**bhag-o-s*) in the IE family, though only in its West- and North-European branches.

Linguistic palaeontology has gone out of fashion because it was realized that its characteristic reasoning tends to be circular. After all, if IE-speakers originated in North-western Europe, they could have forgotten the *beech* word once they left beech-rich territory (as in Tocharian and Indo-Iranian) or given it a new meaning (as in Greek, where the word refers to another tree species, a type of oak); but conversely, if they entered Europe from outside, only those branches settling in Europe would develop a word for the beech, most likely borrowed from the autochthonous population, and assimilate it into their own phonetic system. The latter phase would already account for the differences in the shape the word takes in the various neighbouring branches of IE, where it would undergo all the subsequent developments characteristic of that branch. So, the distribution of the beech word is compatible with both scenarios: of a European and of a non-European origin. Hence Zimmer's (1990) farewell: "The long dispute about the reliability of this 'linguistic palaeontology' is not yet finished, but approaching its inevitable end — with a negative result, of course."

But while many linguists have given up on this approach, some still soldier on. To the extent that linguistic palaeontology is still practised, its early conclusions about the Homeland have not quite been confirmed. Among those who remain more optimistic about its good uses, the most comprehensive and innovative have been Thomas Gamkrelidze & Vyacheslav Ivanov (1995). They have reconstructed PIE forms for the names of the camel, monkey, elephant, lion and leopard in support of a more southerly Homeland hypothesis, viz. south of the caucasus. Thus, they connect Sanskrit *pṛdaku* with Latin *pardus* and Hittite *parsana*, all meaning "leopard", an IE term lost in the northern branches spoken in regions devoid of leopards. Under the hands of the Soviet scholars, "lion" is found to be a native word with regular phonetic correspondences in Greek, Italic, Germanic and Hittite; as well as, with the vaguer meaning "beast", in Slavic and Tokharic. Given the subtropical habitat of this sample of animals, India would be an equally valid candidate (precise quote).

Climate is a tricky factor here, because virtually all IE-speaking areas are familiar with the cold climate and its flora and fauna. In hot countries, the mountainous areas provide islands of cold climate. You don't find palm trees in the foothills of the Himalaya but pine trees. Indians are therefore quite familiar with a range of flora and fauna usually associated with the north, including bears (Sanskrit *ṛkṣa*, cfr. Greek *arktos*), otters (Sanskrit *udra*, Hindi *ūd* or *ūdbilāv*, the latter now also used for the foreign beaver) and wolves (*vṛka*). Elks and beavers do not live in India, yet the words exist in Indo-Aryan form with a different but related meaning. The elk-related word *ṛsa* means a male antelope, and the shift of meaning may have taken place in either direction. As for the name *beaver* and its Sanskrit equivalent *babhru*, thereby hangs an entire tale.

Its un-reduplicated PIE root **bher-o-* means "brown", and has yielded the animal names Skt. *bhallūka*, Eng. *bear*. The reduplicated form **bhebhro-*, roughly "brownie", yields English *beaver*, also ultimately meaning simply "the brown one". Its Vedic form *babhru* is only attested with the meaning "brown", especially as a colour of horses, but in classical Sanskrit it means

6. Dr Koenraad Elst and Dr Girish Nath Jha on a panel

"mongoose" (an English word that is itself derived through Marathi from Draviḍian), or at least a type of mongoose, the ichneumon. Its use in that meaning is not attested in Vedic, but not impossible either. What Allen (1999: 25) says about culture may be valid for word meanings too:

> [M]any have realized the Vedic texts relate to only a small part of the culture of the Vedic period. But it is much less realized how much comparison can do to fill out the picture and identify the material that bypassed the Vedas.

Perhaps the mongoose was already called "brownie" in the Vedic period, but "bypassed" attestation in the Vedic literature, which is finite in volume and capacity after all.

But even if *babhru* only had its core colour meaning in Vedic, that may still tell us something. According to Gamkrelidze & Ivanov (1995: 448),

> . . . reduplicated derivatives of the colour term mean 'beaver' only in a sharply limited dialect group which includes the later European dialects (Baltic, Slavic, Germanic, Italic, Celtic) and Avestan. This is apparently an innovation, one having to do with the particular ecological environment, by speakers of these dialects. It is notable that the Indo-Iranian languages are split by this isogloss: Sanskrit shows the more archaic situation, while Avestan displays the innovation.

Because Sanskrit was still located in the "archaic" environment where once PIE was spoken?

Now, consider another animal name, based on PIE **eghi-* "snake", whence Sanskrit *ahi*, Greek *ekhis*:

> This latter term forms the basis for the term for a species of hedgehog, lit. 'snake-eater' (apparently the reference was to a mongoose, which kills poisonous snakes): Gk. *ekhinos*, 'hedgehog', (. . .) Old English *igil* (German *Igel*), 'hedgehog'.
>
> — Gamkrelidze & Ivanov 1994: 444

This implies that the linguistic ancestors of the Germanic-speakers came from a region where snake-eating mongooses lived, to their historic habitat where this animal is unknown, and there transferred its name to a local animal, the hedgehog. Not quite decisive in the Homeland debate, but a telling indication none the less.

1.4. SENIORITY OF SANSKRIT

The Sanskrit names of many purely Indian animals have IE etymologies: *mahiṣa* "buffalo"; *pṛśati*, "spotted deer"; *hastin, vāraṇa, gaja* "elephant". For the elephant, only *ibha* is accepted in Mallory & Adams (2006: 141) as PIE **yebh*, cfr. Latin *ebur*, "ivory"; the others are Indo-Aryan coinages. Thus, *mahiṣa* is "the strong one", *pṛśatī* is "the spotted one", *hastin* is "the one with the hand", referring to the dextrous elephant's trunk, *gaja* (from *garj-*) is "the trumpeter". The standard pro-AIT analysis is that these "artificial" descriptive coinages indicate a need to give names to new phenomena unfamiliar to the invading Indo-Aryans. However, the procedure is equally common throughout IE.

Thus, as we already saw, *beaver* and *bear* both mean "the brown one"; **kasnos*, English *hare*, Sanskrit *sasa*, means "the grey one"; Slavic *medv-ed* or Sanskrit *madhv-ad* "bear", means "honey-eater"; Latin *homo* "human being" is "the earth-dweller" (cfr. Hebrew: *adam* = "man", *adamah* = "earth"); Greek *ikhthys* "fish" has been analysed as "the netherworld-dweller" (cfr. *khthon* "soil"), while Sanskrit *matsya* "fish" means "the wet one". Surely the PIE-speakers were familiar with fish, let alone with human beings? In Scandinavian poetry, this type of circumlocution is called a *kenning*, and many of these kennings have passed into ordinary language. This procedure must have been used to devise names for new phenomena, but followed established practice for perfectly familiar objects, so that many ordinary words are on closer analysis kennings dusted over by long usage.

Sometimes an animal name is more transparent of its kenning origin in Sanskrit as compared with the other IE languages. This is seen, e.g. in the fact that one term can still denote two different animals which have the same eponymous trait: *pṛdāku* can mean both "snake" and "leopard", from their common trait "spotted", whereas the Latin and Hittite equivalents *"pardus" casu quo "parsana"* refer only to the latter animal and have ceased being transparent of an etymon meaning "spotted".

This is equally true outside the zoological realm, e.g. *nāma* "name", present in most IE branches as a root in its own right, has a yet deeper root in Sanskrit, viz. the verb *nam-āmi*, "to address, greet" (whence the salute *namaste*). Other languages may have verbs *derived* from the "name" substantive, such as Latin *nominare* from *nomen*, but only in Sanskrit can the substantive itself be derived from a simpler verbal root. Here, the relation of Sanskrit to the other IE languages follows the pattern of that between a donor language of loanwords and the receptor languages. Thus, the English word *khaki*, "soil-coloured, green-brown", is not derived from a more basic root within the language; but in the donor language, Persian (through Urdu), it is a derivative of *xāk* "earth, soil". As if the other branches started as the languages of different groups of outsiders who adopted PIE as *lingua franca* but missed some of the finesse of its native users.

In this regard, as in many others (e.g. retaining a complete system of three grammatical numbers, three *genera* and eight cases), Sanskrit seems closer to reconstructed PIE than any other of the latter's daughter languages. This need not prove anything about the Homeland, nor does it prove that Sanskrit is itself the PIE mother language, as Hindu nationalists might eagerly deduce. It may merely mean that Sanskrit is attested at an earlier stage. That at least is the linguistic equivalent of the answer concerning mythology frequently given to the demonstration by Nicholas Kazanas (2009: 116-47), that the reconstructed IE pantheon has been much better preserved in Sanskrit literature than in the other branches. Critics argued: if you consider the Indian pantheon *c.* CE 1000, contemporaneous with the North-Germanic *Edda*, you find that many of the IE and Vedic gods have disappeared from sight, and if you somehow got access to the Germanic pantheon as it was in the Vedic Age, it would very probably resemble the reconstructed PIE situation a lot better than in the medieval accounts.

However, there is nothing "mere" about attesting Sanskrit's higher age. In the common AIT chronology, Vedic is not older than two other preserved IE languages: Hittite (which resembles reconstructed PIE only dimly, both in language and in religion) and Mycenaean Greek. If Sanskrit must be older than those two, implying it was spoken beyond 2000 BCE, that already upsets the established chronology of IE dispersion to a serious extent.

1.5. THE HORSE VOCABULARY

One question where linguistic palaeontology has had an interesting say, is the position of the horse in IE history. The one credible attempt to give **ekwos* roots in the basic PIE vocabulary, is through Greek *ōkus*, and Sanskrit *āśu*, "fast", related to Balto-Slavic *aśu*, "sharp" (Lehmann 1997: 247). This leads to an interpretation of the name of the horse as "the fast one" (Meid 1989: 15), though the derivation could also be reversed. Likewise, the Germanic word *horse* means "the runner", cognate to Latin *currere*, "run". So, those who see artificial coinage of Indian tree and animal names in Sanskrit as proof of the speakers' unfamiliarity with the trees and animals in question, should also deduce that this artificial coinage indicates the foreignness of the horse to the original PIE-speakers in their Homeland.

Another thing remarked about **ekwos* is that it belongs to a younger type of word formation in IE. To take two momentous inventions, the IE words for "fire" (**egni-, *pūr, *āter*) belong to the older category, while the words for "wheel" (**rot-o-s, *kwekwl-o-s*) belong to the younger type, which indicates that the wheel was newly invented or newly adopted from neighbouring peoples by the PIEs, whereas the use of fire was already an ancient heritage.

Coming to livestock: **gwou-* "cow", and **su-* "pig" (whence later the diminutive **su-in-o*, "swine", which is of the younger type) belong to the older category, while **ekw-o-s* "horse", belongs to the younger category. Some scholars deduce from this that the pig and the cow were domesticated earlier than the horse, which happens to tally with the archaeological data. But it might just as well be interpreted as an indication that the horse not only was not domesticated by the earliest PIEs, but was also simply not known to them. After all, the inhabitants of the areas where horses were available for domestication, must have known the horse since much earlier, as a wild animal on a par with the wolf and the deer, and they would have had an ancient name for it. We shouldn't give too much weight to this, since **wlkw-o*, that old "wolf", also belongs to the younger type. But if it matters at all that the term for "horse" is a younger formation (Meid 1989: 14), it would indicate that the horse was not native to the Urheimat, and that the PIEs only got acquainted with it, as with the wheel, around the time of their dispersal. In that case, India was a better candidate for Urheimat status than the horse-rich steppes.

Thirdly, **ekwos* has materialized rather differently and irregularly in the different branches of IE, e.g. with an unaccounted-for initial aspiration in Greek *hippos*. As Witzel says about similar irregularities in the word for "lion": "The *irregular* sound correspondences (. . .) are typical for loanwords, not for original, inherited PIE vocabulary." (Witzel 2005: 391, emphasises this). If these irregularities in the various evolutes of **ekwos* are taken to indicate that it "was borrowed, possibly even independently in some of the dialects" (Lehmann 1997: 247), this would again confirm that the horse was a newcomer in the expanding PIE horizon. This would, however, imply that the related meaning "fast" was derivative from and not the root of the horse word *ekwos*; this is in fact plausible, since the long — or lengthened — vowel in *āśu* tends to indicate derivation.

Add to this the observation by Polomé that no term has come down from PIE for the antler-cheek pieces with the attached bridle, the major implement used in horse-riding and "found in the earliest IE settlements", or at least those which Marija Gimbutas considered *ur*-IE, viz. in the Kurgan culture of the Pontic steppe. Those proverbial Aryan horsemen roaming the Kurgan-studded steppes may not have been IE-speakers at all. And:

> Neither is there a common Indo-European term for 'riding a horse', though 'riding a vehicle' is expressed by **wegh-*, documented in all the major Indo-European languages, also as the common root for a wheeled vehicle. (. . .) No doubt the first carts were drawn by cattle, but these were soon replaced with horses.
>
> — Polomé 1982: 158

The first vehicles predated both the integration of the horse in the IE-speakers' lifestyle and the disintegration of PIE into its daughter languages. The importance of the horse as the defining animal of the IE expansion has been overdone.

1.5. LANGUAGE MEETS LANGUAGE

After this brief consideration of what the relation between languages and the real world can (and cannot) teach us about the language's itinerary, this paper will consider what we can learn from the relation of languages with other languages.

However, here we will not go into the isoglosses of and exchanges between the different branches of the IE family itself. This IE dialectology is one of the main themes of Gamkrelidze and Ivanov's *magnum opus* (1995) and of an important paper by Hock (1999). On the latter, which finds the dialectal distribution far better compatible with an AIT than with an OIT, replies have been written by Elst (2007: 28-35) and Talageri (2009: 205-73).

Instead, we will meditate a little on the exchanges between PIE or early branches of IE with languages genetically unrelated to IE, or related only at an unfathomable time-depth. Even here, we will not take upon ourselves the task of analysing the relation between IE and Uralic. This is admittedly the most important chapter in any treatment of the Homeland-related linguistic evidence, if only because AIT advocates (e.g. Witzel 2003) uphold it as the decisive and unassailable evidence in favour of the AIT. To add substantially to and improve substantively on our earlier discussion of it (Elst 1999: 135-40), we will need to give it our attention in a separate and extensive endeavour.

For now, we will limit ourselves to studying the contacts between IE and some other more peripheral language families. From these sometimes eccentric ventures, modest but real indications can be deduced about the family's Homeland and the early itinerary of its daughter languages.

2. Indo-European and Chinese

Let us start our survey in a far corner of the IE expansion zone: China. The thesis of a close proximity between IE and Chinese was first put forward in 1871 by Joseph Edkins in his work *China's Place in Philology: An Attempt to show that the Language of Europe and Asia have a Common Origin*. (Chang 1988: 1) He presented a number of Chinese words similar to those of IE as being very early loans. Since then, many Sinologists have worked on reconstructing the mediaeval and archaic readings of Chinese characters. The great milestone was Bernard Karlgren's comprehensive phonological and etymological dictionary, *Grammata Serica* (1940). Since the publication of Julius Pokorny's IE etymological dictionary, the *Indo-Germanisches Etymologisches Wörterbuch* (1959), the two came to be laid side by side for the sake of lexical comparison. In 1967, an unaffiliated German scholar, Jan Ulenbrook, published an article that revived the search where Edkins had left it.

2.1. GENETIC OR ADSTRATAL RELATION?

Two distinct lines of thought have developed since then. A handful of scholars try for the more ambitious option, viz. identifying a common origin of Chinese and IE, a kind of "Sino-European" stage in linguistic development from which Chinese and IE went their separate ways. Pulleyblank (1993: 106-07) upholds "the possibility of a genetic connection between Sino-Tibetan and IE" all while admitting that it is "inconsistent with a European or Anatolian homeland for the IEs but it is much less so with the Kurgan theory", especially considering that the *Kurgan* (grave-hill) culture of the steppe "was not the result of local evolution in that region but had its source in an intrusion from an earlier culture farther east". But his and other tentative hypotheses of a deep kinship of Chinese with IE, as also with North-Caucasian and Austronesian, have been refuted in sufficient measure by Vovin (1997) and will not detain us here. Of course, at a time depth of Nostratic or whichever prehistoric kinship, many connections can be thought up, but to the same extent, geographical movements of populations may have taken place over the same millennia. Therefore, even plausible or proven linguistic connections at such time-depth cannot decide the geographical land of origin that interests us here.

More promising is the more modest approach, viz. to identify a much larger number of instances of early borrowing by Chinese from IE. This mainly concerns neighbouring Tocharian, of which seven loans have been identified by Lubotsky (1998) in the sphere of town- and chariot-building. Gamkrelidze & Ivanov (1995: 828-29) give another five from the field of cattle-raising, including the well-known case of *mi* "honey", cfr. Tocharian-B *mit*; and surprisingly also *zhu* "pig" (a very Chinese animal kept by farmers and typically held in contempt by cowherds), cfr. Tocharian-B *suwo*. Rarely the exchange may involve Iranian, for long the *lingua franca* across Central Asia, probably *śer* > *shizi*, "lion". The search for links involving other branches was taken up in right earnest by the late Chang Tsung-tung, a Taiwanese linguist teaching in Frankfurt.

In Chang's list (1988: 5-25, 37-38), we find more items from the IE specialism of cattle-raising, words for swine, sow, goose, cow, goat, bee, etc. Thus, *quan* "dog" < *khuen* (we reproduce his often unorthodox reconstructions), related to **kon*, whence Latin *canis*, English *hound*; and *huang* "yellow", related to PIE **konek*, cfr. Greek *knèkos* "pale yellow", and English *honey*. He connects *ma* "horse" with a PIE form **mark*, whence Irish *marc*, English *mare* (without remarking on the emerging regular correspondence to Sanskrit *marka* "swift"); note that both the Germano-Celtic and the Chinese forms are more usually derived from Altaic, with final *-k* as an Altaic diminutive suffix (Gamkrelidze & Ivanov 1985: 182), though Sergent (1995: 398) derives both the Chinese and Altaic form from IE **mark-*. This sample falls within the conventional wisdom that the Chinese farmers adopted cattle-raising skills from IEs.

2.2. THE FAIR YELLOW EMPEROR

But Chang goes a lot farther and includes hundreds of items from the general vocabulary, both in the material, physiological, genealogical, political and religious sphere, e.g. *gao*, "high", related to PIE **kok*, whence German *hoh*, English *high*; *fu* "belly" < *puk*, related to **bhug-*, Swedish *buk*, German *Bauch*, "belly"; *ge* "song", related to **gā* "to sing", whence Avestan *gāthā*, Sanskrit *gīta* "song"; *an* "peace" < *uan*, related to **ven* "contented, at home, enjoy", whence Dutch *wennen* "to get accustomed", German *Wonne* "pleasure", *Wohnen* "to reside" and Roman goddess *Venus*; *sun* "grandson", related to English *son*; *dao* "lead" < *do:g*, related to **dok* "lead", whence Latin *ducere* "lead", Dutch *(her-)tog*, "duke"; *ting* "royal court", related to Germanic *thing* "council"; *di* "god", related to Sanskrit *deva*, Latin *deus* (further elaborated by Zhou 2005); and even *he* "what" < *huat*, related to PIE **kwad*, whence Germanic *hwat*, English *what*.

Chang (1988: 35-36) finds support in the *Shiji* (Records of the Historian) and *Liji* (Book of Rites) accounts about the legendary Huangdi, the Yellow Emperor. His real name was Xuanyuan, which happens to mean "wagon shaft". Like the pioneers who conquered the Far West, or the Afrikaners colonizing the Transvaal, he "was perpetually on the move with treks of carriages" and "at night he slept in a barricade of wagons". He became emperor after winning a decisive battle in Zhuolu (Deer Ford), on the Mongolian border: "All of this indicates his origin from a stock-breeding tribe in Inner Mongolia", if not farther west. "This emperor must have had an appearance of northern white people, as the epithet [Huangdi] can etymologically be interpreted as 'blond heavenly god'." His traditional date, twenty-seventh century BCE, is close to the attested appearance of the *Longshan* culture characterized by a leap forward in material culture, town-building and, according to Chang, cattle-breeding. Moreover, Huangdi is traditionally credited with devising the Chinese script and specifically with giving many objects and concepts their names.

One of the surprising elements in Chang's thesis, even

more pronounced among some of his followers, is the preponderance of Germanic among the IE sources of purported loanwords in Chinese. Thus, Wei (2005: 19) derives Chinese *de*, "virtue, worthiness, strength" (as in the title of the classic *Daodejing*) from PIE **dhugh* "to be fit, of use, proper; acceptable, achieve", mainly productive in Celtic and esp. in Germanic. Thus English *doughty* "formidable", Dutch *duchtig* "strongly", and German *tüchtig* "efficient"; Dutch *deugen* "to be worthy, fit", *degelijk* "solid"; Dutch *deugd*, German *Tugend* "virtue". Østmoe (1995: 2) even has Germanic influence the Tai languages, situated to the south of the Chinese-speaking area, and explains the Chinese sound change *k-* > *h-* as the impact of Grimm's Law, which effects the same sound change in Germanic.

This could find some support in Gamkrelidze & Ivanov's vision (1995: 473, 832) of the Proto-Germanics moving from the South-Caucasian Homeland around the Caspian Sea to Central Asia, where some may have branched out into China, with the westbound Germanics carrying their Central-Asian itinerary along in the form of loanwords from Ket (*house*) and Altaic (*mare*). If nothing else, the scenario is at least non-conformist.

2.3. A LONG SHOT

Chang's list contains phonologically unconvincing instances, and very long shots such as deriving *wang* "king", from **wanak-*, attested only in Mycenaean Greek. But a few hundred in his list, that ultimately added up to *c.* 1500 items (we had agreed on a visit to discuss his latest findings, when his death intervened), are as plausible and consistent as any putative etymology can be. Given the existing abundance of such exercises between any two languages, where an author could convince himself and some readers of the kinship between the two, this plausibility in itself may fail to persuade.

Thus, Pulleyblank (1193: 106) criticizes Chang as well as his predecessors in this endeavour and implicitly also his followers (who mostly publish their elaborations on Chang's theory in Victor Mair's series of *Sino-Platonic Papers*: Zhu Qingzhi, Julie Lee Wei, Zhou Jixu et al.), for being "quite primitive in their methodology, relying on gathering look-alikes among individual lexical items". This does injustice to Chang, who includes theoretical linguistic considerations, a diachronic analysis of Chinese word structure and the evolution of the tone system, and a typological comparison between Chinese and Tibeto-Burmese among other building blocks of his ambitious thesis. However, Chang's reconstructions are indeed rather sloppy, and there is a complete lack of proper argument for his claims and against foreseeable objections. It is obvious that such a thesis requires a far more thorough basis of proof than has been provided so far. His followers are working on it, but they will need to show more methodological rigour than Chang himself was able to muster.

For the Homeland question, contacts with archaic Chinese will not be decisive in any case. If the Germanics on their way to north-western Europe could make a detour via China, it makes no difference whether they did so coming from Anatolia or from India. From most putative Homelands proposed so far, it would have been a heroic endeavour and indeed an unlikely one.

3. Indo-European and Caucasian

Much less weird than a connection of IE with Chinese is one with Caucasian. Indeed, with a Homeland just north, south or west of the Caucasus Mountains, such a connection should only be expected. A few supporters of these peri-Caucasian Homeland theories have tried to find the traces of the said connection.

There are three distinct Caucasian language groups: Northwest-Caucasian or Adyghian, Northeast-Caucasian or Nakh-Dagestanian, and South-Caucasian or Kartvelian. If PIE originated in their Pontic vicinity, it would make eminent sense if one of these, and especially the northern groups, did show early commonalities with the IE family. Not knowing any of them, we have to scout around for what legitimate experts have said about the matter.

In a typical instance of a non-linguist accepting without question the rumor of a linguistic proof for the Pontic Homeland theory, archaeologist Ratnagar (2006: 172) locates the Homeland "in the steppe region of Eurasia" on grounds of linguistic palaeontology (keywords for certain trees and animals) and the purportedly "mutual" influence on/from Kartvelian and Finno-Ugric.

Linguistic palaeontology can just as well support a more southerly homeland, as argued above. The case of Finno-Ugric deserves a separate treatment, but we can already say that the exchanges were hardly "mutual": it was a one-way traffic with hundreds of words adopted by Finno-Ugric from Indo-Iranian, most of them from plain Iranian but some also from an earlier stage of Indo-Iranian development. If the early Indo-Iranians had traversed Finno-Ugric territory on their way southeast to Afghanistan and beyond, and had such an intimate contact with the natives as to impart that many words to them, one should expect them in turn also to have borrowed a lot from their hosts. In the extant lists proposing Indo-Iranian exchanges with Finno-Ugric, in all a few hundreds, we can hardly find a handful of attempts (notably Blažek 2005) to claim, let alone prove, an arrow from Finno-Ugric and into Indo-Iranian.

As for Kartvelian, notwithstanding the influence it underwent from Armenian, Iranian, Greek and Slavic in successive historic periods, it is much harder to identify loans from PIE, let alone Kartvelian words borrowed by PIE. It did impart a few words to Greek, confirming the impression that the Greeks expressed some ancestral memory in their legends about Colchis, i.e. Georgia.

In her list of tentative correspondences between IE and the three Caucasian groups, Nichols (1997: 144-46), herself an expert on Nakh-Dagestanian, finds hardly any for her north-eastern group (culture words: yoke, honey), practically none for the most Pontic-situated north-western group, but a good handful for South-Caucasian, including words for "yoke", "harvest", "goat", "heart" and the numerals 4 through 7. The IE (minus Anatolian) word for "eight" is an ancient dual form of a word for "four", attested as such in Avestan, *aśti* "four-finger width"; in this very early meaning it was borrowed by Kartvelian, where **otxo* means "four" (Gamkrelidze & Ivanov 1995: 747). Since the Anatolian numerals from 4 upwards are unrelated to those in the other IE languages, it has been argued that these numerals were newly coined or borrowed around the time when Anatolian split off from PIE (Kassian 2009). In that case, we could consider reversing the arrow, with PIE borrowing from Kartvelian, where reconstructed **otxo* is closer to the reconstructed PIE form **okto* than to the Avestan form. If nothing else, it would help Gamkrelidze and Ivanov's purpose of proving a South-Caucasian Homeland. But both directions of borrowing are possible.

Note that all this concerns only the South-Caucasian group, not the two northern ones bordering on the putative Pontic homeland. There seems to have been more contact with south than north of the Caucasus. To be sure, languages may move, as the case of IE itself amply demonstrates, but so far no indications have been dug up to show that Kartvelian was once spoken on the Eurasian steppe. The Middle East may have more to do with early IE history than so far assumed.

At any rate, while borrowing may have taken place on a very modest scale, a common origin is no longer taken into consideration. Gamkrelidze and Ivanov (1982: 177) concede: "If there were enough linguistic data to demonstrate the original unity of IE and Kartvelian, we would have done this a long time ago, because this thesis assumes the original existence of the IE and Kartvelian systems within the boundaries of the northern Middle East", — precisely the South-Caucasian Homeland theory they plead.

As for the northern groups, even a spokesman of the Pontic Homeland Theory, who has unambiguously titled his textbook of IE linguistics *"From the steppes to the oceans"*, denies these eager claims of an IE-Caucasian common origin (Martinet 1985: 21):

> We don't exclude the possibility of contacts between the ancient IEs and their Caucasian contemporaries, but no precise trace has so far been brought forward. The structural similarities that one may envision for a very distant period would not imply a common origin nor a period of symbiosis.

4. Indo-European and Austronesian

In a descriptive paper without explanatory ambitions, Isidore Dyen (1970) has presented some surprising commonalities in vocabulary between Austronesian and IE. Others had noticed some of these, starting with Franz Bopp in the 1840s and Hans Jensen in the 1930s. Dyen's comparisons are sometimes not too obvious but satisfy the linguistic requirement of regularity. They concern not just core vocabulary for "earth", "water", "rice", etc. but even the pronouns (**aku*, cfr. *ego*) and the first four numerals. This is a far more intimate relationship than between IE and any non-IE language in India, whether Burushaski, Muṇḍa, Kusuṇḍa, Nahali, Tibeto-Burman, Draviḍian or Veḍḍa; nor in Europe, whether Basque, Tartessian (a language attested in Spain since 600 BCE; Clackson

2007: 3-4), Caucasian or Finno-Ugric. To be sure, IE has shared its vocabulary lavishly with Draviḍian and Finno-Ugric, but not such central items of the lexicon.

This intimate contact is surprising, because on the face of it, the two language families have had no contact before the early Christian era, when seafarers belonging to the Indo-Aryan branch, already fully distinct as a subgroup of IE since many centuries, must have encountered the Austronesian-speaking populations of Malaya and Indonesia. Dyen does not propose a hypothesis to make sense of it, least of all a common homeland, he merely notices the similarities because they seem just too persistent to explain away.

The language structures of IE and Austronesian differ widely and thus seem to exclude a common origin, leaving only borrowing as the explanation for the common vocabulary. But then, we know that genetically related languages may become completely different in grammatical structure (as exemplified by English, which, from a sternly flectional language like Sanskrit, is developing towards the isolative structure typical of Chinese). Dyen therefore saw no objection to a common genetic origin rather than an early large-scale borrowing.

Not much work has been done to falsify nor to deepen the by now old suspicion of a common origin or early common history of Austronesian and IE. In an Internet discussion we came across the claim that Austronesian *dua*, "two", differs in origin from its IE look-alike by having evolved from **dusa*. Possibly more items on Dyen's list could come up for deconstruction. But if so, the job remains to be done. It seems that people just don't know what to do with this undigested anomaly.

Talageri (2000: 292-93) offers as explanation a somewhat dated theory by the Marxist dean of Indian linguistics, Suniti

Kumar Chatterji (in Majumdar 1951: 150,156), viz. that Austronesian originated in India. This is where not Chatterji but Talageri himself also locates the IE Homeland, thus bringing the two together. Even more eccentrically, Sergent (1995: 398) places the contact between the two language groups in north-eastern China. But it is now generally accepted that the Austronesian Homeland was south-east China, whence it made its spectacular expansion to the island world.

When Bellwood (1994) discusses Dyen's thesis, his focus is not on the IE but on the Austronesian side of the equation: "Dyen's lexicostatistical classification of Austronesian suggested a Melanesian homeland, a conclusion at variance with all other sources of information". This highlights once more that Dyen cannot be accused of an Indian Homeland bias either for IE or for Austronesian. It is in spite of his opinions about the Austronesian and IE homelands (Melanesia *casu quo* the Pontic steppe) that he felt forced to face facts concerning IE-Austronesian similarities.

The dominant opinion is that from south-east China, Anatolian expanded in all seaborne directions spanning between Madagascar and Easter Island, hence its proposed substratum presence even in Japanese, a rather hard nut to crack for an Indian Homeland theory of Austronesian. However, just as the steppe culture is construed by Indian and Anatolian Homeland proponents as a secondary centre of IE dispersal, one could likewise imagine south-east China as a staging area for the naval expansion of an Austronesian population that had freshly arrived there from elsewhere.

It would be special pleading to have the Austronesians sail from afar, say, from India, then regroup in south-east China, then disperse again across the ocean. But they may have expanded from somewhere very near instead. A scenario with this effect is indirectly suggested by Oppenheimer (1998) in his thesis about Sundaland, the now-submerged region south of China and east of Vietnam. He describes it as an *"Eden in the East"* during the final centuries of the Ice Age, more than 10,000 years ago. In his view, the Neolithic Revolution first took place in this warm and fertile part of the world, but people were forced to flee when the ice melted and the sea level rose. During their emigration, they lost part of their innovative achievements but managed to take along others that gave them an edge over the populations they encountered in their lands of settlement. Suppose that some of them stayed in the surrounding lands (south-east China) to become the Austronesians, while others moved west to India where they became the IEs.

This would correspond neatly with the Hindu myth of Manu Vaivasvata: warned by a grateful fish of an impending flood, he built a ship, survived the flood and landed in Ayodhyā, an Indian town that can be reached from the Bay of Bengal by ship via the Gaṅgā River and her tributary, the Sarayū. There he started the Arya dynasties. One of these, the Aila or Lunar branch, spawned the "five tribes" that formed the ethnic horizon of the *R̥gveda*. Of these five, the Druhyu tribe had left India westward within the living memory of the earliest Vedic poets. Talageri (2009: 249, 364) argues they could be the ancestors of the Western branches of the IE family, including at least Anatolian, Tocharian, Italic and Celtic. The struggle between the Paurava tribe, to which the Vedic poets belonged, and the Āṇava tribe, against the background of the latter's expansion to Afghanistan and beyond, forms the *Sitz im Leben* of the *R̥gveda* itself. The Āṇavas would then be the ancestors of the Iranians (whose tribal names can be recognized among Vedic king Sudāsa's opponents in the Battle of the Ten Kings, as well as in the terms *dāsa* and *dasyu*), Armenians and Greeks.

In that scenario, we get India as the well-spring of IE expansion westward, but at the price of positing an earlier

"Aryan invasion": not from the north-west but from the south-east, all the way from Sundaland.

5. Indo-Aryans in West Asia

An Indo-Aryan presence in West Asia is attested through proper nouns in Syria and Palestine since *c.* 1600 BCE, among the Kassites (who conquered Mesopotamia from the north-east) since *c.* 1700 BCE, and in the Mitanni documents since 1500 BCE. At least 68 have been counted in the Hurrian city of Nuzu (near Kirkuk, Iraq), eighteenth-fifteenth century BCE, and 41 in Syria and Palestine (O'Callaghan & Dumont 1948: 57-63, 150-53). For Palestine *c.* 1400 BCE, eight princes with Indo-Aryan names are enumerated (O'Callaghan & Dumont 1948: 65). The adoption of Indo-Aryan names was typical of the upper class. By the way, the list does not include the names Arisena and Somasena, mentioned in a tablet from Akkad dating to *c.* 2200 BCE, cited by Harmatta (1992: 374) and Sharma (1995: 36) as proof of an Indo-Aryan presence in West Asia that early, but re-analysed by Bjarte Kaldhol (Witzel 2005: 390) as being pure Hurrian. Though this Indo-Aryan presence in West Asia comes too late to affect the Homeland question, it does none the less have an indirect impact on it through its implications for Indo-Aryan chronology in India.

5.1. INTERNAL VEDIC CHRONOLOGY

Here, we must turn to the underrated books about the implicit and explicit historical data in the *R̥gveda* and the *Avesta*, by Talageri (2000 and 2009). Talageri's master key is the internal chronology of the *R̥gveda*. Basing himself on two centuries of Western scholarship, from nineteenth-century German Veda scholar Hermann Oldenberg to present-day AIT champion Michael Witzel, Talageri compares the contents of the oldest layer, largely coinciding with books 6, 3 and 7; of the middle layer, books 2 and 4; and the youngest layer, comprising books 1, 5, 8, 9 and 10. Covering every verse and every instance of every data category considered, and comparing the three periods, he finds a shifting focus in the names of animals, plants, rivers, landscape features, technology, ancestors, ethnic groups, and in personal name types and verse forms. His finding is this: the old layer was indubitably composed in the Yamunā/Sarasvatī region, which was to remain the centre of gravity of Vedic culture; the middle layer's horizon expands westwards as far as the Indus; while the youngest parts are also familiar with Afghanistan. This is exactly the opposite of what the AIT predicts. In an "invasionist" scenario, the oldest layer would obviously be based in Afghanistan and be as yet unfamiliar with India's interior, which would then only be settled in the younger period.

What a difference this can make, may be illustrated with the debate on the evidence for horse-drawn chariots in the *Ṛgveda* and in the archaeological records. The pro-AIT argument runs that these are in evidence in the *Ṛgveda*, but don't predate the second millennium in the archaeological record (leaving aside for now that the archaeological record is pretty silent on their first appearance, for none have been dug up from reputedly Indo-Aryan or Indo-Iranian settlements in Kazakhstan's Andronovo culture, the Bactria-Margiana Archaeological Complex or post-Haṛappan India), so that the *Ṛgveda* is definitely younger than 2000 BCE. Against this, Talageri argues that spoked-wheel chariots are not simply in evidence "in the *Ṛgveda*", as the Orientalists have known since the nineteenth century, but are specifically typical of its youngest period. The older parts know of carts, generally with four full wheels, but the chariots with two-spoked wheels are a later development which must have taken place within the period of composition of the *Ṛgveda*, part of which predates their introduction.

5.2. THE PLACE OF WEST-ASIAN INDO-ARYAN IN VEDIC CHRONOLOGY

The material and religious culture, along with the vocabulary and the name-types, allow us to link a number of datable extra-Indian connections to the youngest layer of the *R̥gveda*. According to the AIT, the Indo-Aryans in the West Asia split off from the main Indo-Aryan migration before it entered India, thus definitely predating the *R̥gveda*. However, the remnants of the Indo-Aryan vocabulary in the West-Asian Kassite (seventeenth century BCE) and Mitanni (fifteenth century BCE) culture, bequeathed by Indo-Aryan-speaking emigrant groups of at least several generations earlier, belong to the youngest layer of the *R̥gveda*.

Thus, the word *maṇi* (jewel), in use in Mitanni Indo-Aryan, is absent in the old and middle layer of the *R̥gveda*, and only makes its first appearance in Book 1, one of the youngest of the ten R̥gvedic books. As for personal names, Mitanni-type (MT) names typically end in phonetic adaptations of *-atithi*, *-aśva*, *-sena*, *-bandhu*, *-uta*, or start in *vasu-*, *r̥ta-*, *priya-*, e.g.: Mittaratti (Mitrātithi), Biriassuva (Priyāśva), Biriasena (Priyasena), Subandu (Subandhu), Wasdata (Vasudata), Indarota (Indrota). Some of these names appear literally in the *R̥gveda* as well, and each of their components frequently does. However:

> Not a single MT name is found in the Early Books (6, 3, 7). Only one MT name is found in the Middle Books (4, 2): *Citraratha* in IV.30.18. And it is highly significant that hymn IV.30 is one of the hymns classified by Oldenberg as a late hymn in Book 4. *All* the other MT names are found *only* in the hymns of the Late Books.
>
> — Talageri 2009: 178, (emphasis his)

Likewise, of the composers of the R̥gvedic hymns, we find Mitanni-type names only among those in the Late Books.

Nobody has thus far cared to try a refutation of Talageri's case. One that comes to mind is suggested by the debates among scholars shortly after the discovery of the Mitanni Indo-Aryan vocabulary: is this really Indo-Aryan or could it be Iranian? After all, the prefix *r̥ta-* takes the shape it also has in Iranian, viz. *ar̥ta-*, e.g. in the names Artasumara, Artatama, Artamna. This is probably the effect of the Mitanni cuneiform script being un-adapted to the Indo-Aryan sounds, or of a recrudescence of their pronunciation in the mouths of people who had shifted to Hurrian as their mother tongue.

Some names have the element *-asura*, e.g. the Mitannic general *Kart-aśura*, the name *Biry-aśura* attested in Nuzu and Ugarit, in Nuzu also the names *Kalm-aśura* and *Sim-aśura*, the Cilician king *Shun-aśura*, while in Alalakh (Syria) two people were called *Aśura* and *Aśur-atti* (Sergent 1997: 210). Clearly, the word *asura* had a positive connotation, though the *asura*s are demons in India, while in Iranian, Ahura is God; so couldn't this *-asura* be a phonetic variation on an Iranian name? Indeed, hasn't Szemerényi (1986) argued that the characteristic *s* > *h* shift in Iranian is not older than the eighth century BCE? However, note that some names have the element *-deva*, e.g. *Dewatti* (O'Callaghan & Dumont 1948: 61), for which the situation is reversed: a *deva/daeva* is a demon in Iranian, a god in Sanskrit. Moreover, in the Veda too, *asura* is a word for "god", alongside *deva*; it only got demonized later on, apparently in reaction to the demonization of the *deva*s in the *Avesta*. Some names even have the component *Indra-* (e.g. *Indarota*), hated by the early Zoroastrians. But then again, the Zoroastrian doctrine may not have caught on immediately in the whole Iranian world.

Be that as it may, there would be no problem if the Mitanni IE vocabulary really were Iranian in disguise. For the *Avesta* is in the same situation as Mitanni Indo-Aryan corpus: by the same criteria (plus some that cannot be applied to the Mitanni fragments, especially verse metre), it belongs to the age of the youngest books of the *Ṛgveda*:

> The evidence of the Avestan meters confirms to the hilt the conclusions compelled by the evidence of the Avestan names: namely (. . .) that the Early and Middle Books of the *Ṛgveda* *precede* the period of composition of the *Avesta*.
>
> — Talageri 2009: 80 (emphasis his)

5.3. ZARATHUSTRA'S BATTLE

Indeed, Zarathustra, who was nearly the first composer of Avestan hymns, was the *rājguru* of the Kavi king Viśtaśpa, which in Sanskrit would be *Istāśva*. Following a hint from traditional Parsi scholarship, Talageri (2000: 216) points out that this king is actually mentioned in the *Ṛgveda* I.122.13, in a Late Book but containing miscellaneous material from different periods: "What can *Istāśva, Istarasmi* or any other princes do against those who enjoy the protection [of Mitra and Varuṇa]?".The context of that hymn and of hymns I.100.17 and IV.30.18 (Middle Period) is the Vārsāgira Battle which took place on the Afghan side of the Bolan Pass near Zarathustra's headquarters on the Herlmand River. The protagonists for both sides have been mentioned by name in these Vedic hymns as well as in the *Avesta* and in later Iranian literature down to Firdausi's *Śāhnāmeh*. At that time-depth, it is unique to have an account, no matter how sketchy, from the two sides of a single battle.

The time of composition of Ṛgvedic Book IV

> represents a continuation and culmination of the Indo-Iranian hostilities which commenced in the Early Period. (. . .) this period is contemporaneous with the (. . .) composition of the earliest parts of the *Avesta* (the Gāthās and the earliest core of the Yaśts) and hence the events of this period are contemporary events for the composers of the Early *Avesta*,

> and have a central place in the text. To the *Ṛgveda*, however, these events are more peripheral. — Talageri 2000: 214

This period of hostility accounts for a central feature of the Zoroastrian religion: the abjuring and demonizing of Indra and his band of *deva*s. Possibly both sides had prayed for Indra's help in the battle, and as the losing side, the Iranians spitefully disowned him.

That Avestan is younger than Vedic, is implied in the introduction to an authoritative translation of Zarathustra's *Gāthā*s:

> The prophet's hymns are laden with ambiguities resulting both from *the merger of many grammatical endings* and from the intentionally compact and often elliptical style. . . .
> — Insler 1975: 1 (the emphasis is mine)

Compared with Vedic, Zarathustra's language was already eroded morphologically and phonologically. So, the analysis of both the contents and the language of Veda and *Avesta* teaches us something definite about their relative chronology. For an absolute chronology, however, the evidence from the West-Asian Indo-Aryans is more helpful.

Granting a few generations for the Indo-Aryans to gain a foothold in the West Asia, join the ruling class there, integrate and lose their language, we may estimate that they have left the Indo-Aryan mainstream perhaps two centuries before their well-timed appearance in the West Asia, i.e. in the early second millennium BCE. At that time, that Indo-Aryan mainstream was living the terminal period of the Ṛgvedic age. We need not go into the implications of the shift in Vedic chronology here, but they are inevitably far-reaching.

6. Indo-European and Pre-Sumerian

6.1. THE EUPHRATIC HYPOTHESIS

Another culture entertaining a flood myth, very similar to

that of the Hindus, was that of Sumer in South Mesopotamia. According to both Mesopotamian tradition (as reported by Berosus, third century BCE) and modern linguistics, the Sumerians were immigrants from overseas. They absorbed or displaced an earlier population, which left substratal traces of its language in Sumerian.

While branches of the IE languages have displaced many others languages, sometimes they themselves were overpowered or overwhelmed by others. In Europe, some have been displaced by sister branches of IE, e.g. Lusian, extinct in the first century CE (Clackson 2007: 3-4), Venetic, Messapic, Phrygian, Thracian and purportedly also *Belgian* (or *Nordwestblock*, vide Kuhn 1959, Meid 1986; traceable through loans in West-Germanic, e.g. English *pool*, with un-Germanic initial *p*-). In Central Asia, Iranian and Tocharian lost out to Turkic, though Iranian was preserved elsewhere. In Anatolia, Anatolian was displaced by Iranian, Greek and Armenian, which in turn partly lost out to Turkic. It is reasonable to assume that there must have been more ancient, hitherto undetected dead ends in the expansion of IE languages displaced very early by others.

Was there an IE language in Mesopotamia that predated and influenced Sumerian? A first suspicion of an IE presence in the Sumerian lexicon had already been expressed long ago by Autran (1925: 170-72), e.g.: Sumerian *kur* "mountain", cf. IE **gor-i-s*, whence Slavic *gora* and Sanskrit *giri* "mountain"; *gir* "furnace", cf. IE **gwher* ~ Sanskrit *ghar-ma*, Latin *furnus*, Greek *thermos*, English *warm*; *igi* "eye", *ug* "see", cf. Latin *oculus* "eye"; *tag* "prepare, adorn", cf. Greek *tektn̈n* "builder", *technè*, "skill", Sanskrit *tāṣti*, Latin *texere* "weave". His suggestion was generally disregarded until it was taken up in right earnest by Gordon Whittaker, a British linguist working in Göttingen.

Whittaker has identified in Sumerian the remnants of an IE substratum language which he has provisionally called

Euphratic. While the existence of such a language would fit the hypothesis of a South-Asian origin of IE quite neatly, our first impression was that this would simply be a bit too good to be true. We only started to give him a fair hearing after expressing our doubts on yahoo's forum of IE linguistics (the Cybalist, after the late Cyril Babayev) and being rebuffed by old hands that Whittaker's thorough argumentation deserved better than our cavalier scepticism.

The IE language that he claims to have reconstructed from the presumed loanwords in Sumerian, looks virtually identical to the PIE reconstructed by many others from all the other daughter languages of PIE. If true, it would be a striking vindication of the method of historical and comparative linguistics, but let us not accept that before we have more proof than the promising similarities presented by Whittaker. We are using one of his most recent position papers (Whittaker 2008), in which he answers his critics, along with an even more recent detail study of the Euphratic adjectives (Whittaker 2010).

To sum up:

> It will be argued that the cuneiform writing system, the Sumerian and Akkadian lexicon, and the place names of Southern Mesopotamia preserve traces of an early IE language, indeed the earliest by more than a millennium. Furthermore, this evidence is detailed and consistent enough to reconstruct a number of features of the proposed IE language, Euphratic, and to sketch an outline of Euphratean cultural patterns.
>
> — Whittaker 2008, abstract

The correspondence is either with actual words, or with a peculiar feature of Sumerian, viz. logograms that represent a sound and show a picture with visible reference to a known object, following the rebus principle. In some cases, the sound of the logogram does not correspond to the name of the object shown in Sumerian, but does fit its name in IE. Thus, the logogram *pes* "wide", shows a fish, IE **peisk*, whence Latin *piscis*, English *fish*.

Among the words that seem borrowed, we may mention: *lik* < **wlkw* "wolf"; *ku* ~ *kuon* "hound"; *hu* < **$h_2$av-i* "bird", cf. Latin *avis*; *lib* < **wlp-eh*$_1$ "fox", Latin *vulpes*; *irib* "ram", cf. Latin *aries*; *gilis* "mongoose, rat", cf. Latin *glis* "dormouse", Skt. *giri* "mouse"; *gud* "bovine", cf. Skt. *go*, Eng. *cow*; *uwi* "sheep", cf. Lat. *ovis*, Eng. *ewe*; *sukur* "spear", cf. Latin *securis*, "axe" < **sek* "cut"; *ner* "lord, man" < **$h_2$ner*, cf. Skt. *nr̥*, *nar-*, Gk. *aner* "man"; *gara.pa.te.si* "city governor" < IE **ghrdh-o-pot-is* "lord (Gk. *potès*, Skt. *pati*) of the enclosure (Russian *gorod*, *grad*, Germanic *Gard*)"; *mel* "flour", cf. Dutch *meel*, related to English *mill*; *agar* < **$h_2$agro*, cf. Latin *ager* and Dutch *akker* "field", English *acre*; *ag*, "axe" < **$h_2$ag-s-ih$_2$*, cf. English *axe*.

Moreover, "most of the toponyms in southern Mesopotamia are neither Sumerian nor Semitic" (Whittaker 2008: 163, quoting Michalowski with approval). Here too, IE is called upon to provide the answers: *Kalama* "the land of Sumer", marshy southern Mesopotamia, cf. **kolh$_2$-m-* "reed"; *Nibru* "Nippur", city dedicated to the wind and weather god Enlil, cf. **nebh-ro* "cloudy"; *Lagas*, translated in Akkadian as *Nakamtu* "storehouse", cf. **legh-os-*, "storehouse"; *Tintir* "Babylon", translated in Akkadian as *Bab-El* "gate of the gods", cf. **deiu-om dhur*, Sanskrit *devānām dvāra*.

Critics including Vanséveren (2010) have objected that there is no systematic, exception-free phonetic correspondence between the Sumerian terms and their purported IE equivalents. It must be admitted that the phonetic correspondences are not as neat and systematic as they are between, say, Germanic and Sanskrit via IE. But this is only what one could expect if the scenario of Sumerian borrowing from a substratal Euphratic does apply: the process of borrowing is less organic than a language's internal evolution (say, from PIE to Germanic or to Sanskrit), more piecemeal, more susceptible to uneven correspondence with the original.

6.2. EUPHRATIC'S WESTERN BIAS

For neighbouring Semitic, it has been remarked that most words shared with IE actually appear only in the latter's Western branches, e.g. Akkadian *śukurru* "javelin", Hebrew *segor* "axe", cfr. Latin *securis* "axe", Old Slavic *sekyra* "hatchet"; *ard* "earth"; *gedi* "goat"; *waynu* "wine"; *fellah* "farmer", related to *plough*; *taur*, Latin *taurus*, cfr. *steer*. In the case of Sumerian too, the set of loans "betrays a strong lexical affinity to that area of the IE dialect continuum from which the Western (or north-western) languages emerged" (Whittaker 2008: 159).

Since Euphratic was a very early branch and could not yet have undergone the *kentum* > *satem* shift or other isoglosses characterizing the historically attested branches, it naturally must have been closer to PIE than the latter. However:

> I am not, and have never been, claiming that the IE language in contact with Sumerian was PIE itself, but rather a very early IE dialect from the area of the IE continuum, out of which the Western dialects emerged.
>
> — Whittaker, 2010: 132

One way to make sense of Whittaker's "data", is that the Euphratic population was a branch of a broader migratory movement westward, started in the vicinity of Mesopotamia. Whether this should be South Caucasus, Bactria, the Indus Valley, not to mention distant Sundaland, is a matter for further speculation. If Whittaker is right, his theory has more importance for the IE Homeland debate than he himself lets on. He observes that for today's main contenders for Homeland status, south-west Russia and Anatolia, the presence of an early colony in Mesopotamia can be explained with more or less equal ease. Both scenarios require a migration, but not quite as spectacular as, say, from northern Europe, a major pre-war Homeland candidate. They require no special pleading. It may be added that both Bactria and India were just as close and had well-documented trade relations with Mesopotamia. Meluhha, roughly coterminous with Sindh, even had trader settlements there. Seals with Haṛappan inscriptions have been found in Mesopotamia, and depictions of the Indian humped bull have shown up as far west as Palestine. No such attestation exists for similar contacts with the Pontic people. However, Meluhha lay outside the more northerly Vedic area, and cursory Mesopotamian information about the Meluhhan language indicates that it did not belong to IE or to any known language family. At any rate, both the Sumer-Meluhha trade and the Haṛappan urban high culture belong to the third millennium BCE, while the "Euphratic" people must have lived in Mesopotamia in the fourth millennium BCE, if not earlier.

6.3. A PATTERN OF MISPLACED LANGUAGES

Euphratic as the proposed pre-Sumerian branch of the IE family does not stand on its own. If verified, it would already be the third "Western" IE language that shows up deep in Asia. The first one was Tocharian, found unexpectedly in Xinjiang (*c.* 1895). The second one was Proto-Bangani: a *kentum* IE substrate found in the Bangani language in Himachal/ Uttarakhand in the western Himalaya by Zoller (1988, 1993). It is close to the westernmost branches of IE not just because of its *kentum* features (18 words identified by Zoller, e.g. *kôtrô* "fight", where Sanskrit has *satru*) but also because of its vocabulary. Thus, *dṅkru* "tear", instead of the expected Indo-Aryan *aśru*, shares the initial dental with Greek, Latin and Germanic, unlike Baltic, Indo-Iranian and even Tocharian. It also has *lôktô* for "milk", cfr. Greek *galakt-*, Latin *lact-*; and *gṅsti* "guest", cfr. Latin *hostis*, English *guest*.

After Zoller's sensational announcement, his findings were checked by Van Driem and Sharma (1997: 177), negatively:

> The purpose of our mission to Bangan was to be able to provide independent attestation of the existence of vestiges of Kentum IE in the Himalayas or, alternatively, to demonstrate their non-existence. We had hoped to be able to do the former, if only because that task would probably have proved less labour-intensive, but we did the latter.

The debate was marred by personal acrimony and most linguists and Indologists who cared to comment declared Proto-Bangani still-born, until Delhi-based field linguist Anvita Abbi did more thorough research on the spot and settled the matter by confirming Zoller's findings and noticing

> retention of perhaps Pre-Vedic Sanskrit words, some going as far back as PIE and its branches of languages which are extinct now (such as Kentum languages like Tocharian and Anatolian.
>
> — Abbi 1997

Zoller's and Abbi's position was defended by Hock (1998) and passed into the conventional wisdom when Witzel (2003: 55) acknowledged that there must have existed "speakers of the non-Indo-Iranian, Western-IE group now represented in the substrate of Bangani".

Witzel adds that they must have come from either Afghanistan or straight across the mountains from Xinjiang, where they may have been neighbours of the Tocharians. But that is precisely the point: did the speakers of Proto-Bangani come from outside or did they preserve the original language of north-west India? There is no material reason to insist on the former scenario, except for AIT bias. Rather than claiming that these Oriental but Western-looking languages were the product of an early expansion from the West, it is becoming less implausible that the Western branches got to their historical habitat from an area close to the habitats of these three extinct languages, Tocharian, Proto-Bangani and Euphratic.

Looking at the map, we find that Bactria, the Oxus River basin in north Afghanistan and south Uzbekistan, is close enough to all three. Nichols (1997) has already argued on other grounds that this must be the origin of the spread of the IE languages. Even the critique by Simon (2009) of her method does not contain arguments against a Bactrian origin *per se*. Bactria did have the kind of economical importance and demographic weight that could make it the well-spring of consequential migrations. But lying on the historic crossroads of army movements and migrations, it may also have been the staging area for populations from elsewhere. That is the role assigned to Bactria in the scheme presented by Witzel (2003) of steppe-based tribes regrouping and updating their skills in the Bactria-Margiana complex before invading (or "immigrating" into) India. His scheme may well be right, but the provenance and direction of the migratory movement may have been different, even the very opposite.

6. Conclusion

Purely linguistic evidence is a fairly soft type of evidence. It is not compatible with just any state of affairs in real-world history, bendable any which way depending on personal whims or political compulsions, as sceptics might blurt out. But it is none the less fairly elastic. Linguists should think twice before claiming to have "proved" anything, especially in a nebulous domain like the distant PIE past. So, it would be inappropriate to base any grim conclusions on our little survey of the well-attested or as yet hypothetical contacts of the fledgling IE family with other ancient languages.

However, we hope to have pin-pricked a few premature certainties, in particular about the Pontic rootedness of early IE. The steppe-based horsemen riding triumphally into Europe and South Asia were a better story than the more complicated picture that is emerging here. And it could still prove accurate one day, but it is wrong to claim that it has been proven by linguistic evidence, as many non-linguists and some linguists still assume. Thus far, no neighbouring language has been found to equal the distant Austronesian family in sharing a central part of the vocabulary with IE. Yet, no linguist jumps to the conclusion that IE originated in Austronesia, and the same prudence should be exercised with regard to the more conventional Homeland claims.

We have reason to urge flexibility in interpreting the linguistic data, especially when we find linguistic opinion to conflict with harder types of evidence: textual testimonies (including their astro-chronological data) and archaeological findings. If the absence of an archaeological trail of Aryans moving into South Asia can at all be compensated for by intangible linguistic evidence, the actual linguistic data we have are not such that they provide this hoped-for overriding evidence. We are still dealing with plural possibilities for a Homeland, and the discipline of linguistics can only slowly narrow down the spectrum of possibilities.

References

Abbi, Anvita, 1997: "Debate on Archaism of Some Select Bangani Words", *Indian Linguistics* 58, pp. 1-14.

Alinei, Mario, 1996: *La Teoria de la Continuità*, Bologna: Mulino.

Allen, Nicholas, 1998: "The Indo-European Prehistory of Yoga", *International Journal of Hindu Studies*, April 1998, pp. 1-20.

———, 1999: "Hinduism as Indo-European: Cultural Comparitivism and Political Sensitivities", in Bronkhorst & Deshpande, 1999, pp. 19-32.

Arvidsson, Stefan, 2006: *Aryan Idols: Indo-European Mythology as Ideology and Science*, Chicago and London: The University of Chicago Press.

Autran, C., 1925: *Sumérien et Indo-Européen: L'aspect Morphologique de la Question*, Paris: Librairie Orientaliste Paul Geuthner.

Bellwood, Peter, 1994: "An Archaeologist's View of Language

Macrofamily Relationships", *Oceanic Linguistics*, December 1994, pp. 391-406.

Blažek, Václav, 2005: "Indo-Iranian Elements in Fenno-Ugric Mythological Lexicon", *Indogermanische Forschungen* 110, pp. 162-95.

Bronkhorst, Johannes, and Madhav Deshpande, 1999: *Aryan and Non-Aryan in South Asia. Evidence, Interpretation and Ideology*, Cambridge MA: Department of Sanskrit and Indian Studies, Harvard.

Bryant & Patton, 2005: *The Indo-Aryan Controversy. Evidence and Inference in Indian History*, New York: Routledge.

Cardona, George, et al., eds., 1970: *Indo-European and Indo-Europeans*, Philadelphia: University of Pennsylvania Press.

Chang, Tsung-tung, 1988: *Indo-European Vocabulary in Old Chinese*, Sino-Platonic Papers # 7, Philadelphia: Department of Oriental Studies, University of Pennsylvania.

Clackson, James 2007: *Indo-European Linguistics, An Introduction*, Cambridge: Cambridge University Press.

Dani, A.H., and V.M. Masson, eds., 1992: *History of Civilizations*, vol. 1, Paris: UNESCO Publ.

Deo, S.B. and Suryanath Kamath, eds., 1993: *The Aryan Problem*, Pune: Bharatiya Itihasa Sankalana Samiti.

Dyen, Isidore, 1970: "Background 'noise' or 'evidence' in Comparative Linguistics: The case of the Austronesian languages", in Cardona 1970.

Elst, Koenraad, 1999: *Update on the Aryan Invasion Debate*, Delhi: Aditya Prakashan.

———, 2005: "Linguistic Aspects of the Aryan Invasion Theory", in Bryant & Patton 2005, pp. 234-81.

———, 2007: *Asterisk in Bharopiyasthan: Minor Writings on the Aryan Invasion Debate*, Delhi: Aditya Prakashan.

Erdosy, G., 1995: *The Indo-Aryans of Ancient South Asia*, Berlin: Walter De Gruyter.

Gamkrelidze, Thomas, and Vyacheslav Ivanov, 1985: "The Problem of the Original Homeland of the Speakers of Indo-European Languages (in response to I.M Diakonoff's articles in Vestnik Drevnej Istorii, 1982 #2 and #3)", *Journal of Indo-European Studies*, pp. 175-84.

———, 1995: *Indo-European and the Indo-Europeans*, Berlin: Mouton De Gruyter (Russian original 1985).

Harmatta, Janos, 1992: "The Emergence of the Indo-Iranians: The Indo-Iranian Languages", in Dani & Masson 1992.

Hoch, Hans Heinrich, 1998: "To Anyone Concerned with the Question of Bangani", http://www-personal.umich.edu/~pehook/bangani.hock.html .

———, 1999: "Out of India? The Linguistic Evidence", in Bronkhorst & Deshpande 1999, pp. 1-18.

Insler, S. 1975: *The Gathas of Zarathustra*, in *Acta Iranica*, 3rd series vol. 1, Leiden: Brill.

Kalyanaraman, Srinivasan, 2010: *Indus Script Cipher: Hieroglyphics of Indian Linguistic Area*, Chennai: Sarasvati Research Center.

Kassian, Alexei, 2009: "Anatolian **meyu*- '4, four' and Its Cognates", *Journal of Language Relationships*, pp. 65-78.

Kazanas, Nicholas, 2009: *Indo-Aryan Origins and Other Vedic Issues*, Delhi: Aditya Prakashan.

Kuhn, Hans, 1959: "Vor- und frühgermanische Ortsnamen in Nord-Deutschland und in den Niederlanden", *Westfälische Forschungen* 12, pp. 5-44.

Lal, B.B. 2008: *Why Perpetuate Myths? A Fresh Look at Ancient Indian History*, Delhi: NCERT.

Lincoln, Bruce, 1999: *Theorizing Myth: Narrative, Ideology, and Scholarship*, Chicago: University of Chicago Press.

Lubotsky, Alexander, 1998: "Tocharian Loanwords in Old Chinese: Chariots, Chariot Gear and Town Building", in Mair 1998, pp. 379-90.

Mair, V.H. ed., 1998: *The Bronze Age and Early Iron Age Peoples of Eastern Central Asia*, Washington D.C.: Institute for the Study of Man.

Majumdar, R.C. 1951: *The History and Culture of the Indian People*, vol.1: *The Vedic Age*, Mumbai : Bharatiya Vidya Bhavan.

Mallory, J.P. and D.Q. Adams, 2006: *The Oxford Introduction to Proto-Indo-European and the Proto-Indo-European World*, Oxford: Oxford University Press.

Martinet, André, 1986: *Des Steppes aux Océans. L'Indo-Européen et les "Indo-Européens"*, Paris: Payot.

Meid, Wolfgang, 1986: "Hans Kuhns 'Nordwestblock' Hypothese:

zur Problematik der Völker zwischen Germanen und Kelten", in *Germanenproblemen in heutiger Sicht*, Berlin, De Gruyter.

———, 1989: *Archäologie und Sprachwissenschaft: Kritisches zu neueren Hypothesen der Ausbreitung der Indogermanen*, Innsbruck.

Misra, Satya Swarup, 2005: "The date of the Rigveda and the Aryan Migration: Fresh Linguistic Evidence", in Bryant & Patton 2005, pp. 118-33.

Müller, Friedrich Max, 1883: *India: What Can It Teach Us?*, London: Longmans.

O'Callaghan, Roger T., S.J. and P.E. Dumont, 1948: *Aram Naharaim: A Contribution to the History of Upper Mesopotamia in the Second Millennium B.C.*, Rome: Pontificium Institutum Biblicum.

Oppenheimer, Stephen, 1999: *Eden in the East: The Drowned Continent of Southeast Asia*, London: Phoenix.

Ostmoe, Arne, 1995: *A Germanic-Tai Linguistic Puzzle*, Philadelphia: Sino-Platonic Papers 64.

Parpola, Asko, and Christian Carpelan, 2005: "The Cultural Counterparts to Proto-Indo-European, Proto-Uralic and Proto-Aryan. Matching the Dispersal and Contact Patterns in the Linguistic and Archaeological Record", in Bryant & Patton 2005, pp. 107-41.

Polomé, Edgar C. 1982: "Indo-European Culture, with Special Attention to Religion", in Polomé, ed., 1982, pp. 156-72.

Polomé, Edgar C. ed., 1982: *The Indo-Europeans in the Fourth and Third Millennium*. Ann Arbor, MI: Karoma.

Pulleyblank, Edwin, 1993: "The Typology of Indo-European", *Journal of Indo-European Studies*, vol. 21.

Rajaram, Navaratna S., 1995: *The Politics of History*, Delhi: Voice of India.

Schlegel, Friedrich von, 1808: *Über die Sprache und Weisheit der Indier*, Köln.

Sergent, Bernard, 1995: *Les Indo-Européens. Histoire, Langues, Mythes*, Paris: Payot.

———, 1997: *Genèse de l'Inde*, Paris: Payot.

Sharma, Ram Sharan, 1995: *Looking for the Aryans*, Chennai: Orient Longman.

———, 1999: *Advent of the Aryans in India*, Delhi: Manohar.

Simon, Zsolt, 2009: "Some Critical Remarks on the Recent PIE Homeland and Ethnogenesis Theories", *Indogermanische Forschungen* 114, pp. 60-72.

Szemerényi, Oswald, 1986: "Armenia between Iran and Greece", in Pieper & Stickel, eds.: *Studia Linguistica Diachronica et Synchronica Werner Winter sexagenario anno MCMLXXXIII gratis animis ab eius colleges, amicis discipulis oblata*, Berlin: Mouton de Gruyter, pp. 783-99.

Talageri, Shrikant, 2000: *The R̥gveda: A Historical Analysis*, Delhi: Aditya Prakashan.

———, 2009: *The R̥gveda and the Avesta: The Final Evidence*, Delhi: Aditya Prakashan.

Trautmann, T.R., 1997: *Aryans and British India*, Delhi: Vistaar.

Van Driem, George, and Suhnu Ram Sharma, 1996: "In search of Kentum Indo-European in the Himalayas", *Indogermanische Forschungen*, vol. 101, pp. 107-46.

———, 1997: "Some Grammatical Observations on Bangani", *Indogermanische Forschungen*, vol. 102, pp. 179-98.

Vanséveren, Sylvie, 2010: "Euphratique: Indo-Européen au pays de Sumer?", in Vanséveren, ed., 2010.

———, ed., 2010: *Calliope. Mélanges de Linguistique Indo-Européenne Offerts à Francine Mawet*, Leuven: Peeters.

Van Soldt, Wilfred, 1998: "Het Kassitisch", *Phoenix*, Leiden, pp. 90-93.

Voltaire, 1777: *Lettres sur l'origine des sciences et sur celle des peuples de l'Asie*, Paris.

Vovin, Alexander, 1997: "The Comparative Method and Ventures beyond Sino-Tibetan", *Journal of Chinese Linguistics*, vol. 25, pp. 308-36.

Waradpande, N.S., 1993: "Fact and Fiction about the Aryans", in Deo & Kamath 1993, pp. 14-19.

Wei, Julie Lee, 2005: *DAO and DE: An Inquiry into the Linguistic Origins of Some Terms in Chinese Philosophy and Morality*, Philadelphia: Sino-Platonic Papers 165.

Whittaker, Gordon, 2008: "The Case for Euphratic", Bulletin of Georgian National Academy of Sciences, vol. 2, no. 3, 2008. http://www.science.org.ge/2-3/Gordon%20Whitteker.pdf

———, 2010: "Some Euphratic adjectives", http://

www.scribd.com/doc/45690416/Some-Euphratic-Adjectives.

Witzel, Michael, 2003: *Linguistic Evidence for Cultural Exchange in Prehistoric Western Central Asia*, Philadelphia: Sino-Platonic Papers 129.

———, 2005: "Indocentrism: Autochthonous Visions of Ancient India", in Bryant & Patton 2005, pp. 341-404.

Zhou, Jixu, 2005: *Old Chinese "*tees" and Proto-Indo-European "*dues": Similarity in Religious Ideas and a Common Source in Linguistics*, Philadelphia: Sino-Platonic Papers 167.

Zimmer, Stefan, 1990: *Ursprache, Urvolk und Indogermanisierung*, Innsbruck.

Zoller, Claus Peter, 1988: "Bericht über besondere Archaismen in Bangani, einer Western Pahari-Sprache", *Münchener Studien zur Sprachwissenschaft* #49, pp. 173-200.

———, 1993: "A Note on Bangani", *Indian Linguistics* #54, pp. 112-14.

4

The Origin of Indian Civilization
Critical Analysis of the Contribution of Linguistics

Angela Marcantonio

Abstract

There are two linguistic paradigms available to account for the origin of Sanskrit, corresponding to two different scholarly traditions: (a) the Eastern tradition, according to which Sanskrit is an autochthonous language, perhaps bearing connections to other Indian languages, such as Draviḍian [Misra (2005), Aiyar (1975); see Bryant (2001) and Bryant & Patton (eds. 2005) for a review of the debate]; (b) the Western tradition, according to which Sanskrit is a member of the Indo-European (IE) language family, and the bearers of the Sanskrit language and civilization therefore originated somewhere in the West — having moved at some point of time into the north-western part of India (today Pakistan). How it is possible for such diametrically opposed theories to sustain themselves? It is as if the Western scholars observed the "hits", the correlations, between Sanskrit and (say) Latin or Greek, whilst the Eastern scholars observed the "hits" with (say) Draviḍian. This is a well-known phenomenoxn, called: "confirmation bias", whose recognition dates back at least as far as Sir Francis Bacon, a pivotal figure in the development of the scientific method: "The general root of superstition is when men observe when things hit, and not when they miss; and commit to memory the one and forget the other" (Goldacre 2008: 176). This paper shall argue that confirmation bias has strongly affected the IE theory, that is, the establishment of the IE language family, and, as a consequence, its model of the Western origin of Indian civilization.

1. Introduction

In this article I shall investigate the effect of confirmation bias in the Western linguistic scholarly tradition (I will not investigate possible bias in the Eastern tradition). In the Western tradition it is believed (e.g. Fortson 2004: 9) that the IE paradigm has been firmly established as a "science unto its own", through the so-called "comparative method" of historical linguistics. On the other hand, several linguists, such as Clackson (2007: 2) and Nichols (1996), claim that the similarities identified among the languages belonging to the IE family (including Sanskrit), are obvious, self-evident (at least at the grammatical level, and to the naked eye of the trained scholar). This in turn means that the belonging of Sanskrit to the IE language family has also been established "scientifically", and that, as a consequence, the bearers of the Sanskrit language and civilization must have originated in the West.

I can also report anonymous personal communication with several Western scholars, who believe that the thesis of the local origin of Sanskrit is (also) a consequence of the fact that Indian scholars "are not familiar with the methods of historical linguistics, including the comparative method", and, as a consequence, are unable to observe the hits between Sanskrit and the (Indo-)European languages.

I shall argue that confirmation bias has become endemic in the Western tradition, since there are, in fact, also many "misses" within the IE theory — and in the methods of historical linguistics in general — that are however systematically minimized, or swept under the carpet. In other words, we shall see how it almost does not matter what counter-evidence is put forward against the mainstream, Western paradigm: this counter-evidence is always "explained away" using various means of justification — if all else fails, it is still possible to label the disobedient datum as not relevant. All of these processes are embodiments of confirmation bias.

In order to illustrate this, I shall review some of the key linguistic evidence as well as key tenets underpinning the IE theory, whilst at the same time also pointing out the misses, the items of counter-evidence. It will become apparent even from this brief outline that the counter-evidence — if properly labelled as such — outweighs the evidence, whose prominence is indeed the result of "cherry-picking" the data. In reviewing the relevant data, I shall focus on the following themes: the IE lexical comparative corpus; the sound Laws, with particular reference to Verner's Law; the neo-grammarian model of language change, and related family tree diagram; the concepts of "variation", "lexical diffusion" and the nature of (sound-) change; the laryngeal hypothesis as a (supposed) example of fulfilled prediction within the IE theory; the borrowing *vs* inheritance interpretation in lexicon and grammar; the issue of the reliability (or otherwise) of the reconstructions in general and within IE.

In the past, the belief in the scientific nature of the IE theory has "crowded out" other possible models brought forward to trace back the origin of Sanskrit and the Indian civilization — including the thesis of a local origin. However, the results of my research suggest that the IE theory has *not* been scientifically founded. This in turn means that the thesis of the IE origin of Sanskrit has not been scientifically demonstrated either. Therefore, alternative paradigms should be taken into consideration and evaluated on their own merits, rather than merely be rejected because they contradict the mainstream linguistic theory, whose reliability can in fact be called into question.

2. The Indo-European Comparative Corpus

2.1. QUANTITATIVE ANALYSIS OF A SAMPLE OF THE INDO-EUROPEAN LEXICAL CORPUS

Let us start with the issue of the quantity and distribution of the IE cognates. For this purpose, Marcantonio (2009 b) has examined a substantial sample of the IE comparative corpus: all the verbal roots listed in the ***LIV*** dictionary, edited by Rix (1998), a modern and (supposedly) much more rigorous dictionary than the previous existing ones. The investigation involved simply counting the reconstructed roots, and the following are the results (for more detail see Marcantonio 2009b):

- ***Result 1***: 32 per cent of the of the 683 "safely reconstructed" verbal roots ("safely" according to the dictionary itself) are only evidenced (according to the dictionary) in one single branch[1] of the IE family. This suggests that these roots may be of local, or other origin. However, the assumption is made that they are of IE origin and reconstructions are proposed. It is then self-evidently circular to conclude that these words are of IE origin just because of the establishment of a reconstruction.
- ***Result 2:*** 34 per cent of the roots are reconstructed on the basis of data drawn from two language branches only. It is also accepted within the linguistic community that reconstructions based on just two witnesses are unsafe, because the possibility of chance resemblance or of borrowing rates are quite high in these

1. By "branch" I mean the various branches of the IE family as conventionally established: Germanic, Balto-Slavic, Italic, Indo-Iranian, Anatolian, Tocharian, Armenian, Albanian, Greek and Celtic. Here I refer only to the evidence (or purported evidence) reported in the dictionary.

circumstances. At least three witness language branches would be required to be relatively safe. In spite of this, the assumption is made, again, that these roots are of IE origin, and reconstructions are proposed. However, once again, it would be circular to conclude that the attested verbs are inherited just because of the establishment of reconstructions.[2]

- ***Result* 3:** This means that 66 per cent of the verbal roots listed in ***LIV*** are reconstructed on the basis of just one or two branch witnesses only.

Thus, 66 per cent of the verbal reconstructions in ***LIV*** cannot be relied upon because they lack statistical significance, and it is hard to imagine on which quantitative basis they can be considered as reflections of genuine IE correlations.

2.2. THE INDO-EUROPEAN LEXICAL CORPUS AND THE LARYNGEAL THEORY

Discounting those unreliable roots whose reconstruction does not meet the "three-witnesses criterion", this leaves us with 34 per cent of the roots whose reconstruction is supported by three or more witnesses and are therefore worth examining as the basis of a genuine IE comparative corpus. Of this 34 per cent roots, nearly half have been reconstructed using laryngeal segments, whose number and phonetic/phonological status is still disputed, and whose development is fraught with irregularities[3] (see Clackson (2007: 53-61) for a review of the situation and discussion in section 5. below). A further and

2. Most reconstructions of the verbal roots in ***LIV*** consist not just of a single reconstruction, but of a set of alternative "sub-reconstructions", a set of alternating starting-point roots. This fact too raises a problem of (lack of) significance (Marcantonio 2009b).

3. Clackson (2007: 61) states that: "PIE laryngeal may provide an example of where reconstruction is possible without the assumption of rigid sound-laws".

more serious problem connected with the laryngeal theory is the (seemingly) unknown number of extra parameters, extra rules that need to be added to the system in order for the laryngeal to operate and produce the outcomes expected from them. This being the case, it is obvious that making recourse to these segments strongly increases the flexibility, the power of the overall explanatory system. If — to play safe — we discount the roots reconstructed with the help of laryngeals, we are left with only 126 roots (i.e. 18 per cent of all the roots listed in *LIV*), that could form evidence, in principle, for genuine linguistic correlations. However, within these 126 verbal roots there are only a very small number that are widely represented across the IE linguistic area, occurring in four/five or more IE branches, as shown in the diagram reported below in *fig.* 4.1 (from Marcantonio 2009b: 15):

Thus, only a lamentably small minority of the traditionally established verbal correlations (as listed in ***LIV***) can be considered as potentially genuine. As to the nature of these correlations, there is no compelling reason to assume that they are inherited (see discussion in section 6. below).

3. The Indo-European Sound Laws

3.1. INTRODUCTION

In this section I shall discuss the issue of the validity, or otherwise, of the IE sound Laws. It has been noticed for long that the neo-grammarian model of sound change, according to which they proceed in a mechanical, linear, and exceptionless way (like the "laws" of nature) is amply contradicted by the evidence (see Alinei (2005) for a review of the situation, and discussion below). As a consequence, many (but not all) linguists nowadays interpret the traditional IE laws in terms of a "majority rule": sound changes can be seen as sound laws if they apply to a statistically significant majority of the relevant data. This is a fair claim; however, is this really the case? To

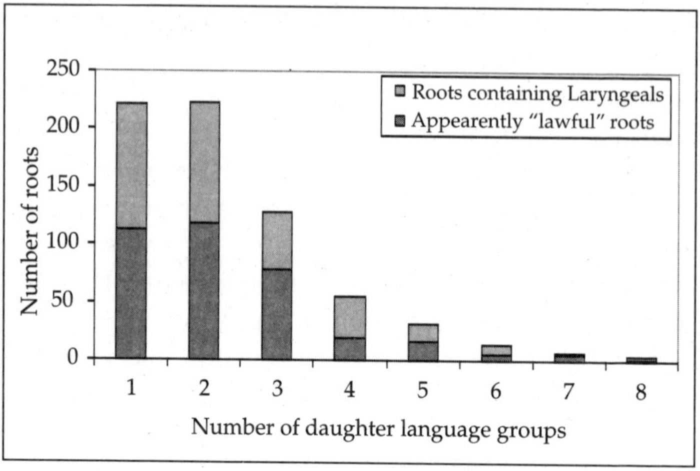

fig. 4.1: The number of verbal roots listed in ***LIV***. Only 18 per cent of these meet "three witnesses" criterion and do not contain laryngeal segments. The label "lawful" refers to the roots reconstructed without laryngeals.

find out, let us examine one of the most revered IE laws, Verner's Law.

3. 2. VERNER'S LAW

It is received wisdom in historical linguistics that sounds evolve over millennial timescales according to systematic sound Laws. This paradigm is illustrated by Grimm's Law (1819, 1822-37), which states (among others) that the hypothesized IE obstruent sounds **p*, **t* and **k* evolved into the Germanic sounds *f*, θ and *h* ~ χ respectively. Initially there was a significant body of counter-evidence to Grimm's Law (three groups of exceptions), and Verner (1877/1978) tried to explain one of these groups of exceptions. He argued that the exceptions he was investigating were only "apparent", since it could be demonstrated that they were triggered by special contextual conditions, as discussed below.

Verner observed that the obstruents resulting from

Grimm's Law become "voiced"[4] when occurring in the final position of a Germanic nominal or verbal root, unless the corresponding obstruent in the hypothesized IE ancestor noun or verb is preceded by an accent [for further discussion see Collinge[5] (1985) and Ringe (2006: 93ff.)]. Verner assumes that the accent system and the accent position(s) in Sanskrit can be equated to that of the hypothesized IE language. By operating his Law on certain Sanskrit nouns Verner predicts whether:

- **(A)**: the etymologically correspondent Germanic nominal root contains a voiceless or voiced sound in the relevant position, that is: *f*, θ, *h* ~ χ or the corresponding voiced *b*, *d* ~ ð, and *g* respectively;

By operating his Law on several Sanskrit verbal conjugations, Verner predicts whether:

- **(B)**: the etymologically correspondent Germanic verbal conjugations contain the relevant voiceless or voiced sound in the expected contexts, that is: *voiceless* in all the present tenses and the singular persons of the past tense indicative *vs* voiced in the other verbal forms (including past tense plural, past participle, etc.). The occurrence of the voiceless or voiced variant through the conjugation creates the so called Germanic "voiceless *vs* voiced sound/grammatical alternations".[6]

---

4. The original formulation of Verner's Law is quite complex; here we can give only a brief outline, grossly simplifying the supporting data and argumentations. For a detailed analysis see Marcantonio & Brady (2017).

5. Collinge (1985) lists all the established major and minor IE Laws and tendencies, also providing for each of them comments and criticisms.

6. Compare for example the Germanic root **slah* "to hit", whose relevant forms in Old Saxon, for example, are as follows: *slahan* (infinitive present, voiceless), *slōh* (past tense singular, voiceless) *vs slōgun* (past tense plural, voiced), *slagan* (past participle, voiced); see Verner (1978:38-39). Compare also →

Verner goes on to show that attested Germanic nouns and verbal conjugations match these predictions perfectly in the distribution of the expected sounds. Today, this perfect match is widely reported in textbooks as compelling evidence for Verner's Law (**VL**), and his article is (often) highly regarded: for example, Lehmann (ed., 1967: 132) says it "may be the single most influential publication in linguistics".

However, there are serious problems with Verner's demonstration of his Law, as shown in Marcantonio & Brady (2012). In fact, although Verner declares that he will use methods of analysis acceptable even in rigorous mathematics, these methods actually differ substantially from those of math, and from what one might expect. In fact, Verner's methods are biased, because the "matches" between the voiceless or voiced outcomes (in nouns), or the voiceless *vs* voiced alternations (in verbal conjugations) and his predictions are recognized, but the "mismatches" are not. In fact, Verner systematically states that he will "ignore" these mismatches (without however providing an explanation for this procedure); alternatively, various *ad hoc* explanations are supplied to explain them, or they are not mentioned at all [there is a substantial literature on the "bias" that results from procedures like this; see again Goldacre (2008)]. Marcantonio & Brady (2012) have re-analysed the same data using standard, quantitative unbiased methods. This analysis shows that a large majority of Verner's reported (attested) nouns and verbal conjugations do not match his predictions relating to the

---

→ Modern German: *ziehen* "to pull" (infinitive present, voiceless) *vs ge-zogen* (past participle, voiced). Actually, in the singular person of the past tense, as well as in other forms, we find a lot of variation. Regarding the above reported verbal conjugation, for example, the voiced variant *slōg* is more frequent than the predicted voiceless *slōh*. However, Verner disregards this fact (see Marcantonio & Brady 2012).

relevant, voiced or voiceless outcomes. It follows, to a high level of statistical confidence, that Verner's claimed correlation between the IE accent positions (in reality, the Sanskrit accent positions) and the distribution of voiced and voiceless alternations is false.[7] In other words, Verner's Law is not valid: it is not even a "majority rule". The authors further observe that Verner's biased method of analysis has propagated into historical linguistics. When examining the evidence for a given law (not just **VL**), the matches are typically cited in favour of the Law, but the mismatches may be minimized or not counted: they are "explained away" to be the result of various factors, such as "conditioning environments", "dialectal mixture", "borrowing", "secondary changes", "analogy", etc. (see Durkin 2009: 182). These explanations may appear to be reasonable, and they may well be correct in many cases; however, they introduce a bias because they are applied selectively. This has the effect of "cherry-picking" the forms that match a given Law and explaining away or disregarding the rest.

7. The reader might ask: if Verner's Law is not the triggering factor for the Germanic voiceless *vs* voiced alternations, what is it then? As discussed in Marcantonio & Brady (2012), the alternations are an intrinsic Germanic phenomenon that goes well beyond the scope of Grimm's Law. In fact, voicing may be implemented also in segments that are *not* the outcome of Grimm's Law, being a natural process of lenition that *may* take place when voiceless sounds occur in a voiced context, such as intervocalic position. Furthermore, alternations of this or similar type occur in many different languages, including, for example Italian (see section 4.5): Italian *ospedale* from Lat. *hospitālis* "hospital", but *lato* from Latin *latus*. Compare also Vulgar Latin *focu* > Spanish *fuego* but Italian *fuoco* "fire". See also similar alternations in some Sayan Turkic languages (Ragagnin 2010), etc. One may also compare the so-called consonantal gradation in Finnish, of which there are many types; for example: stem *varpaa- vs* basic form (nominative singular) *varvas* "toe", stem *hitaa- vs* basic form *hidas* "slow", etc. although here the basic factor that triggers the alternation is the structure of the syllable (Karlsson 1983).

Applying an unbiased analysis to Verner's data, the actual matches between Verner's predictions and the expected outcomes (that is: voiceless *vs* voiced alternations in verbal conjugations according to point (**B**) above), are summarized in Table 4.1 below (from Marcantonio & Brady 2012: 296):

Table 4.1: The percentage of conjugations (with their labial, dental and velar alternations, respectively) matching Verner's predictions: only 22.6 per cent of the total number of the relevant conjugations match Verner's predictions

Language	**Labial** conjugations (f *vs* b)%	**Velar** conjugations (h ~χ *vs* g)%	**Dental** conjugations (θ *vs* d ~ð)%	**Estimated** Total* %
Gothic	0	0	0	**0**
Old Norse	0	63	0	**20**
Old Saxon	0	13	0	**4**
Old English	0	69	67	**49**
Old Frisian	0	40	33	**18**
Old High German	0	47	50	**35**
Estimated Total*	**0**	**42**	**24**	**22.6**

3.3. CONCLUSION

If it were to become widely accepted in historical linguistics that it is necessary to use procedures that are designed systematically to identify and control potential sources of bias, then all the traditionally established IE sound Laws should be revisited, to verify whether or not they really meet the "majority rule" criterion. If this kind of analysis were widely carried out, it is possible that a number of established results in the field will come to be regarded as unsafe.

4. The Neo-grammarian Model of Language Change is Not Supported by the Evidence

4.1. INTRODUCTION

We have seen in the previous sections that the majority of the verbal roots listed in ***LIV*** and one of the major IE Laws, **VL**, are fraught with the same problem: they lack statistical significance. This should suffice to call into question the validity of the IE theory. Even if this were not the case, the IE theory should still be revisited because, in general, there is a body of evidence that consistently contradicts the neo-grammarian paradigm of language formation and development, that is, the fundamental tenet upon which the theory is based. This body of evidence has long been known and debated, without however having had any significant impact on the traditional IE paradigm, most probably because of the process of confirmation bias. In what follows, I shall briefely review major aspects of this debate.

4.2. ALTERNATIVE INTERPRETATIONS FOR IDENTIFIED CORRELATIONS

It is well known within historical comparative studies that when several related languages share a common feature this does not necessarily mean that it has been inherited from a common source. Inheritance is only one of the processes by which languages may share a common feature: (a) the languages may develop the feature(s) in question independently of one another (a process often called "parallel development"); (b) these features may emerge and develop in one language, in a centre of cultural/economic power (and therefore a centre of creation of innovations), and then diffuse into nearby languages like the concentric waves that form in a pond when a stone is thrown into it (Schuchardt (1866-68) and Schmidt[8] (1872); see also Jakobson (1942) for a general discussions of these issues); (c) chance resemblances, etc. It is also well known that: (d) *relatively* regular and systematic sound/word correspondences — often claimed to hold mainly among "cognates" (words inherited from a common source) — may in fact also hold between original and borrowed elements (either from different,[9] but ultimately related dialects/languages, or from unrelated languages); therefore it may not be always possible to verify whether similar/correspondent elements have been borrowed or inherited. More in general: (e) it may be difficult or even impossible to find out which of the above-listed processes, or other processes may be responsible for the shared features of a given group of languages (unless clear linguistic or extra-linguistic "proofs" are available at this regard).

These results, achieved by detailed studies of modern languages and dialects, contradict the neo-grammarian model

---

8. This "diffusion" model — the *Wellentheorie* — was propagated by Schmidt (1872), although it was actually Hugo Schuchardt who first envisaged this in his work of 1866-68. This process is well documented in dialectological studies; see for example, Chambers & Trudgill (1980).
9. A classical example is given in Jolivet & Mossé (1946: 62): some Latin words that entered the Old High German (OHG) languages underwent the Old High German Consonant Shift (OHGCS), as in Lat. *pālus* → OHG *pfāl* "pole", but others did not, as in Lat. *poena* → OHG *pīna* or *bīna*"pain". Supposedly, this different outcome in the Latin words borrowed into Germanic reflects the different times of borrowing, that is: during or after the implementation of the OHGCS, respectively. Notice, however, that Lat. *p* is *often* rendered as *b* or *p* in Germanic: Lat. *praedicare* → OHG *bredigōn* and *predigōn* "to preach"; see also the example above. This in turn shows that sound changes as well as sound substitutions may well not be regular.

of language change and formation. In fact, they show that (partial) similarities or correspondences among related languages can well be explained not by making recourse to abstract changes that would proceed blindly and mechanically, but through the actual, real behaviour of the various, relevant innovations, innovations that may spring up, singularly but in parallel with other changes, in various parts of a given speech community. This in turn means that the concept of proto-language dissolves into a multitude of different "isoglosses", each isogloss defining the geographical boundary of a certain shared feature, such as the pronunciation of a sound, the meaning of a word, the use of some syntactic constructions or grammatical elements, etc. Indeed, major dialects are typically demarcated by whole "bundles" of isoglosses that can, however, only be identified and described a posteriori.

For example, there is evidence that gold was traded between Italy and the Baltic coast in exchange for amber before the time of Christ. This trade appears to coincide with the isoglosses of the Latin word for gold, *aurum* < **ausom* (see Sabine *ausom*; Pisani 1954-55: 348; Ernout & Meillet 1954 at the lexical entry *aurum*). This suggests that the trade was the vector for the spread of the word. Indeed, *ausom* is found today in Baltic languages such as Lithuanian *áuksas* (with an unexplained -*k*-) and Old Prussian *ausis*, but it is not present either in the nearby Germanic languages (see, e.g. Gothic *gulþ*) and the nearby Slavic languages or in other IE territories, where again different terms are used. The conventional explanation, however, does not appear to take this evidence into account: supposedly, there was an original IE proto-word, which spread throughout the IE territories but became lost in those territories where it is not observed today (having been replaced by other, different terms). No independent explanation is given (or apparently required) for the loss of the original word in the languages where it is not observed

— such an explanation is obviously able to match almost any observed distribution. The only reason to favour this interpretation of the data appears to be "confirmation bias" — that is, picking the evidence that supports one's favoured theory (in this case the theory that the word is of IE origin) and ignoring the rest.

4.3. AN ALTERNATIVE INTERPRETATION FOR "RYE"

In this section I'll show an example of how the adoption of the traditional family tree model — on which the concept of proto-language and inheritance is based — typically trumps the adoption of alternative models of interpretation, despite the fact that the relevant data do not appear to support the inheritance interpretation. Compare the following two diagrams, showing the distribution of the terms indicating "rye" within the IE linguistic area and across the bordering Finno-Ugric (FU) area (from Marcantonio 2010: 2):

These parallels are mostly found in Northern Europe. Their distribution suggests that they "emerged" locally (whatever the exact point or points of origin might have been), amongst the people living around the Northern Europe and the Baltic Sea, who probably grew and traded this commodity [for more details see Marcantonio (2010)]. However, this plausible explanation does not fit in with the dominant family tree model and related classification of the languages in question, whereby Finnish and Estonian are classified as FU languages. How is then a linguist (historical linguist, or etymologist) to reconcile the above-reported evidence with the widely accepted presumption that the origin of words is to be traced back to one well-defined source through a clear-cut line of descent (in this case, ultimately, either from IE or FU)? The answer in this case has been to impose an IE origin onto the Germanic, Baltic as well as Fennic terms for "rye", as

English rye, Finnish ruis

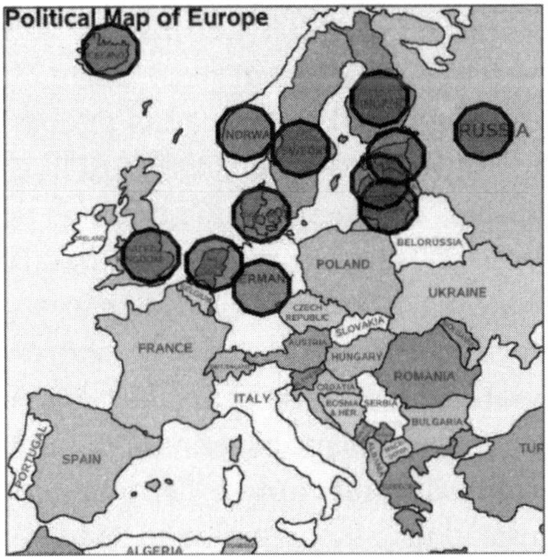

- All bordering the sea in northern Europe
  - — Crop grows in cold temperatures
  - — North European trading community
- Distribution suggests "rye" emerged from this community

Received wisdom: Indo-European origin

- Textbooks say "rye" is Probably of IE origin and borrowed into Finnish (*OED*)
  - — Rye is present in three IE language groups (Russian Germanic, Baltic) so must be IE!
  - — Reconstructed IE god *Deiwos caused rye fields to ripen (Mallory & Adams 2006, p. 408)
- Even though the distribution indicates local origin/diffusion
- **Local emergence never considered**
- **Confirmation bias**

seen in the *Oxford English Etymological Dictionary* (**OED**-on-line)[10] for the lexical entry *rye* and the Finnish etymological dictionaries for the lexical entry *ruis* (**SSA** and **SKES**).[11] The occurrence of the various parallels of *rye* in most Germanic languages, in the Baltic languages and in Russian is the basis for assuming that the word "must have" originated most likely in the Germanic linguistic area, although a Baltic origin is not excluded. This in turn "implies" that the presence of parallel terms in Finnish and Estonian "must" be the result of borrowing from Germanic into FU (more precisely, into the Fennic branch), probably at an early time of contact among the two language families. This is a plausible assumption, but an assumption nevertheless, and not a "proven", a documented fact, as it is instead usually presented in textbooks and dictionaries. The alternative assumption that the term(s) for "rye" originated just as "local" terms, is equally plausible. Actually, the latter interpretation appears to be more plausible if one takes the following factors into consideration. First, the term has a restricted, localized distribution. Second, this is one of those linguistic situations where we cannot tell apart borrowed from inherited elements, as is evident from the many — more or less regular — "variants" of this term occurring both within and across the IE and the FU area.[12] Third, even if

---

10. Early editions of the dictionary say that the word is ultimately of IE origin. Following a change of policy, later editions, including *OED*-on-line, omit to refer to high level node reconstructions, and limit themselves to actual attestations and lower level nodes. The earliest attestations of this word are in Germanic.

11. Both the *SSA* and *SKES* dictionaries state Finnish *ruis* (genitive stem *rukii-*) and related Estonian form, may be of Germanic origin (from a form reconstructable as **rugiz*), although a Baltic origin cannot be excluded.

12. Compare the following variants (from *OED*-on-line): Old Icelandic *rugr*, Norwegian *rug*, Old Swedish and Old Danish →

a process of borrowing could be assessed, it would be nevertheless impossible to establish its direction and timing. The "local emergence" interpretation in turn implies that the precise origin, or origins, of this term and related clear-cut classification as (ultimately) either IE or FU is simply beyond our reach.

On a similar basis, one could revisit the classification of those Sanskrit words whose etymology is still debated. In fact, in the (R̥g)-Vedic texts there are many words whose origin has been interpreted differently by different scholars. For example, they have been explained at the same time as being:[13]

- inherited from IE
- borrowed (mainly from Draviḍian, but also from Muṇḍa languages);
- the result of chance resemblance or other unclear processes

In this regard Hock (1996: 38) observes: "A non-partisan appraisal would have to be that, given the multiple different possible explanations, no explanation can be considered certain enough [. . .]". This being the case, one cannot exclude the alternative, simpler interpretation that the words in question emerged and spread locally, within the so-called "South Asia linguistic area" / *Sprachbund* [Emeneau (1956 & 1994) and Masica (1976)]. These potentially "autochthonous" words would have simply diffused bypassing the borders of the three major language families existing in India: IE, Draviḍian and Muṇḍā

→ *rugh*, Dutch *rogge*, Old Saxon *roggo*, *rokko*, Old High German *roggo*, *rocco*, German *Roggen*, † *Rocken*, etc., Old Prussian: *ru(g)gis*, Lithuanian *rugiai* (plural, denoting the "grain of rye" collectively), Latvian *rudzi* (plural), and Russian *ro* .

13. See Hock (1975 & 1996: 38-41); Southworth (1979); Kuiper (1955, 1991 & 1992); Burrow (1973), etc., for this intense debate.

(according to mainstream classification), their precise origin or *origins* being beyond our reach.

4.4. VARIATION AND LANGUAGE CHANGE

Examples like the terms for "rye" (with its variants bypassing the border of conventional language families), are not at all isolated. Actually, variation, that is, the existence of competing linguistic forms of the same linguistic element within a speech community[14] is the normal state of a language. This fact on its own strongly contradicts the traditional tenet that a language is essentially homogeneous and invariant at any point in time, this tenet in turn underpinning the other traditional tenet that language change is basically a systematic, abrupt shift from one steady state of language to another (see discussion below for the nature of language/sound change). This state of variation — and the vital role it plays as a vehicle of change — is seen clearly in "words histories", reported in dialectal and etymological studies. In fact, words and other linguistic elements, with their more or less numerous variants, typically form, dissolve, diffuse, change or get extinguished through an intricate, often unpredictable and unique path, or *paths*, of development. Along this path(s) there may also appear at some point some sound change(s) that have been implemented (*relatively*) regularly, but this does not change the fundamental variable nature of language. A clear example of this is the word history of the Middle and then Modern English term *poke*, that displays at least three paths of development (as traced back by Durkin (2009: 64-65):

14. That variation is the normal state of language was already observed by dialectologists and etymologists, who in fact have since long been fierce opponents of the neo-grammarians. However, it has been the pioneering work of the socio-linguists in the 1960s that has confirmed and brought into prominence the concept of variation, by showing that the choice among variants may have various causes, including ethnic and social connotations.

Path 1: "Middle English *poke /pokə/* > *pōke /pɔ : kə/* (by open syllable lengthening) > *pōke / pɔ:k/* (with loss of the final *-e*, which remains in spelling) > early Modern English */po:k/* (with vowel raising as a result of the Great Vowel Shift) → Modern English *poke / pəʊk /*" (Durkin 2009: 64)

Despite this sequence of seemingly regular changes, the actual documentation on the spelling history provided by the **OED** (at the lexical item *poke* n.1) reveals "a large number of different forms in different varieties of English, all of which developed from Middle English forms with a long vowel as a result of open syllable lengthening" (see Durkin (ibidem) for the forms in question, too numerous to be reported here). However, next to these forms, where at least the "open syllable lengthening" sound change appears to have operated fairly regularly, the ***OED*** reports another set of forms pointing to the existence of other paths of development, arising this time from a variant with a short vowel, that is: the variant *pok*, where the expected Middle English "open syllable lengthening" change has failed to materialize:[15]

Path 2: Middle English *poc, pok, puc, pokke, pocke, pock, pok*, etc.

This is, however, not yet the full form history, since there is in ***OED*** a third group of spelling for *poke* that points to the existence of yet another pathway of development, arising again from the short vowel variant: along this pathway a further change (diphthongization before velar plosive *-k*) has taken place in Scots:

Path 3: Scots: *polk > pouk > powk*

Durkin (2009: 65-66) comments on the situation as follows:

> We can already see that the development from Middle English *poke* to Modern English *poke* via Middle English open syllable lengthening and the Great Vowel Shift is

15. As is evident, the situation is complex, and I cannot report here all the details.

> paralleled by a number of other historical pathways in different varieties of English. Most of the variation displayed by *poke* is regionally based [. . .]. However, we also find formal variation that is not regionally based in origin.

Word histories can be so complex and unpredictable that it is quite possible to come up with a wrong etymology even when we are able to apply the methods of historical linguistics with a certain degree of confidence (enough knowledge about the history of the elements involved being available). This is the case of *Harvington,* the name of an English village, as traced back again by Durkin (2009: 269-71). English names with the ending *-ing-ton* are quite common,[16] whereby the element *-ton* is the antecedent of Modern English *town,* whilst *-ing-* ultimately reflects a Germanic element with the meaning "belonging to, descendent from, etc."; see for example *Paddington* "settlement named after, connected with *Padda*". Thus, judging from the modern form only, and relying on the (correct) etymology of the elements *-ing-* and *-ton,* it is more than reasonable to assume that *Harv-ing-ton* means something like "settlement/town connected to someone whose name might reflect a form of the term *Harv-*". However, if we investigate the old records relating to this noun, we get a different picture: *Herwyn-ton* (1275, etc.), *Herewin-ton* (1275, etc.), *Horin-ton* (1323), *Herwyn-g-ton* (1325), *Harwyn-ton* (1545).

The balance of the earliest forms suggests that *-g-* is not original[17] and that therefore this noun is not, as previously assumed, an "*-ing-ton*" type of noun. Rather, the forms suggest simply a "*-ton*" type of noun, something like: "a settlement/ town connected to somebody named *Her(e)wyn*". Indeed,

16. Like in the previous examples drawn from Durkin (2009), I grossly simplify the narrative, due to restriction of space and easiness of exposition.

17. The non original *-g-*, according to Durkin (*ibidem*) is probably a spelling resulting form the frequent occurrence of *-in* as a variant of *-ing*.

there exists a personal name *Herewynn*: it is an old Germanic name, in turn probably consisting of two elements (*here* "army" and *wynn* "joy"), each with their own complex histories.[18]

Regarding word histories of the type reported above, Di Giovine (1984) observes that the correct application of the methods of analysis may still not guarantee the possibility of tracing back the correct origin and pathway of development of a given word. What is needed is "the burden of proof", that is an actual "demonstration", an actual linguistic element that proves that the assumed etymology is correct. The author adds that, "sometimes", this proof may unexpectedly come up, as in the case of Venetian *apalto* and Italian *appalto* "agreed amount of money for a job to be done". In fact, like in the case of *Harvington*, here too the burden of proof was eventually found. Venetian *apalto* was supposed to derive from Late Latin **appactum*, although it was known that Venetian/Italian *-lt-* does not usually derive (at least directly) from **-ct-*. But the riddle was eventually solved when the Old French form *apaut* (**-act-* → *-aut*) was found in some thirteenth century administrative texts: this form in *-aut* constitutes the missing link between the assumed **appactum* and the attested *a(p)palto* [for many other examples of etymological issues of the sort presented here see Manco & Silvestri (eds., 2010/2011)].

The lesson to be learned from these case studies (of which there is plenty, for example in Germanic and Romance studies) is, ultimately, that reconstructions cannot be fully trusted (even if the correct criteria of analysis have been applied), unless, of course, we have the burden of proof. This being the case, one must be particularly cautious with the IE reconstructions — including the statistically significant ones — for which it is

18. There is actually another village with this name, with an equally surprising history, yet again not connected to the assumed *-ing-ton* type of name. See Durkin (2009: 270-71) for details.

much more difficult to find the burden of proof, due to the time depth involved.

4. 5. THE NATURE OF SOUND CHANGE: LEXICAL DIFFUSION

According to the neo-grammarian model, sound changes are regular, systematic and mechanical, in the sense that they are necessarily implemented every time the appropriate phonetic environment is met, irrespective of other factors. However, sounds do not occur and change in a *vacuum* — as it were. On the contrary, they are inserted in words, grammatical elements, nominal and verbal phrases, morphological constructions, sentences, speech acts that are different in different peoples, and even by the same person at different times, etc. It is therefore hard to believe, a priori, that sounds can remain totally unaffected by the events affecting the linguistic units and the speech acts they are embedded in. Indeed, sound changes, like word histories (as discussed in the previous paragraph), do not and cannot proceed regularly and mechanically, since their development is typically the result of all sorts of interacting factors: descent, contact, accidental historical events, ethnic, cultural and socio-linguistic stratification, etc., as amply demonstrated in detailed linguistic research [see, e.g. Chambers & Trudgill (1980), Labov (1994), etc.; see also the "*Lautgesetz* Controversy" (Wilbur 1977)].

This being the general scenario, it has been clearly observed for some time now *how* sound changes are actually implemented: they are introduced suddenly (for whatever reason) into just a few words of the relevant form and then they *may* spread over time to more and more (classes of) words, and possibly, but not necessarily, to all of the relevant words — in this way contributing to the building up of variation. Thus, sound changes are "phonetically abrupt" but "lexically gradual". This is contrary to the basic assumption of the neo-grammarian model, according to which sound changes are instead phonetically gradual but lexically abrupt, applying absolutely and simultaneously to every single relevant form [see, e.g. Fortson[19] (2004: 5)]. The process of gradualness in the diffusion of sound changes into the relevant lexical items (first pointed out by dialectologists) is nowadays referred to as "lexical diffusion" (Chen & Wang 1975). Thus, for example, according to the neo-grammarian model, if in a given language there comes up a sound change that transforms an inter-vocalic *-t-* into its correspondent voiced *-d-*, this change will apply regularly and systematically so as to convert every single intervocalic *-t-* occurring in that language into *-d-* (given the appropriate context). However, as mentioned, dialectological, etymological, and, more recently, socio-linguistic and "lexical diffusion" studies have shown that this is patently *not* the case; see below some examples of variation and slow diffusion of sounds, including intervocalic *-t-* and *-d-*.

Regarding the issue of whether the phonetic change itself is abrupt or gradual, the traditional view of the "organic, mechanical" nature of change implies that linguistic change also has a "duration" of some sort. However, as mentioned, observations in the field show that phonetic changes do not have a measurable duration, on the contrary, they are instantaneous. For example, when a new word is introduced into a speech community, it is not the case that it is introduced as a single, invariable form which then slowly differentiates and develops into its (dialectal and/or social) varieties; on the contrary, its variation (in one or more sounds, or other linguistic aspects) is implemented immediately (Alinei 2005: 23 ff.).[20] Equally, the process of sound substitution (if the

19. Fortson claims that: "Sound changes, importantly, are *regular* and *exceptionless* — that is, they affect all the relevant examples of the particular sound(s) in the language" [italics in original].

20. Here is a very simple and well-documented example. When →

process is implemented at all) that takes place when we pronounce a word from a foreign language, is abrupt (Alinei (1996: 173-94). As is obvious, the fact that sound changes do not proceed according to an assumed, although not well-specified "biological clock", being instead instantaneous, clearly contradicts the assumption that the IE sound changes took millennia to be implemented.[21]

It is within the above-drafted framework of language development — lexical diffusion and variation — that one can also bring into the equation the neo-grammarian principle of the (*relative*) "regularity of sound change", as pointed out by Pisani (1954-5; see also 1957). Compare, for example, the

---

→ the Italian term *televisione* (television) was first introduced, in the second half of the last century, it was immediately pronounced differently in the various Italian regions, that is: its dialectal variants were instantaneously created. For example: in the north-western dialects it was pronounced, approximately, /*televizj'un*/, in the north-eastern dialects /*televizj'ɔn*/ and in the southern dialects /*televizj'ɔn∂*/ (Alinei 2005: 24).

21. At this point one might ask how the thesis of the abrupt nature of sound change would apply to well-established sound changes and correspondences of the type: Sanskrit *bhárāmi*, Latin *ferō*, Greek φέρω, Gothic *baíra*, etc. (see section 6.2). Assuming the inheritance (and not the borrowing) interpretation, the answer may be as follows, as proposed by Alinei (2005). It is not the case that, for ex., *bh- (and/or the other sounds forming the root *bher-) has taken millennia to convert into the various sounds in question; on the contrary, the single sound change itself has been abrupt (at some point in time). However, the words containing this/these sounds have been transmitted from one generation to another unchanged, since "change" is not the only force operating in languages, the opposite tendency, "conservativism", being another strong force too, particularly in written languages, as is the case here. It is the interplay of these (and other) phenomena that give the (false) impression that sound change takes long time to be implemented.

variation in the occurrence of (late) Latin *fede*(*m*) next to, or instead of *fide*(*m*) "trust", *pece*(*m*) next to *pice*(*m*) "pitch" and *menu* next to *minu*(*s*) "minus" (probably somebody, at some point in a given speech community pronounced a closed *e* instead of short *i*). At some other point, other speakers have learned and imitated the new pronunciation through isolated words. At this point at least two different directions of development might have been possible: (a) the sound change (the new pronunciation) could have occurred only in those words where it was first noticed, for example in *fede*, *pece* but *minu*, or (b): it could have extended elsewhere (perhaps by another group of speakers), encompassing also *minus*, thus yielding *fede*, *pece* and *menu*. As it happens, eventually closed *e* substituted short *i* in almost all the territory where Latin was spoken. However, this *almost regular* change took place because of a (probably) conscious imitation on behalf of groups of speakers, or because of other historical/social factors [for which see again Labov (1994)], and not because of the operation of mechanical and exceptionless laws. That this is indeed the correct analysis is confirmed by the fact that the change in question took place through slow diffusion and variation from one group of words to another, a diffusion observable also in the variable pronunciation of the same single individual.

To take another example, in some Latin inscriptions (Diehl 1910, n. 153) somebody writes *avetat* instead of *habitat* (he/she lives) with *e* instead of *i* in non-accented syllable, as well as *anemola* instead of *animula*, where *i* bears the accent this time (the change being triggered perhaps by the model of *anema* instead of *anima* (soul) with *e* once again in non-accented syllable). Compare also "aborted" sound changes, such as the "partial" diffusion of a new pronunciation, coming from the north of Italy into Tuscany and therefore into literary Italian, that is: the voiced counterpart of the voiceless consonants in intervocalic position: *ospedale* from Latin *hospitālis* (hospital), *lago* from Latin *lacus* (lake), as against *lato* (side), *maturo* (ripe, mature) and *oca* (goose) from Latin *lātus, matūrus* and *auca* respectively [see again Pisani (1954-55)]. Another clear example of lexical diffusion is the change *th* (~ *dh*) > *d* in various Germanic languages, as seen in English *brother* and *three vs* German *Bruoder* and *drei*. This change started from about the second half of the eighth century in the (southern) Old High German dialects (Bavarian and Alemannic), and diffused slowly, and partially, into the central (Franconian) dialects, but did not reach the (northern) Saxon dialect, for example, where in fact *th* ~ *dh* is the norm. In addition, where the change did take place, it was implemented in a highly messy way. In fact, the two variants often co-occurred in the same dialect or text in certain words and/or certain positions in the words but not in others, or one variant became prominent at the expense of the other in a few dialects for a certain period in certain words, or the shifted sound (*d*) advanced and then receded (aborted) altogether in some words in some dialects, etc., until it became the "norm" (see below) in standard and literary German (Braune 1975: 162-67).

These examples also show that sound changes are not specific of a given language/language group, as traditionally assumed, but are instead a set of single phenomena, a set of isoglosses that take place each on its own accord, spreading in different ways and encompassing all sort of exceptions. However, when a sound change diffuses so much at the point of achieving the status of a "generally accepted variant" (as in the case of intervocalic *-d-* in the Italian literary language, as illustrated above, through the prestige of the Tuscany dialect), then it typically ends up to be considered as the "norm" within the territory included in the isogloss in question. This norm, often determined by socio-economic factors (as socio-linguistics has shown), is the result of a "chosen variant" within a set of possible variants — it should be stressed — *not* the result of a systematic, mechanical sound law, not even in its modern interpretations in terms of "majority rule"!

5. Laryngeals: A "Truth Scientifically Demonstrated"?

5. 1. INTRODUCTION

It is widely reported that the IE theory underwent "a paradigm shift in the Kuhnian sense" (Clackson 2007: 53). Allegedly, "the most spectacular coup" occurred in 1927, a coup that "transformed the laryngeal hypothesis into a truth scientifically demonstrated" (Szemerényi 1987: 207, 209; my translation). This is a strong claim about scientific validity. Is it true or is this another instance of confirmation bias?

5.2. THE LARYNGEAL THEORY

The laryngeal hypothesis can be traced back to 1879, when Saussure tried to match the vowels of the various IE languages as well as to reconstruct one single type of root in IE.[22] He found that the vowels and vowel alternations in the attested languages did not match according to his assumptions. In order to correct these mismatches, he hypothesized the existence of certain phonological segments in proto-IE, which he labelled *A and *O, calling them: *coefficients sonantiques*. These segments would have affected the syllable nuclei in various ways, according to their various positions in the root,[23] in this manner producing the desired outcome (matches in vowels, vowels

---

22. In line with the assumptions of the day, Saussure thought that uniformity of root structure had to be achieved. Assumptions like this are not so fashionable today, as it is recognized that "variation" is the norm in language.

23. Laryngeals can occur in the following positions in the root: (1) inter-consonantal position, (2) post-vocalic position, (3) word-initial (pre-vocalic) position, (4) post-resonant position, (5) word-initial (pre-consonantal) position, and, finally: (6) position after a voiceless stop in Indo-Iranian.

alternations and syllable structure) before disappearing.[24] This hypothesis has subsequently been modified in various ways: for example, Saussure (1879: 184) was clear that the postulated coefficients were vowels or semi-vowels, not consonants,[25] but today they are usually regarded as consonants, on the basis of some observations and claims first made by Möller (1880) and later confirmed by Cuny[26] (1912). The "spectacular coup" was (supposedly) the discovery by Kuryłowicz (1927) that Saussure's postulated segment **A* in IE is represented in Hittite by a symbol, of uncertain phonetic value, that in the cuneiform script is written as *h* (often written *ḫ* in the literature). This discovery would have fulfilled the "prediction" made by Saussure — the existence of the IE *coefficients* — whilst also confirming their consonantic value, as envisaged by Möller and Cuny (see discussion below).[27]

24. It is clear from this that, strictly speaking, Saussure was not trying to make any prediction (at least not explicitly), but only to cope with difficult mismatches, by postulating *ad-hoc* segments.

25. Saussure states that the coefficients belong to the class of *'sonantes'*, together with *i, u, n, m, r* (l), and are to be distinguished from consonants; see also (Szemerényi 1987: 200), who points this out.

26. The consonantic value of the coefficients was first proposed by Möller (1880: 150 and 151 fn.), followed by Cuny (1912). Möller did not back up his proposal with any real evidence; instead he made (cautious) suggestions about the possibility that these segments might have been consonatic, more precisely, "laryngeal" (*"kehlkopfspirants ?"*, or *"kehlkopf-r ?"*; p. 151; fn.). As to Cuny, he supported Möller's proposal by observing that, given certain contexts, these segments behaved as if they were less sonorous than vowels and resonants, and must have been, therefore, probably, fricative. In other words, the "coefficients/laryngeals" were less sonorant than the resonants. However, nowadays there appears to be a going back to the vocalic interpretation of the coefficients, as discussed in the text.

27. The story of the origin and development of the laryngeal →

5.3. A FULFILLED PREDICTION?

Disregarding the fact that Saussure was making no proper predictions (see footnote 24), and that his coefficients were not conceived as "consonantic" in any case (see footnote 25), the reality is that Kuryłowicz claimed nothing of the sort usually reported in the specialist literature and textbooks. Kuryłowicz (1927) lists 23 sets of (supposed) Hittite *vs* other IE cognates, often with related reconstructions (most of which are not referenced). This list contains 14 sets of words (that is, 14 sets of supposed cognates) where, the Author observes, **A* in the reported IE cognates is "never represented by *h* in Hittite" (p.104, my translation), and 9 sets of words (9 sets of supposed cognates) where, instead, the assumed **A* in the IE cognates "is represented by *h* in Hittite" (pp.101-02) — compare the "Appendix" for the full lists of these 23 sets of cognates.

This amounts to the *unsurprising* observation that IE **A* either is, or is not represented by *h* in Hittite. Logically, this

→ theory is long and complex. Its supposed advances and set backs include competing elements, some of which appear to be contradictory (such as the question of whether the coefficients are consonantic in nature or not). Here we highlight only those steps that are "key steps" to the alleged scientific demonstration. For more detail see Szemerényi (1987), Clackson (2007: 55-61), Lehmann (1955: 22-35, 85-98, 103-08), Reynolds, West & Coleman (1998), etc. For a critical review of the laryngeal theory see, for example, Gusmani (1979), Misra (1977), Di Giovine (2005) and Marcantonio (2009b: 14-15, 30-33). See also Bonfante (1944), who rejects the laryngeal theory altogether, mainly because of the following shortcomings: (a) the "protean character" (p. 54) of these segments, that is, their extreme flexibility in quality, quantity and mode of operation, in this way being able to solve any identified problems of reconstruction, this analysis being confirmed in Marcantonio (2009b: 14-15, 30-33); (b) the fact that alternative, simple solutions are in fact available to solve the observed mismatches, some examples of which are given on pp. 53-54.

does not establish the claim that *A is represented by h in Hittite (in some environments). More generally, see Law (2011: 75-80) for what is needed to establish a theory in the usual practice of science. For instance, a theory must make predictions that would not be expected anyway. However, Kuryłowicz's observations would not be a *surprise*, almost whatever model one subscribes to. For example, the evidence presented (as reported in "Appendix") does not even allow one to distinguish between the following two possible models of interpretation (although the fact that the expected match between *A and h is missing in the majority of cases might suggest "model 2" as more appropriate):

(Model 1): IE *A *is* represented by Hittite h (with 14 exceptions)

(Model 2): IE *A *is not* represented by Hittite h (with 9 exceptions)

Kuryłowicz does not discuss this issue. He simply introduces a new hypothesis: that Saussure's coefficient *A has a *double valeur* (p. 95). He writes the symbol ∂_1 where there is no h in Hittite, and ∂_2 where there is an h in Hittite. This is, of course, nothing more than a description, in symbols, of the mere fact that IE *A and Hittite h match in some cases and do not match in other cases (in fact, they do not match in the majority of cases). Contrary to what is reported in most textbooks, it is not the confirmation of a "prediction" made by Saussure, but simply an amendment to his theory after the fact (a "post-diction").

How can we understand the process which has led to these observations becoming elevated, in the published literature, into an alleged "spectacular coup" that has supposedly demonstrated the theory as a "truth scientifically demonstrated"? When later authors examined Kuryłowicz's evidence, it appears to have become common practice to highlight the 9 sets of words that match the proposed model, and to downplay the 14 sets of words that do not match it. No independent criterion is suggested for making such choices. See Law (2011: 176) for a description of what is required for a criterion to be independent of the model proposed, and why such procedures are not accepted in the normal practice of scientific research, because they can amount to "cherry-picking" the data.

If one were to attempt to make the best of this "discovery", one might nowadays apply statistical reasoning. This approach would depart from that of the original authors, who believed in the exceptionless nature of sound change. Any attempt to apply statistical reasoning to this data would immediately run into the difficulty that a sample of 23 sets of cognates is likely to represent insufficient data to make strong conclusions. For example, assuming a "null hypothesis" that the matches were the result of a random event (such as in a coin toss), there would be 11.5 matches with a standard deviation of 2.4. The value observed by Kuryłowicz is close to one standard deviation of this expected value. This means there is insufficient data to establish the claimed correlations. A valid statistical analysis would also need to ensure that the data, that is, the reported attestations from Hittite and the other IE languages quoted, were independently chosen. Similarly, the proposed reconstructions should be independently made, in order to avoid confirmation bias (see Law 2011: 176). This task faces the difficulty that Kuryłowicz does not consistently make a reference either to his reported attestations or his proposed reconstructions (see again "Appendix" for details).

5. 4. CONCLUDING REMARKS ON LARYNGEALS

From what has been highlighted thus far, it is clear that

Kuryłowicz's (1927) essay does not contain any data and/or demonstrations that can be hailed as a paradigm shift of the Kuhnian type. This would still be the case even if Saussure had made a specific, *surprising* prediction by assuming the consonantic/fricative nature of his postulated coefficients.

It is worth noting at this point that the thesis of the consonantic/fricative nature of the laryngeals has recently been called into question. As anticipated in footnote (26), Cuny (1912) argued that the Saussurian "coefficients" must have been consonantal, and not vocalic segments, because, in his view, they were less sonorant than the resonants. More specifically, Cuny (1912: 102-3) observed that if the coefficients **A* and **O* (as well as the later added coefficient **E*) were followed by a resonant (*r, l, m, n*), it was the resonant, and not the postulated "laryngeal", that became a vowel. In other words, a resonant occurring adjacent to a laryngeal forms a syllable nucleus, in preference to the laryngeal; this in turn would mean that the laryngeals, originally, were less sonorous, *moins facilement vocalisable* (p. 102) than the resonants. However, Reynolds et al. (1998) argue that there is no need to refer to the notion of "sonority" to explain this process of vocalization. According to their analysis:

> The fact that the resonant precedes the "laryngeal" is sufficient to make it a syllable head. In fact, it is problematic to deduce relative sonority on the basis of syllabification, because syllable structure often does not respect sonority sequencing generalizations. —p. 99

The Authors also show how all the assumed developments of the laryngeals and their (supposed) consequent effects on adjacent sounds may equally well, if not better, be explained by classifying them as: "metrically weak vocalic segments within orthodox syllable theory" (p. 99). Thus, Reynolds et al. conclude that, if one analyses the evidence for the laryngeals in the light of generative phonology[28] (p. 84), the consonantal/fricative hypothesis does not stand up to scrutiny. In fact, "the internal evidence for it is restricted to a few words in individual languages, and the rather stronger external evidence is based on unusual typological parallels" (p. 84). In contrast, the analysis of the IE "laryngeal" interpreted "as a vowels subsystem fits all of the internal evidence" (p. 102) — compare also Bonfante (1944) for alternative interpretations to account for the (assumed) effects of laryngeals.

The results of Reynolds et al. analysis can be interpreted in two ways: (A) the coefficients were claimed to be consonantic in nature, but now they turn up to be vocalic. In this case the "prediction" was wrong. (B): it does not matter whether the coefficients turn up as vowels or consonants, what matters is the very fact that "a" segment was postulated in proto-IE in the relevant positions (for which see footnote 23), and it did turn up. In this case, no "scientific" prediction has really been made, since a scientific prediction has to be specific and surprising in order to be verified, or falsified. Either way, the laryngeal hypothesis cannot be hailed as a truth scientifically demonstrated, since it is so flexible that it is capable of "predicting" almost any outcome.

Last, but not the least, the following problems are worth mentioning. First, the "particularly puzzling [. . .] paradox that laryngeals are lost nearly everywhere" (Clackson 2007:

28. The Authors analyse the IE laryngeals in the light of contemporary phonological theory, by this meaning mainstream generative phonology as presented in textbooks, such as Kenstowicz (1994). There is no room here to illustrate this framework. It suffices to say that this approach is driven by the search of universals of phonological structure, including those universals relevant to the analysis of laryngeals, that is: syllable structure, metrical weight and categories such as vowel, consonants, glides, etc.

59). Indeed, the "fact" that laryngeal segments are nowhere to be found in the other IE languages (part of them having been (allegedly) lost even in Hittite[29] and the other Anatolian languages) is hard to justify. Second, the curious fact that the laryngeal theory is now widely (although not universally) accepted, whilst the basic assumption that suggested the "laryngeal value" of the *coefficients sonantiques* is, instead, widely rejected, that is: the genetic relationship of IE and Semitic. Indeed, Möller (1880 & 1906) and the other, early proponents of the laryngeal hypothesis came up with the thesis of the consonantic/laryngeal value of the Saussurian coefficients by applying the principles of Semitic phonology to the IE data, in the attempt to prove the genetic connection among the languages in question.

6. Borrowed or Inherited?

6.1. THE BORROWING INTERPRETATION IN LEXICON

There are several ways in which correlations among (related or non-related) languages can be explained (see in section 4.2 above). In particular, in explaining possible correlations among languages believed to be related, scholars should also take into account the possibility that some (/many?) of the identified lexical correspondences (after one has removed those that have no significance) may be the result of borrowing. That this is indeed a real possibility appears to be widely recognized. For example Fortson (2004: 12), after stating that reconstructions are more difficult to achieve, the further back in time one goes, says that:

> Borrowing becomes indistinguishable from native words, semantic changes make it difficult to reconstruct word meanings, and morphological analogies and levelling processes erase evidence of earlier inflectional patterns.

29. Melchert (1994: 6-74) gives an account of the (supposedly) "lost" laryngeal segments.

Clackson (2007: 6) observes that: "Lexical and phonological developments are too easily shared through linguistic convergence". Garret (2006), in his study of Old Greek dialects, concludes that: (a) it is not possible to construct a unified, invariant entity that could be labelled as proto-Greek; (b) the true historical filiation of the IE family is unknown; (c) the familiar IE branches arose not by orderly, subsequent differentiation of earlier, higher order subgroups, but by convergence among neighbouring dialects in dialectal *continuum*. Jakobson, already in (1942) had pointed out the "importance" of the "acquired" similarities, both among related and not-related languages. He further observed (1942: 352) that the similarities shown by two forms could be secondary, recently acquired features whilst, in contrast, their differences could be primary, inherited features, so that the distinction of organisms in "related" and "not-related" loses its relevance

> *Ainsi «les ressemblances que deux formes présentent dans leur organisation peuvent être un fait secondaire acquis récemment, et au contraire les différences être un fait primaire hérité». Dans ces conditions la distinction des organismes en apparentés et non-apparentés perd son caractère décisif.*

This being the state of the art, the obvious question arises: how can we be so sure that all the identified IE lexical correlations are inherited, rather than borrowed?

6.2. THE BORROWING INTERPRETATION IN GRAMMAR

The borrowing interpretation can apply also to the grammatical/morphological correlations — traditionally considered to be one of the pillars[30] underpinning the IE theory, because of their alleged resistance to borrowing.

30. There is no room here to discuss the role of grammar in assessing genetic correlations, or the extent at which grammatical borrowing may occur; for a review see Marcantonio (2009a).

It has been known for quite some time that (mutual) grammatical borrowing (between genetically related and not-related languages), including case and verbal stems and endings, derivational suffixes, etc., does occur — given the appropriate contact circumstances and length of time. Compare for example Pisani (1954-55), Gusmani (1986), Alinei (1996: 172 ff.), Durkin (2009: 133 ff.), Thomason & Kaufman (1988); Johanson (2002), etc. On the other hand, Matras (2009) presents evidence that case and verbal inflections in Romani (a mixed language) tend to be borrowed "wholesale", if they are borrowed at all. For example, the Greek-derived tense markers in Romani are characterized by a wholesale import of the entire paradigm, rather than of individual markers. Compare also Levin (1995), who lists numerous, at times striking, examples of lexico-grammatical, "wholesale correlations" between IE and Semitic languages (whatever their interpretation may be).[31] On the other hand, Greenberg (1953/2005: 15), for example, has observed that when forms, in general, are "too similar" (whatever the measurement for this would be), they could be the result of borrowing, rather than inheritance, because the "historical remoteness of the assumed relationship" is likely to have disrupted such a close similarity (see also the quote by Jakobson reported in the previous paragraph; for general issues on how (possibly) to distinguish between borrowed and inherited features see Croft (2005)). There are some instances of "wholesale correlations" within IE, at times spanning entire paradigms. For example, textbooks frequently cite tables illustrating the verb "to carry, to bear", which shows amazing correspondences across Sanskrit, Greek,

31. Levin (1995: 11) states: "This volume presents the main etymological evidence upon which to rest a comparative grammar of Semitic and Indo-European. For the five long chapters contain the key examples of morphological correspondences, afforded by nouns, verbal roots, pronouns, prepositions, and numerals."

Latin, Gothic, Old Irish, etc., in most forms of the declension of the (thematic) present tense, as well as in the lexical forms (compare Sanskrit *bhárāmi*, Latin *ferō*, Greek φέρω, Gothic *baíra*, etc.). The verb "to be" also shows striking similarities in lexicon and morpho-phonological alternations, across the present tense paradigm [Fortson (2004: 87); Sihler (1995: 548); Clackson (2007: 124-25), etc.], as shown below:

IE	$*h_1$*és-mi*			$*h_1$*és-ti*			$*h_1$*sénti*	
Lat.	*sum*	'I am'	*vs*	*est*	'he/she is'	*vs*	*sunt*	'they are'
Gk.	*eimí*	"	*vs*	*estí*	"	*vs*	*eisí*	" (Attic)
Skt.	*ásmi*	"	*vs*	*ásti*	"	*vs*	*sánti*	"

The traditional interpretation is that these patterns can only be inherited. However, in the light of recent research on language in contact (as outlined above), it is legitimate to wonder whether these patterns might represent, instead, instances of wholesale borrowing — although the answer to this question is difficult. For example, there do not appear to be instances of borrowing of the verb "to be" within or across other language families.[32] Furthermore, Romani is a mixed language, and, as pointed out by Matras, the imported verb paradigm exists in complementary distribution alongside the inherited inflection paradigm. This is certainly not the case within IE, even if (it can be objected), here we are dealing with written records that might well have eliminated any instances of variation, of competing forms.

Whatever the case, the major problem in assessing grammatical correlations is that applying consistently the comparative method is even more difficult at this level of language than at the level of phonology and lexicon, because

32. For example, there is no borrowing of the copula within Uralic, within Altaic or across Uralic and Altaic, although there are many correlations among these two (traditionally estabilished) families.

of several factors, including the disruptive operation of analogical levelling (indeed, it is often claimed that grammatical correlations are simply "self-evident"). Harrison depicts the situation as follows (2003: 223):

> Grammatical objects fair poorly as evidence for genetic relatedness [. . .]. There can be no regularity assumption for grammatical objects to provide a measure of similarity, because grammatical objects are unique.

As a matter of fact, if we look at the various forms and paradigms of the verb "to be" a little closer, for example, we discover that there are several problems, in the sense that the correlations are not, after all, that clear-cut and "self-evident". In the present tense the Latin forms pose some difficulties, because, as pointed out by Sihler (1995: 549), "despite appearances, none of the forms [. . .] with the exception of *sunt* are directly inherited, no matter how simple a development like **esti* > *est* looks on its face". As to the imperfect tense, "there is no historical connection between the G[reek] and the L[atin] paradigms called the imperfect" (Sihler 1995: 550-52), the explanation being that: "the PIE imperfect was lost without a trace in Italic" (Fortson 2004: 250), as well as in the other IE languages, as an original, separate category. As to the perfect tense, for example, we find in Latin the following forms: *fuī, fuistī, fuit* ("I was", etc.). These (suppletive) forms are claimed to be based on the aorist tense of the IE root **bhū-* (~ **bhuH*, with laryngeal notation), the same root seen in Vedic aorist *á-bhū-t* and Greek aorist *ἔ-φῦ* "he/she has become, was, etc." (Sihler 1995: 552; ***LIV*** 83-85). However, in Sanskrit the root *bhū-* is fully productive in all sort of tenses and moods, including the perfect *ba-bhū́-va* (and many more other forms of perfect; Macdonell (1995: 402-03); see also Marcantonio (2009b: 23 ff.)]. In contrast, Latin *fu-* is only used in a bunch of forms, in addition to the above listed ones.[33] Similarly, the root *h_1*es*- is much more productive in Sanskrit than in Latin and Greek, having also a full imperfect and perfect conjugation (Macdonell 1995: 370-71). Last, but not the least, it must be pointed out that the two IE roots in question (*h_1*es*- and **bhuH*-) have been reconstructed with the help of laryngeal segments, whose intervention is critical in achieving the desired match among several of the (assumed) sound correspondences and derivations. It could be objected, correctly, that here there are also some regular sound correspondences that have been established without making recourse to laryngeal segments and that are supported by other (although not numerous) sets of cognates, such as Sanskrit *bh* *vs* Latin *f* (< IE **bh*). However, we do not have the "burden of proof"; furthermore, the development of the voiced aspirates in Latin (**bh* > *f*, **dh* > *f* and **gh* > *h*) is complicated and still a little controversial (Szemerényi 1990: 55-56). Thus, it may well be possible that Sanskrit *bhū*- and Latin *fu*- have nothing to do with one other, being an artefact of the method of analysis.

To summarize and conclude: the forms of the various IE languages relating to the widely reported present paradigm of "to be" are so close that could be interpreted *also* as the result of borrowing. In contrast, the forms/paradigms of the perfect and imperfect tense are not so close at all, suggesting instead a long process of divergence from the assumed proto-language. In other words: the picture is messy (as expected), and the evidence appears to be inconclusive as to the nature of the connection. However, probably because of confirmation bias, a clear cut, well-ordered picture is typically presented in textbooks, whereby the genetic connection is given as a "proven fact", rather than for what it is: a plausible (but also

33. See for example the plus-perfect *fu-eram* "I had been", Latin future perfect *fu-erit* and Umbrian *fu-s-t*, both meaning "he will have been", the subjunctive *fu-at*, etc. (Fortson 2004: 250-51; Sihler 1995: 552).

arguable) interpretation of the data. Actually, from the evidence and argumentations outlined above it follows that the paradigm of the perfect and imperfect would be more appropriate than that of the present in support of the genetic interpretation.

7. Summary and Conclusion

In the previous paragraphs I have highlighted the following:

- the traditionally established (lexical and grammatical) IE correlations, at an unbiased, statistical analysis, turn out to be much less numerous, less "compelling" than usually believed;
- the highly idealized neo-grammarian model, encompassing the nature of language and language change, the sound Laws and the family tree diagram, is not supported by the actual evidence of how languages form, develop, change and diffuse in the real world. In particular, one major law of IE, Verner's law, at a closer investigation, does not even meet the "majority rule" criterion;
- data contradicting the IE theory, of which there is plenty, are hardly ever labelled as "counter-evidence"; on the contrary, they are ignored, or minimized, or justified at any cost, as we have seen with Verner's Law;[34]
- even if a high number of statistically significant (lexical and/or grammatical) correlations could be eventually

---

34. This process of confirmation bias is at work also in more modern research. For example, recently many computer-generated IE family trees have been proposed, that are supposed to be more reliable than traditional ones because (thanks to computers) they are designed on the basis of a large amount of data and statistical techniques. However, the Germanic branch does not fit the expected results in this

→

identified within the traditional IE comparative corpus, and even if it could be demonstrated that most IE laws do meet the "majority rule" criterion, inheritance would not be the only possible explanation.

It is true to say that several linguists nowadays do recognize that contact and other factors are an integral part of the life of any language, at least at the lexical/phonological level (see section 4 above). Some other scholars (particularly in the last century) have positively interpreted IE as a *Sprachbund*, meaning that the identified correlations are basically "acquired". Compare in this regard Trubetzkoy (1939), who first proposed this (see a detailed discussion of his views in Clackson's article in this volume); Pisani (1954-55, 1957, 1974, etc.); Alinei (1996), etc.; see also the quoted paper by Jakobson (1942) regarding the general issue of the various, possible origins of the "phonological affinities".[35]

As to the sound laws, as mentioned, several scholars nowadays interpret them in the sense of "majority rule"; but see Fortson (2004), who still embraces the thesis of the "exceptionless" nature of sound change (see footnote 19). However, as far as I know, this "majority rule" interpretation has only been "assumed" and not "verified", a part from the study on Verner's Law by Marcantonio & Brady (2012). Thus, at the moment, we do not really know whether or not the other traditional laws of IE meet this criterion.

Several scholars also recognize that there are further methodological issues within this context. For example,

---

→ exercise, and it has therefore been discarded from the computer-generated tree proposed by Ringe et al. (2002), with the explicit justification that there is no "best-fit tree" if Germanic is included.

35. N.S. Trubetzkoy is the founder of modern, structural phonology; R. Jakobson is the founder of the phonological analysis in terms of "distinctive features".

Clackson (2007: 3) points out that the application of the comparative method

> . . . does not guarantee a language's place in the family: only the initial recognition that two or more languages are related can do that. [. . .] There is no absolute set of criteria [to classify a language as IE] beyond the general rule that the evidence must convince both the individual linguist and the majority of the scholarly community.[36]

Nevertheless, probably because of the process of confirmation bias, the results of this stimulating debate do not appear to have had any significant impact on the IE theory and the every day practice of reconstruction.[37]

I personally believe that it is time to call into question the validity of the IE theory, because, as we have seen, it has not been scientifically founded — contrary to common belief. Actually, a theory of this sort may be regarded as "not even wrong",[38] in the sense that it is built up in such a self-consistent way that it cannot be either verified or falsified. It is true that

---

36. Clackson (2007: 2) also observes that: "There has been no advance on Jones' criterion for relatedness between languages of the [IE] family: greater similarity in verbal roots and morphological paradigms than might be expected by chance".
37. For example, there is ambiguity as to whether the concept "IE family" should be interpreted as a "pre-historical fact" or purely and simply as a theoretical construct. For example, Fortson (2004), Mallory (1989) and Mallory & Adams (2006) assume the existence of a real, IE-speaking community — on this issue compare also the article by Clackson in this volume. In contrast, for example, Harrison (2003: 231) states that: "Too many comparative historical linguists want to dig up Troy, linguistically speaking [. . .]. I do not consider comparative historical linguistics a branch of prehistory".
38. These words are attributed to the eminent physicist W. Pauli, with regard to a theory within physics, according to Rees (1999/2000: 76).

there are some statistically significant correlations among the IE languages; but, according to the analyses carried out thus far, they too represent a small percentage of the overall comparative corpus to be of any significance — a quantitative analysis of all the areas of the IE comparative corpus would be required before trying to assess the nature of the identified correlations. Even if it could be demonstrated that there are many more statistically significant correlations and that these correlations are inherited — as argued by Clackson in this volume, on the ground that this is the most economical interpretation — the existence of an actual IE proto-language still could not be proven. In fact, as argued by Pisani (1957), what we reconstruct is only single forms, single bits, single elements of a language or language group, or, at best, single isoglosses (whose origin may be difficult to ascertain) and not the entire language/language group. Compare also Kazanas (2002, 2009 and in this volume), who argues that IE is not reconstructable (mainly because of the intrinsic irregularity of sound change and the flawed application of the methods of historical linguistics), although the author accepts the thesis of a genetic relation among the IE languages on different grounds.[39]

This being the state of the art, I also believe that there is no reason to uphold the thesis that Sanskrit is "genetically" connected to the other (supposed) IE languages, and that, therefore, its origin is to be found somewhere in the West. The origin of the Indian civilization definitively needs revisiting, and not only on the basis of linguistic data and

39. According to the Author, the IE language family must have existed — Sanskrit being part of it — because there are many lexical and grammatical "similarities" (as against "correspondences"), as well as, and most importantly, cultural correlations among the IE languages which could not be explained if not assuming a genetic relationship.

analysis, but also through the contribution of the other disciplines typically engaged in tracing back the origin of peoples and civilizations, such as archaeology, palaeo-anthropology and genetics.

Appendix

In what follows, I shall list all the Hittite *vs* other IE languages cognates exactly as reported by Kuryłowicz (1927), without further comments. Nevertheless, I shall translate the meaning of the reported examples, if provided, and add the missing meaning of some other examples, if necessary [according to the dictionary Walde (1954), the dictionary mostly used by Kuryłowicz; see also Frisk (1960)]. The reader will form his/her own opinion on the quality and quantity of these data.

The 9 sets of cognates where IE *A is represented by *h* in Hittite (p. 101) are the following:

(A) *h* in initial position: Hittite. *hantezzi* "the first" *vs* Latin *ante*, Armenian *andrank* and Greek ἀντί; Hittite *henkan* "death" *vs* Latin *neco* "to kill", Greek. ἀνάγκη "constraint, necessity", Breton *ankou* & Welsh *angeu* "death"; Hittite *hūiš*(*u*) "to live" *vs* Sanskrit *vásati*, Greek ἰαύω "to spend the night", Old High German *wësan* "to be" and Armenian *goy* "he exists"; Hittite *hark-* "to shine" *vs* Greek ἀργής "shining" and Old Indian *árjuna-* (there is one final set of cognates in this batch, but I do not report them because the Author considers them as uncertain).

(B) *h* in internal and final position: Hittite *išhiia* "to bind" *vs* Latin *saeta* "little bristle"; Hittite *šuhh* "to throw, pour, etc." *vs* Old Indina *sūváti, sūté* (*savitár-*); Hittite *pahš* "to take care, look after" *vs* Latin *pāscor* (< *pā*(s) + *scor*) "to graze" (*pāstor* "shepherd"); Hittite *wah-nu* (~ *weh*) "to turn, twist" *vs* Latin *vārus* "bent outwards"; Hihhite *pahhur* "fire" *vs* Gothic *fōn* (< *pā-un*) – in this batch too there is one final set, whereby, however, the single Greek word corresponding to the Hittite attestation is considered to be of non-IE origin.

The 14 sets of cognates where IE **A* is never represented by *h* in Hittite (p. 104) are the following (quoting from Hittite):

> *eš* "to be"; *eš* "to sit down"; *ed* ~ *ad* "to eat"; *-a-* third person enclitic pronoun; *anda*(*n*) "inside" *vs* Greek ἔνδον; *ar* "to come, go" *vs* Latin *erro*, Sankrit *ṛṇóti*, *ṛccháti*; *apiia* "there" *vs* Greek ἐπί; *dâ* "to put (down)"; *it* "go!"; *aššuš* "good" *vs* Greek ἐύς; *lâ* "to undo"; *arraš* "anus" *vs* Irish *err*, Greek ὄρρος and Old High German *ars*; *ug*(*g*)*a* "I" *vs* Latin *ego* and Greek ἐγώ; *veš* "to *dress*" *vs* Latin *vestis* and Greek ἕννυμι.

Kuryłowicz (pp. 102-03) attempts to support his thesis also by establishing three sets of Hittite *h vs* IE **A* correspondences at the grammatical level, that is: (1) Hittite *h* as a frequent final element of verbal root, after a nasal or liquid; (2) as a suffix forming denominal verbs; and (3) as a component of the present singular verbal endings *-hi*, *-ti* and *-i*. However, the supposed IE cognates and/or related endings are hardly reported, so that it is difficult to make sense of this "evidence".

References

Aiyar, R.S., 1975, *Draviḍian Theories*, Madras Law Journal Office.

Alinei, M., 1996, *Origini delle Lingue d'Europa, La Teoria della Continuità*, I, Bologna: Il Mulino.

———, 2005, "Conservation and Change in Language," *Quaderni di Semantica* 26/1: 7-29.

Bonfante, G., 1944, "Review of E.H. Sturtevant 1942", *The Indo-Hittite Laryngeals*, Baltimore: Waverly, *Classical Philology* 39: 51-7.

Braune, W., 1975, *Althochdeutsche Grammatik* [13th edn.], Tübingen: Niemeyer.

Bryant, E.F., 2001, *The Quest for the Origins of Vedic Culture: The Indo-Aryan Migration Debate*, Oxford University Press.

Bryant, E.F. & L.L. Patton, 2005 (eds.), *The Indo-Aryan Controversy: Evidence and Inference in Indian History*, London: Routledge.

Burrow, T., 1973, *The Sanskrit Language*, London: Faber & Faber [revised edn.].

Chambers, J.K. & P. Trudgill, 1980, *Dialectology*, Cambridge: Cambridge University Press.

Chen, M. & W. Wang, 1975, "Sound Change: Implementation and Actuation", *Language* 51: 255-81.

Clackson, J., 2007, *Indo-European Linguistics: An Introduction*, Cambridge: Cambridge University Press.

Collinge, N.E., 1985, *The Laws of Indo-European*, Amsterdam: Benjamins.

Croft, W., 2005, "Introduction", in J. H. Greenberg, *Genetic Linguistics: Essays on Theory and Method*, ed. by W. Croft, Oxford University Press, 2-55.

Cuny, A., 1912, "Indo-européen et sémitique", *Revue de Phonétique* 2: 101-32.

Di Giovine, P., 1984, "Italiano *appalto*", in *Studi Latini e Romanzi in Onore di Antonino Pagliaro*, Roma: Il Calamo. 187-229.

———, 2005, "Le laringali indo-europee: un fantasma della ricostruzione?", in R. Bombi, G. Cifoletti, F. Fusco, L. Innocente & V. Orioles (eds.), *Studi in Onore di Roberto Gusmani*, Alessandria: Edizioni dell'Orso, 4-30.

Diehl, E., 1874-1947, *Vulgärlateinische Inschriften*, Bonn: Marcus & Weben.

Durkin, P., 2009, *The Oxford Guide to Etymology*, Oxford University Press.

Emeneau, M., 1956, India as a linguistic area, *Language* 32: 3-16.

———, 1994, *Draviḍian Studies: Selected Papers* (ed. Bh. Krishnamurti), Delhi: Motilal Banarsidass.

Ernout, A. & A. Meillet, 1959, *Dictionnaire tymologique de la Langue Latine*, Paris: Klincksieck.

Fortson IV, B.W., 2004, *Indo-European Language and Culture: An Introduction*, Oxford: Blackwell.

Frisk, H., 1960, *Griechisches Etymologisches Wörterbuch*, Heidelberg: C. Winter.

Garret, A., 2006, "Convergence in the Formation of Indo-European Subgroups: Phylogeny and Chronology", in P. Forster & C. Renfrew (eds.), *Phylogenetic Methods and the Prehistory of Language*, Cambridge: McDonald Institute for Archaeological Research. 139-51.

Goldacre, B., 2008, *Bad Science*, London: Harper & Collins.

Greenberg, J.H., 1953/2005, "Historical Linguistics and Unwritten Languages", in A.L. Kroeber (ed.), *Anthropology Today*, University of Chicago Press. 265-86. [Reprinted in W. Croft (ed.). 2005: 1-31].

Grimm, J., 1819/1822-37, *Deutsche Grammatik*, I-IV. Göttingen: Dieterich.

Gusmani, R., 1979, "Ittito, teoria laringalista e ricostruzione", in E. Neu & W. Meid (eds.), *Hethitisch und Indogermanisch, Vergleichende Studien zur historischen Grammatik und zur dialektgeographischen Stellung der indogermanischen Sprachgruppe Altkleinasiens*. Innsbruck: Institut für Sprachwissenschaft der Universität Innsbruck.

———, 1986, *Saggi sull'Interferenza Linguistica* [seconda edizione], Firenze: Le Lettere.

Harrison, S.P., 2003, "On the Limits of the Comparative Method", in B.D. Joseph & R.D. Janda (eds.), *The Handbook of Historical Linguistics*, Oxford: Blackwell, 213-43.

Hock, H.H., 1975, "Substratum influence on (R̥gvedic) Sanskrit?", *Studies in the Linguistic Science* 5/2: 76-125.

———, 1996, "Pre-R̥gvedic Convergence between Indo-Aryan (Sanskrit) and Draviḍian? A Survey of the Issues and Controversies", in J.E.M. Houben (ed.), *Ideology and Status of Sanskrit: Contributions to the History of the Sanskrit Language*, Leiden: Brill. 17-58.

Jakobson, R., 1942, "Sur la théorie des affinités phonologiques", Appendix to Principes de Phonologie, by N.S. Troubetzkoy, Paris: Klincksieck. 351-65. [Reprinted in Jakobson, R. 1962-88. Selected Writings I. Paris/Mouton: The Hague, 234-46].

Johanson, L., 2002, *Structural Factors in Turkic Language Contacts*, Richmond: Curzon.

Jolivet, A & F. Mossé, 1946, *Manuel de l'allemand du moyen age (des origins au XIVe siècle)*, Paris: Montaigne.

Karlsson, F., 1983, *Finnish Grammar*, Helsinki: WSOY.

Kazanas, N., 2002, "Indigenous Indoaryans & the R̥gveda", *Journal of Indo-European Studies* 30: 275-334.

———, 2009, "Indo-European Linguistics and Indo-Aryan Indigenism", in A. Marcantonio (ed.). 9: 1-60.

Kenstowicz, M.J., 1994, *Phonology in Generative Grammar*, Oxford: Blackwell.

Kuiper, F.B., 1955, "Ṛgvedic Loanwords", in O. Spies (ed.), *Studia Indologica: Festschrift für Willibald Kirfel zur Vollendung seines 70. Lebensjahres*, Bonn: Orientalistisches Seminar der Universität, 137-85.

———, 1991, *Aryans in the Ṛgveda*, Leiden Studies in Indo-European 1, Amsterdam/Atlanta: Rodopi.

———, 1992, "Rigvedic Loanwords", *International Journal of Dravidian Linguistics* 21: 1-49.

Kuryłowicz, J., 1927, "*ə* indoeuropéen et *h* Hittite", in *Symbolae grammaticae in honorem Ioannis Rozwadowski*, Cracow: Uniwersytet Jagiellonski.

Labov, W., 1994, *Principles of Linguistic Change: Internal Factors*, Oxford: Blackwell.

Law, S., 2011, *Believing Bullshit: How Not to Get Sucked into an Intellectual Black Hole*, New York: Prometheus Books.

Lehmann, W.P., 1955, *Proto-Indo-European Phonology*, Austin: University of Texas Press.

Lehmann, W.P. (ed.), 1967, *A Reader in Nineteenth Century Historical Indo-European linguistics*, Bloomington: Indiana University Press.

Levin, S., 1995, *Semitic and Indo-European: The Principal Etymologies, (With Observations on Afro-Asiatic)*, Amsterdam: Benjamins.

LIV = Rix, H. *et al.* (eds) 1998.

Macdonell, A.A., 1995, *A Vedic Grammar for Students*, Delhi: Motilal Banarsidass.

Mallory, J.P., 1989, *In Search of the Indo-Europeans, Language, Archaeology and Myth*, London: Thames & Hudson.

Mallory, J.P. & D.Q. Adams, 2006, *The Oxford Introduction to Proto-Indo-European and the Proto-Indo-European World*, Oxford University Press.

Manco, A & D. Silvestri, (eds.) 2010/2011, *L'Etimologia*, Atti del XXXV Convegno della Società Italiana di Glottologia (21-23 ottobre 2010), Napoli: Il Calamo.

Marcantonio, A., 2009a, "Introduction", in A. Marcantonio (ed.), I: 1-71.

———, 2009b, "Evidence that most Indo-European Lexical Reconstructions are Artefact of the Linguistic Method of Analysis", in A. Marcantonio (ed.), 10: 1-46.

———, (ed.) 2009, "The Indo-European Language family: Questions about its Status", *Journal of Indo-European Studies*, monograph series 55, Washington DC: Institute for the Study of Man.

———, 2010, "The Use of Reconstructions and Attestations in the 'Oxford English Dictionary'," *Proceedings of the Fifth International Conference on Historical Lexicography and Lexicology* (**ICHLL5**); Oxford: 16-18 June 2010, Oxford Research Archive (on-line).

Marcantonio, A & R. Brady, 2012, "The Evidence to Support Verner's Law", *Vedic Venues* 1: 236-306.

Masica, C.P., 1976, *Defining a Linguistic Area: South Asia*, University of Chicago Press.

Matras, Y., 2009, "Defining the Limits of Grammatical Borrowing", in A. Marcantonio (ed.), 11: 1-25.

Melchert, H.C., 1994, *Anatolian Historical Phonology*, Amsterdam/ Atlanta: GA: Rodopi.

Misra, S.S., 1977, *The Laryngeal Theory: A Critical Evaluation*, Delhi: Chaukhambha Orientalia.

———, 2005, "The Date of the R̥gveda and the Aryan Migration", in E.F. Bryant & L.L. Patton (eds.), 181-233.

Möller, H., 1880, "Review of: Kluge, F. 1879, *Beiträge zur geschichte der germanischen Conjugation*", *Englische Studien* 3: 148-64.

———, 1906, *Semitisch und Indogermanisch*, Teil I: *Konsonanten*, Copenhagen: Hagerup.

Nichols, J., 1996, "The Comparative Method as Heuristic", in M. Ross & M. Durie (eds.), *The Comparative Method Reviewed: Regularity and Irregularity in Language Change*, Oxford University Press, 39-71.

Pisani, V., 1954-55, "August Schleicher und einige Richtungen der heutigen Sprachwissenschaft", *Lingua* 4: 337-68.

———, 1957, "L'indo-européen reconstruit", *Lingua* 7: 337-48.

———, 1974, *Indogermanisch und Europa (Ars Grammatica*, Band 2), München: Fink Verlag.

Ragagnin, E., 2010, "Some Observations on the Fortis *vs.* Lenis Opposition of Consonants in Sayan Turkic", in H. Boeschoten & J. Rentzsch (eds.), *Turcology in Mainz/Turkologie im Mainz* (*Turcologica* 82), Wiesbaden: Harrassowitz. 201-08.

Rees, M., 1999/2000, *Just Six Numbers*, London: Phoenix.

Reynolds, E., P. West & J. Coleman, 1998, "Proto-Indo-European 'Laryngeals' were Vocalic", *Oxford Working Papers in Linguistics, Philology and Phonetics*, vol. 3: 84-104.

Ringe, D.A., T. Warnow & A. Taylor, 2002, "Indo-European and Computational Cladistics", *Transactions of the Philological Society* 100: 59-129.

Ringe, D., 2006, *From Proto-Indo-European to Proto-Germanic*, vol. I. Oxford University Press.

Rix, H., et al. (eds.) 1998, *Lexikon der indogermanischen Verben, Die Wurzeln und ihre Primärstammbildungen*, Wiesbaden: L. Reichert.

Saussure, F. de (1879), *Mémoire sur le système primitif des voyelles dans le langues indo-européennes*, Leipsick: Teubner.

Schmidt, J., 1872, *Die Verwandtschaftsverhältnisse der indogermanischen Sprachen*, Weimar: H. Böhlau.

Schuchardt, H.E., 1866-68, *Der Vokalismus des Vulgärlateins*, Lepizig: Teubner.

Sihler, A.L., 1995, *New Comparative Grammar of Greek and Latin*, Oxford University Press.

SKES = *Suomen Kielen Etymologinen Sanakirja*, E. Itkonen & A.J. Joki (eds.), Helsinki: Suomalais-Ugrilainen Seura I-IV; 1980.

Southworth, F.C., 1979, "Lexical Evidence for Early Contacts between Indo-Aryan and Draviḍian", in M. Deshpande & P.E. Hook (eds), *Aryan and non-Aryan in India*, Ann Arbor, MI: Centre for South and Southeast Studies, 191-233.

SSA = *Suomen Sanojen Alkuperä. Etymologinen Sanakirja*, eds. T. Itkonen & U.-M. Kulonen, Helsinki: Suomalaisen Kirjallisuuden Seura, 1992-2002.

Szemerényi, O., 1987, "La théorie des laryngales de Saussurre à Kuryłowicz et à Benveniste: Essai de réévaluation." in O. Szemerényi, 1987, *Scripta Minora. Selected Essays in Indo-European, Greek and Latin* [ed. P. Considine & J. T. Hooker], vol. I: *Indo-European*.191-215.

———, 1990, *Introduction to Indo-European Linguistics*, Oxford University Press [4th edn.].

Thomason, S.G. & T. Kaufman, 1988, *Language Contact, Creolization, and Genetic Linguistics*, Los Angeles: University of California Press.

Trubetzkoy, N.S., 1939, Gedanken über das Indogermanenproblem, *Acta Linguistica* 1: 81-89.

Verner, K., 1877/1978, "An Exception to Grimm's Law" [English tr. by R. Stanley]", in P. Baldi & R.N. Werth (eds.), *Readings in Historical Phonology*, University Park Pa: Pennsylvania State University, 32-63.

Walde, A., 1954, *Lateinisches Etymologisches Wörterbuch*, vols. I-II. Heidelberg: Winter.

Wilbur, T.H., 1977, *The* Lautgesetz *Controversy, A Documentation*, Amsterdam: Benjamins.

5

Ṛgveda
Its Chronology on the Basis of Astronomical References

B.N. Narahari Achar

Abstract

It has been well known that more than a hundred years ago Jacobi and Tilak independently arrived at the conclusion that astronomical references in *Ṛgveda* can lead to a determination of its chronology. The astronomical methods indicated a rather high chronology compared with the low chronology indicated by the dominant Aryan Invasion Theory approach to the historic study of *Ṛgveda*. This paper re-examines the astronomical evidence in the light of simulations using planetarium software. A consistent picture in the chronology which smoothly flows from the Vedic times to the time of Mahābhārata war and to the later Vedic texts is presented.

I. Introduction

The study of Vedic literature and of the *Ṛgveda* in particular from a historical point of view originated with the Western scholars, and evolved with Western thought and research. The date of about 1500 BCE proposed for *Ṛgveda*, a date favoured by most Western scholars is the direct outcome of the so-called Aryan Invasion Theory (AIT) (see Bryant & Patton 2005 for a comprehensive discussion), now discredited (Singh 2010; see also Kazanas 2009). This chronology is in direct conflict with the traditional Indic chronology on the one hand and with the chronology based on astronomical data derived by Tilak (1893), and Jacobi (1894) and their modern counterparts, Elst (2007), Frawley (1991), Kak (1994) and Rajaram (1997), among others. The high chronology based on astronomical data was denied by the esteemed scholars of the day such as Winternitz (1927) with concomitant misrepresentation of the astronomical knowledge of the Vedic times and was never recognized by the scholarship. This paper was prompted by a recent work by Talageri (2008) which gives a relatively low chronology for the *Ṛgveda*.

It is the purpose of this paper to re-examine the astronomical data in the *Ṛgveda* using the planetarium software and to present the chronology based on the astronomical references. Astronomy is considered to be the foremost of sciences, and has played an important role in India since the Vedic times. Astronomy was essential in determining the proper times for performing the ritual *yajña*. It is generally accepted that the *ṛgjyotiṣa* (*RJ*) recension of *Vedāṅgajyotiṣa* (*VJ*) is the earliest codified text of astronomy in India. Western scholars (Pingree 1973) have assigned a date of about 400 BCE for this text, in addition to attributing a Babylonian origin for it. It is an understatement to say that there is bias among the Western scholars in describing the state of science in ancient India and that there is misrepresentation in accounting the chronology of India. The accounts of history of astronomy in ancient India that are currently available have to be revised in view of the developments discussed here.

The author had presented a paper in the first symposium on the origin of Indian civilization as to how the date of the event of the Mahābhārata war can be determined on the basis of astronomical references using the Planetarium Software

(Achar 2010). Here, a summary of how the dates of certain texts, such as *Śatapatha Brāhmaṇa*, and *VJ* will also be presented. The paper concludes by showing that a consistent chronology for the Vedic India based on astronomical methods can be given.

The plan of the paper is as follows. Since the paper is based on astronomical methods and the earliest known text of astronomy is the *VJ*, about which there exist a lot of misconceptions and misrepresentations, the first section is devoted to a study of *VJ*. This section will dispel any doubts about its Vedic origin and throw some light about its date. This is followed by a discussion of a number of misrepresentations about the concepts of astronomy in *Ṛgveda*. After presenting a new list of identification of Vedic *nakṣatra*s with modern names of asterisms using simulations with planetarium software, the dates of *Śatapatha Brāhmaṇa* and the Mahābhārata war are discussed. Finally, the dates associated with astronomical references in *Ṛgveda* are discussed. This is followed by a discussion of several other Vedic texts whose dates can be determined using the astronomical method and simulations with the planetarium software and a consistent chronology for Vedic literature is presented.

2. Vedāṅgajyotiṣa

It is universally accepted that of the three recensions of *VJ*, *RJ* is the earliest text of astronomy of Ancient India. In this paper terms *VJ* and *RJ* are used inter-changeably and refer to *RJ* only. The knowledge codified in this text is attributed to Sage Lagadha, but the composition of the text which has preserved this knowledge is attributed to Śuci, a disciple of Lagadha. *RJ* is more like a pocket reference rather than a detailed treatise of astronomy and gives all the knowledge of astronomy essential for the performance of Vedic rituals, codified in a form akin to the style of *sūtra*s in 36 *śloka*s, easy for memorization, but sometimes difficult for understanding. *VJ* is declared to be the science of time, as its primary purpose is to determine the proper time for the performance of Vedic rituals. Some of the important concepts of *RJ* include *tithi*, *nakṣatra* (defined as a division of the Ecliptic), *aṁśa*, *kalā*, *aṣṭaka* and *parvan*. Units of time, and measurement of time, *ṛtu*, *ayana*, and *adhimāsa* and a five-year period called *yuga* are all described in *RJ*. Pingree (1973), in his eagerness to show that *VJ* was derived from Mesopotamian origin, assigned a date of about 400 BCE for it, while Sastry (1985) and others had assigned a date of about 1200 BCE, based on the reference in *RJ* that the winter solstice occurred at Dhaniṣṭhā, and on the identification of Dhaniṣṭhā with β-Delphini.

2.1 INAPPROPRIATENESS OF THE ASSUMPTION OF BABYLONIAN ORIGIN FOR RJ

The author has argued (Achar 1998 a) that it is inappropriate to assume a Babylonian origin for *RJ* in view of the intimate connection of astronomy with the Vedic ritual *yajña*. In fact, every astronomical concept in *RJ* can be traced to *Ṛgveda* and other Vedic texts. For the concept of *tithi*, for example, there are several well-known quotations from *Ṛgveda* which show that the year nominally of 360 days is divided into 12 months of 30 days each, thus alluding to *tithi*, the 30th part of a lunar month:

> *dvādáśāraṁ na hi tajjarā́ 'ya varvárti cakraṁ paridyāmṛtasyá* |
> *āputrā ágne mithunā́so atrá saptaśatā́ní vimśatiścá tasthuḥ* ||
>
> — *ṚV* I.164.11

Formed with twelve spokes, by the length of time, unweakened, rolls round the heaven this wheel of enduring order. Herein established, joined in pairs together, seven hundred sons and twenty stand, O Agni.[1]

1. Translations of verses from *Ṛgveda* are mostly taken from Griffith (1973).

samā́nāṁ māsa ākṛ́tiḥ || — *ṚV* X.85.5

The moon is the one who shapes the year.

Aitareya Brāhmaṇa (32.10) defines the *tithi* and the *Taittirīya Brāhmaṇa* gives the names of the fifteen tithies of the waxing phase:

etāvánuvākau pū́rvapakṣasyā́horātrāṇā́ṁ nāmadheyā́ni ||
— *TB* 3.10.10.2

These are the names of days of the first side (of the month).

The concepts of equinoxes and solstices, the scheme of *adhimāsa*, (the intercalary month), the five-year *yuga* system can all be traced to Vedic sources (Achar 1998 a). For example, *Aitareya Brāhmaṇa* (18.22) shows the knowledge of the equinox and the period between two solstices:

yathā vai puruṣa evaṁ viṣuvā́ṁstasya
yathā dakṣiṇordhá evaṁ pūrvordho |
viṣuvató yathottarordhá evamuttarordho
viṣuvatástasmāduttara ityācakṣaté ||

The *viṣuvant* (equinox) is like a man. The first half of the *viṣuvant* is like the right half of a man. The second half of the *viṣuvant* is like the left half. Therefore they call it the latter.[2]

The practice of inserting an intercalary month is adduced to in

veda māso dhṛtavráto dvādáśa prajāvátaḥ |
vedā ya upajā́yate || — *ṚV* I.25.8

He knows the twelve moons with their progeny (the twelve months with the days which are their offspring). He knows the moon of later birth (the thirteenth intercalary month).

2. Translations of *mantras* from *Aitareya Brāhmaṇa* are taken from Keith (1919).

2.2 NAKṢATRA SYSTEM IS KNOWN IN ṚGVEDA

Nakṣatras, variously translated as asterisms or lunar mansions with an enduring list of 27 (sometimes 28) in number have been the hallmark of Indian astronomy. They refer to stars, which lie near the path of the Sun or the Moon as markers, while in *RJ* they refer to the divisions of the ecliptic. Explicit mention of the names of only a few of the 27 *nakṣatras* is found in the *Ṛgveda* although complete list of 27 (or 28) *nakṣatras* can be found in other Saṁhitā and Brāhmaṇa texts. This has led scholars, both Western and Indian, to believe that not all the *nakṣatras* were known at the time of *Ṛgveda* and the development of the full list occurred later. The author has shown (Achar 2002a) that the entire list of *nakṣatras* can be found in the *Ṛgveda*, contrary to the scholarly pronouncements that such an entire list came to be recognized only at the time of *Taittirīya Saṁhitā*. The clue is that there is a presiding deity for each *nakṣatra* and the *nakṣatra* can be denoted either by its own name or by the deity representing it. Such use was common is demonstrated by a verse from *RJ* 14, which lists the *nakṣatras* at the end of *parvas*.

jau dra ghaḥ khe śve ahī ro ṣā
cin mū ṣa ṇyaḥ sū mā dhā ṇaḥ ।
re mṛ ghāḥ svā apo ajaḥ kṛ ṣyo
ha jye ṣṭhāiti ṛkṣā liṅgaiḥ ॥ — *RJ* 14

Each *nakṣatra* is indicated by a single letter, either the first letter or the last letter of its own name (*jau* for *āśvayujau*, *dra* for *ārdra*, *ro* for *rohiṇī*, etc.). It can also be denoted by the first letter or the last letter of the deity representing it (deity Āpaḥ for Pūrvāṣādhā, or *mā* for Aryamā representing Uttara-phālguṇī). There is another place in *RJ* where there is a list of *nakṣatras* at the beginning of *ayanas*, given entirely in terms of the names of deities:

vasus tvaṣṭā bhavo ajaśca mitraḥ sarpo aśvinau jalam
dhātā kaśca ayanādyāśca artha pañcama bhastu ṛtuḥ — *RJ* 9

> Vasu, Tvaṣṭā, Bhava, and Aja; Mitra, Sarpa, Aśvinīs, *jala*; Dhātā and *ka*, are at the beginning of *ayana*. Four and a half segments of *nakṣtra* constitute one *ṛtu*.[3]

Here, for example, the deity Vasu stands for Śraviṣṭhā, and the deity Tvaṣṭā for Citrā etc. Nobody can question the authenticity of *VJ* as an astronomical work. Therefore the list of deities can only represent the list of *nakṣatras*. Now the deities for Kṛttikā, Ārdrā, Proṣṭhapadā, Uttaraphālguṇī, Mṛgaśiras and Punarvasu are, respectively, Agni, Rudra, Ajaekapat, Bhaga, Soma and Aditi. These are listed in *Ṛgveda* (V.51.13-14):

> *agniḥ svastayé* | . . . *svasti nó rudraḥ* . . .
> *svasti na indráścāgniścá svasti nó adite kṛdhi* | etc.

> May Agni be beneficient . . . may Rudra bless. . . .
> May Indra and Agni prosper us. Prosper. Os, O thou Aditi. . . .

It is made abundantly clear that it is the *nakṣatra*s that are being referred to here, by *svasti panthāṁ anúsaṁcarema sūryācandramasā'viva*, "May we pursue in full prosperity our path like the Sun and the Moon in theirs" referring to the path of the sun and the moon, the ecliptic. One *nakṣatra* is explicitly mentioned: *svati páthye revatī*: "May Revatī in the path prosper us". In fact, as discussed in the author's papers referred to, the deities of all the *nakṣatra*s and more occur in this single *sūkta*. This destroys the myth that the entire list of *nakṣatra*s are not known in *Ṛgveda* and the lists suddenly appear in *Taittirīya Saṁhitā*. Authors of history of ancient astronomy of India should note that the knowledge of all *nakṣatra*s is derived from *the Ṛgveda*.

2.3. NAMES OF THE MONTHS CAITRA ETC. ALREADY KNOWN IN ṚGVEDA

One of the characteristic features of the Hindu calendar is the

3. Translations of verses from *Vedāṅgajyotiṣa* are taken from Sastry (1985). The word *nakṣatra* stands for the arc segment of the ecliptic as well as the bright star near the segment which is the marker.

naming of the month on the basis of the *nakṣatra* near which a full moon may be taken to have occurred. These are the well-known Caitra, Vaiśākha, Jyeṣṭha, etc. for the months with full moons near Citrā (Spica), Viśākhā (Zubenelgenubi), Jyeṣṭhā (Antares), etc. The names of the months in the Vedic texts, however, are *madhu, mādhava, śukra, śuci, nabhas, nabhasya, iṣa ūrjā, sahas, sahasya, tapas* and *tapasyā*. Some scholars have conjectured that the names of the months based on the *nakṣatras* was not known during the Saṁhitā times, but came into vogue much later. In fact, Dixit (1969) surmises that this scheme came into vogue when the vernal equinox actually took place in Caitra. Using the Planetarium software, the author has shown that there is no basis for this argument to establish a chronology. The scheme of naming the months called the *caitrādi* system has also been traced (Achar 2000c) to *Ṛgveda* on the basis of the connection between *yajña* and the important role of *agni* in it.

3. Time and Its Measurement

Astronomy is an observational science. *RJ* propounds a five-year luni-solar year called the *yuga*, comprising of ten *ayanas*, subdivided into *ṛtu* (two-month season), *māsa* (month), *ardhamāsa* (half-month), *ahorātra* (day and night), *kalā, muhūrta* (48 minutes), and *kāṣṭā*. These concepts can be traced to Vedic sources, for instance, as listed in *Mahānārāyaṇopaniṣat* (*MNU*):

> *kalāmúhūrtāḥ kāṣṭā́ścāhorātrāścá sarvaśaḥ* ।
> *ardhamāsā māsā́ ṛtávassaṁvatsaraścá kalpantāṁ* ॥
> — *MNU* 1.2.3-4

The author has shown that the method of measuring time with a water clock can be traced to *Atharvaveda* (Achar 1998 b), and the method of Gnomon can also be traced to Vedic sources. In short, the entire astronomical knowledge of *VJ* is traceable to *Ṛgveda*.

4. Identification of the Vedic Nakṣatras

Although in *RJ* the *nakṣatras* refer to divisions of the ecliptic, and the names of the divisions correspond to bright asterisms also known by the same names, there must have been a time when only the asterisms and not the divisions of the ecliptic were used as the markers for the observation of movements of the sun and the moon. It is essential to identify the Vedic *nakṣatra*s (the bright stars) with their modern names, for the lists that are available in the literature are not satisfactory, some of the asterisms being more than 30° away from the ecliptic and could not have been used as markers for the motion of the sun and the moon. The author has used the simulations using the planetarium software, SkyMap Pro, of nearly 900 new moons and full moons occurring around 2297 BCE, when Kṛttikās (identified with Pleiades) were on the celestial equator and around 2220 BCE, when the vernal equinox occurred at Kṛttikās and has produced (Achar 2002b) a table for identification of the *nakṣatra*s, which is reproduced below. This identification is based on the view of the sky as the Vedic people themselves would have seen as simulated by the Planetarium Software. On the new moon days and full moon days, there is absolutely no question about the relative positions of the Sun and the Moon, and hence of the *nakṣatra,* which describes the moon's position. The details of the identification procedure can be obtained from the reference cited above. The Planetarium Software produces the view of the sky by an extrapolation of the positions of the stars in a modern catalogue. The stars identified as a particular *nakṣatra* will therefore retain the identity. This is in contrast to the procedure adopted by Pingree (1989), where the polar coordinates of stars given in a Siddhānta text are first converted to equatorial coordinates, then extrapolated to modern epochs to compare with the coordinates of stars in a modern catalogue and then make the identification.

The present list is believed to be the correct one as it is based on the view of the sky the Vedic people themselves would have observed. It agrees with most of the stars in the list

Table 1: Identification of the Vedic Nakṣatras

Nakṣatras	No. of stars	Identification of the Principal star		Presiding Deity
		RCRC	Present	
Kṛttika	6	η-Tau	η-Tau	Agni
Rohiṇī	1	α-Tau	α-Tau	Prajāpati
Mṛgaśirā	3	λ-Ori	β-Tau*	Soma
Ārdrā	1	α-Ori	γ-Gem*	Rudra
Punarvasu	2	β-Gem	β-Gem	Aditi
Puṣyā	1	δ-Cnc	δ-Cnc	Bṛhaspati
Āśleṣā	6	ζ-Hya	ζ-Hya	Sarpa
Makhā	6	α-Leo	α-Leo	Pitṛ
Pūrvaphālguṇī	2	δ-Leo	δ-Leo	Aryamā
Uttaraphālguṇī	2	β-Leo	β-Leo	Bhaga
Hastā	5	δ-Crv	γ-Vir*	Savitā
Citrā	1	α-Vir	α-Vir	Indra
Svāti	1	α-Boo	π-Hya*	Vāyu
Viśākhā	2	α-Lib	α_2-Lib	Indrāṇī
Anūrādhā	4	δ-Sco	δ-Sco	Mitra
Jyeṣṭhā	1	α-Sco	α-Sco	Indra
Mūlā	7	λ-Sco	λ-Sco	Pitṛ
Pūrvāṣāḍhā	4	δ-Sgr	δ-Sgr	Āpaḥ
Uttarāṣāḍhā	4	σ-Sgr	σ-Sgr	Viśvedevāḥ
Śravaṇā	3	α-Aql	β-Cap*	Viṣṇu
Dhaniṣṭhā	5	β-Del	δ-Cap[4]*	Vasu
Śatabhiṣā	1	λ-Aqr	λ-Aqr	Indra
Pūrvābhādrā	2	β-Peg	α-Peg	Ajaekapāt
Uttarābhādrā	2	γ-Peg	γ-Peg	Ahirbudhnya
Revatī	1	ζ-Pis	ζ-Pis	Pūṣā
Aśvinī	2	β-Ari	β-Ari	Aśvin
Bharaṇī	3	41-Ari	δ-Ari	Yama

4. The list of identifications is taken from Achar (2002b). The identifications marked with * differ from the usual lists such as the one from the Calendar Reform Committee. These stars →

given in the Report of the Calendar Reform Committee (Saha and Lahiri 1955); but there are six cases, where there is disagreement. The new identification is based on stars, which are very close to the ecliptic and hence better suited as markers for the motion of the Sun and the Moon. Besides, the new identification easily explains a controversy (Achar 2002b) that had plagued the *nakṣatra* system, namely classification into *Deva* and *Yama nakṣatras*.

5. Date of Vedāṅga Jyotiṣa

The author has shown (2000 a) that the date for the *Lagadha* recension of *VJ* must be revised to about 1800 BCE, rather than the previously accepted date of 1200 BCE. The date of *VJ*, as discussed by Sastry (1985), is based on the calculation of the time when winter solstice occurred at Dhaniṣṭhā. The date of 1200 BCE is based on the identification of Dhaniṣṭha with β-Delphini according to the old identification scheme derived from the *yogatārās* of the *siddhāntas*, and may not correspond to what the Vedic people themselves had observed. Based on the identification scheme proposed by the author in Table 1, Dhaniṣṭhā corresponds to δ-Capricorni. Fig. 1 shows the star map for Delhi on 3 January 1752 BCE, the day of winter solstice. It is clearly seen to be the month of Māgha in fig. 2, as per the description in *RJ* verses 5 and 6. It can be noted that β-Delphini is more than 30° away from the Ecliptic and could not be a marker star, whereas δ-Capricorni is right close to the Ecliptic and would be suitable as a marker star. Thus, it follows that the date of *Lagadha* recension of *VJ* is to be dated around 1800 BCE. That there must have been versions of *VJ* much older than the *Lagadha* recension, as for example that followed at the time of the Mahābhārata war.

→ are closer to the ecliptic, and are brighter and better markers for the motion of the Sun and the Moon.

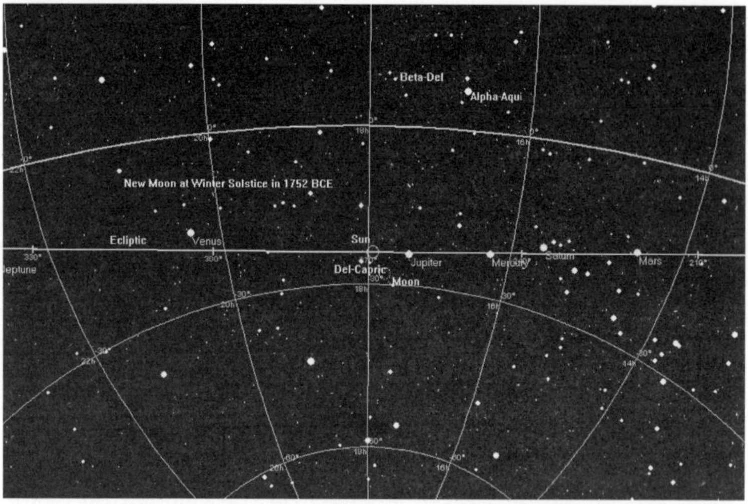

fig. 1: Winter Solstice in 1752 BCE

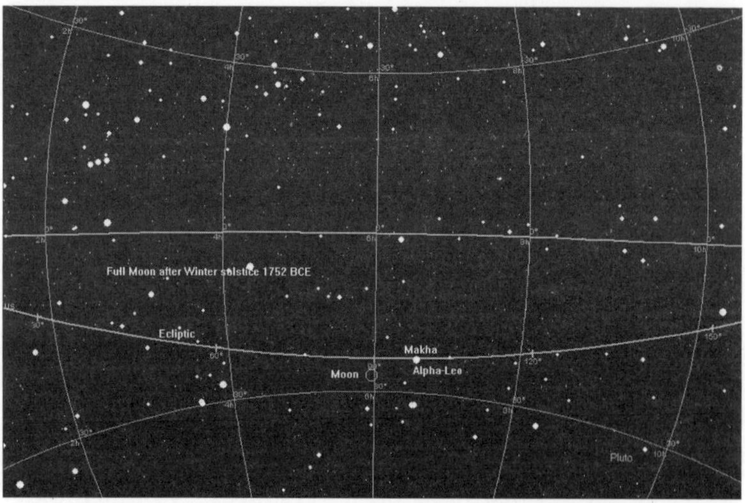

fig. 2: Full Moon after the Winter Solstice in 1752 BCE

6. Date of Śatapatha Brāhmaṇa

It is a well known fact that there are many references to astronomical phenomena contained in the Brāhmaṇa texts and in fact these references have been used in the past by scholars such as Tilak (1893) and Dikshit (1895) to determine the dates of the events mentioned in these texts. A prime example of such investigations is the dating of the *Śatapatha Brāhmaṇa* by Dikshit on the basis of the following lines referring to Kṛttikās

etā ha vai prācyai diśo na cyavante. . . — *ŚB* II.1.2.3

and again they do not move away from the eastern quarter[5]

amī hy uttarā hi saptarṣayaḥ udyanti purā etāḥ. . . — *ŚB* II.1.2.4

these latter, the seven *ṛṣis* rise in the North and they (the Kṛttikās) in the East

These lines occur in the second *brāhmaṇa* of the first *adhyāya* of the second *kāṇḍa* of *ŚB*, in connection with choosing a suitable time for *agnyādhāna*, the establishment of the ritual fires for the first time by a householder. It is suggested that the new householders should establish the traditional *gārhapatya* and the *āhavanīya* fires on the day of Kṛttikā *nakṣatra*, for their presiding deity is Agni. The Kṛttikās never swerve from the East and they alone consist of many stars. He who performs *agnyādhāna* on the day of Kṛttikā is blessed with "abundance" and a "steadfast family". But, the second line quoted above argues against this proposition; for, *saptarṣis*, who were married to Kṛttikās are constantly separated from the latter as they rise only in the East, while the *saptarṣis* stay in the North, implying a similar fate befalling the new householder. However, counter-arguments are presented and finally, it is argued that Kṛttikās are the most auspicious, but some other *nakṣatras* are also suggested as equally auspicious for the purpose of *agnyādhāna*.

The astronomical importance of these lines was recognized by Dikshit, who interpreted "they do not move away from the eastern quarter" to mean that the "Kṛttikās rise exactly at the east point" and used this fact to determine the date of *ŚB*

5. Translations of *mantras* from *Śatapatha Brāhmaṇa* are taken from Eggeling (1963).

as about 3000 BCE. With the advent of the so-called planetarium software, the author (2000 a) reinvestigated this particular issue by simulations of the view of the sky and confirmed that Dikshit was essentially correct in his dating of *ŚB*.

One interesting thing came out of the simulations. The simulations showed that all the members of the *saptarṣi maṇḍala* were circumpolar in 3000 BCE. The translation given above for *ŚB* (II.1.2.4) cannot be correct. Being circumpolar, the seven *ṛṣi*s do not rise or set. The *padavibhāga* of this verse should be

amī hi uttarāhi (santi) saptarṣayaḥ ।
udyanti purā etāḥ ।।

and *udyanti* cannot go with *saptarṣayaḥ*. This mistake was traced to the commentary by Sāyaṇa who could not have known from his latitude in the fourteenth century that the *saptarṣi*s were circumpolar in Kurukṣetra in 3000 BCE. All scholars have simply followed Sāyaṇa.

7. Date of the Mahābhārata War

According to tradition, the war between the Kauravas and Paṇḍavas took place at the transition between Dvāpara and Kaliyugas, around 3000 BCE:

antare caiva samprāpte kalidvāparayorabhūt ।
samantapañcake yuddhaṁ kurupāṇḍava senayoḥ ।। — *MB*. I.2.9

and when the juncture of Kali and Dvāpara occurred, the war between the armies of Kurus and Pāṇḍavas took place at Sāmantapañcaka.

However, ever since the Western scholars showed interest some hundred years ago in the epic and began to discuss its "historicity", a lively debate (or rather a war of dates!) has been going on. While some scholars (Sircar 1969) declare that the whole epic is a myth denying any historical truth to the story of the epic, many (Gupta & Ramachandran 1976; Sathe

1983) do believe that the war actually took place, but are divided as to the magnitude of the event and as to the date when it took place. A plethora of dates ranging from before 5000 BCE to around 1000 BCE have been proposed (Vedavyas 1986) on the basis of estimates arrived at by using diverse methodologies.

Among the diverse methodologies used, one methodology based on astronomical references (of which there are more than 150 in number, and occur scattered throughout the epic) deserves special mention. More than 40 per cent of all the articles (totalling more than 120 in number) dedicated to determining the date of the war, are based on the astronomical references (Sathe 1983). Although the astronomical references are scattered throughout the epic, most of them pertaining to the war occur in Udyogaparvan and Bhīṣmaparvan of the epic Books V and VI). Practically all scholars have characterized the references in Bhīṣmaparvan (Book VI) as astrological omens (Sengupta 1947) and inconsistent and not suitable for a "scientific" analysis. Some scholars have introduced[6] *ad hoc* hypotheses in attempting to find some degree of coherence among the apparently "inconsistent" astronomical references. The author (2004) has clearly shown that such *ad hoc* hypotheses are totally unnecessary and that

(i) The astronomical references in the Bhīṣmaparvan are not merely "astrological effusions fit for mother goose's tales" (as once characterized by Professor Sengupta), but follow a Vedic tradition of omens and describe mostly comets and not planets as generally assumed,

(ii) The few true planetary references in this *parvan* are identical to those in Udyogaparvan,

---

6. It has been common to make ad hoc assumptions to fit whatever model one is proposing and to bring some degree of consistency in the astronomical references in the epic. For example, Sengupta (1947) assumed that a pair of eclipses had →

(iii) These common references lead to a unique date for the war, 3067 BCE,

(iv) All other astronomical references in the epic are consistent with the date,

(v) The date agrees with the date given earlier by Professor Raghavan and is consistent with the traditional date of about 3000 BCE,

(vi) Using the planetarium software, it can be easily demonstrated that all other dates proposed by different authors are inconsistent with the planetary configurations referred to in (ii) above.

7.1. ASTRONOMICAL REFERENCES IN UDYOGAPARVAN

Kr̥ṣṇa's mission for peace is so important that astronomical events in reference to that mission are recorded.

(i) Kr̥ṣṇa leaves for Hastināpura in the *maitrī muhūrtta* in the month of Kārttika on the day of Revatī *nakṣatra.*

(ii) On the way he halts at a place called Vr̥kasthala and reaches Hastināpura on the day of Bharaṇī *nakṣatra.*

(iii) The meetings and discussions for peace go on till the day of Puṣyā *nakṣatra,* when Duryodhana rejects all offers of peace. War becomes imminent.

(iv) Kr̥ṣṇa leaves Hastināpura on the day of Uttaraphālgunī. Karṇa accompanies him in his chariot and has a long conversation with him.

(v) During the conversation Karṇa describes some omens

→ occurred two years before the war (2449 BCE, his date for the war) and later inserted into the text. Sharma (1986, 2004) assertains that Vyāsa met Dhr̥tarāṣṭra not just once on the eve of the war, but several times before the war. Hence the planetary positions refer to different times. Iyengar's (2003) model would yield better consistency for planetary positions if part of the text in Bhīṣmaparvan is taken over to a chapter in Sabhāparvan.

he has seen that indicate a great harm to the Kuru family which include the following: Śani is afflicting Rohiṇī, Aṅgāraka has performed a retrograde motion before reaching Jyeṣṭhā and is prograde again having past Anurādhā, the Moon had lost all its lustre on the full moon of Kārttika and a solar eclipse would appear to take place next new moon day.

(vi) At the end of the conversation, Kṛṣṇa sends a message to Bhīṣma and Droṇa through Karṇa that seven days from that day there is going to be an *amāvāsya* of Jyeṣṭha and that war rituals be started on that day.

Except for Professor Sengupta (1947), these astronomical references are generally agreed to be genuine and pertinent by most scholars. Professor Sengupta does not have "faith in the astrological omens" described by Karṇa in (v) above. However, he does believe that the reference to "Jyeṣṭha *amāvāsya*" is extremely important, but considers the reference to two eclipses occurring within thirteen days as interpolation.

7.2. ASTRONOMICAL REFERENCES IN BHĪṢMAPARVAN

Sage Vyāsa meets with Dhṛtarāṣṭra just prior to the war and describes the omens he has seen. Among these omens described in seventy-six verses in two chapters, are some forty astronomical references given in four different segments. These are some of the most misunderstood astronomical references. On a superficial reading, and assuming that the astrological references to *graha* pertain to planets as most scholars have done, the references appear to be confusing and contradictory. Since they also occur in four different segments, scholars have characterized them as unreliable and even as interpolations. But, by a careful analysis the author has shown that Vyāsa is very systematic in his description and follows a very genuine Vedic tradition of omens. The omens occur in four segments because they pertain to four different aspects of the impending disaster: (a) an imminent war, (b) great harm to the Kuru family, (c) destruction of both armies, and (d) disaster to the entire population. Most of the omens pertain to comets and not the planets. The only true planetary positions are described in segment (b) as the omens describing harm to the Kuru family they are identical to those described by Karṇa earlier in Udyogaparvan.

7.3. THE IMPORTANT PLANETARY CONFIGURATIONS

The important references to planets consist of those that are common to both Udyoga and Bhīṣmaparvans and include the following:

(i) conjunction of Śani with Rohiṇī

(ii) retrograde motion of Aṅgāraka just before reaching Jyeṣṭhā

(iii) a lunar eclipse on the Kārttika *pūrṇimā*, followed by

(iv) a solar eclipse at Jyeṣṭha.

These events lead to a unique year for the war. All other references in the epic are consistent with this date.

8. Simulations Using Planetarium Software and the Date of the War

A search is made for the years in which there is a conjunction of Saturn (Śani) with Aldebaran (Rohiṇī) between 3500 BCE and CE 500. As Saturn takes an average of 29.5 years to go around the sun once, the event also repeats with the same period. There are 137 such conjunctions during the interval specified above. A search is then made for those years from among these 137 dates when Mars (Aṅgāraka) is retrograde before reaching Antares (Jyeṣṭhā). Since the retrograde motion of Mars repeats with the same period as its synodic period, a spread of two years on either side of each of the dates was considered in the search. The search reduced the set of dates to just seventeen: 3271 BCE, 3067 BCE, 2830 BCE, 2625 BCE, 2388 BCE,

2183 BCE, 1946 BCE, 1741 BCE, 1503 BCE, 1299 BCE, 1061 BCE, 857 BCE, 620 BCE, 415 BCE, CE 28, CE 233 and CE 470, when Saturn was near Aldebaran and Mars executed a retrograde motion before reaching Antares. A search was then made for those years in which there was a lunar eclipse near Pleiades (i.e., on the Kārttika pūrṇimā). This reduces the set to just two, 3067 BCE and 2183 BCE. It turns out that in both of these years the lunar eclipse is followed by a solar eclipse at Jyeṣṭhā. A sequence of "two eclipses within a period of 13 days" also occurs in the two eclipse seasons. When one considers the fact that Bhīṣma passed away on the Māgha *śukla aṣṭamī*, after the occurrence of winter solstice, a unique date results, for the winter solstice in 13 January, 3066 BCE occurred on *śukla pañcamī*, whereas the winter solstice in 2182 BCE occurred on *Kṛṣnacaturthī*.

Thus a unique date of 3067 BCE for the date of the war emerges. The author has shown that this date is consistent with all the other astronomical references in the epic in several publications with the help of copious illustrations of star maps generated by Planetarium software. Some of them will be included as part of this essay by way of illustration

8.1. ILLUSTRATIONS

The star maps in *figs*. 3-6 show that the astronomical events are reproduced. In *fig*. 3, the day Kṛṣṇa starts on his diplomatic mission, it is clearly seen that Moon is near Revatī, and Śani is at Rohiṇī. *Fig*. 4 shows the star map for *Jyeṣṭha amāvāsya*, the new moon day at Antares, which is also a solar eclipse day. The retrograde loop of Mars in that year is also shown superposed in the figure. The retrograde motion of Mars before reaching Jyeṣṭha had occurred several months earlier. *Fig*. 5 shows the day the war starts: moon is at Bharaṇī. *Fig*. 6. shows the day of Bhīṣma's expiry: *śukla aṣṭamī*, Rohiṇī *nakṣatra*.

The author's papers (2004, 2010) may be consulted for more details. The sheer volume of astronomical data and the

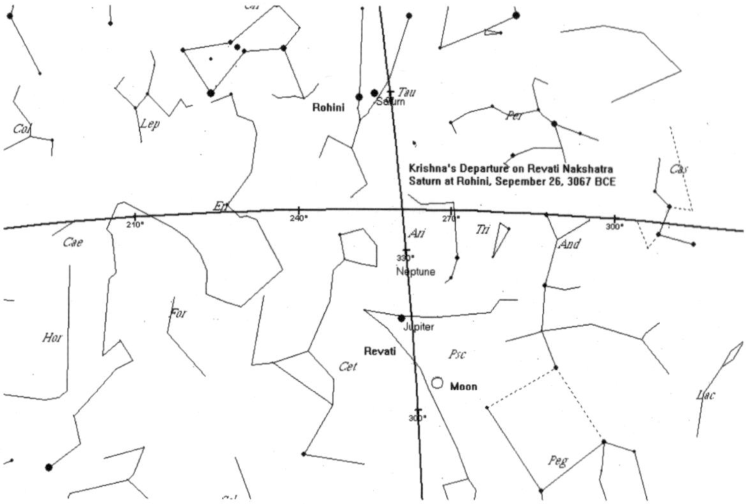

fig. 3: Kṛṣṇa's Mission for Peace: Departure on 26 September 3067 BCE.

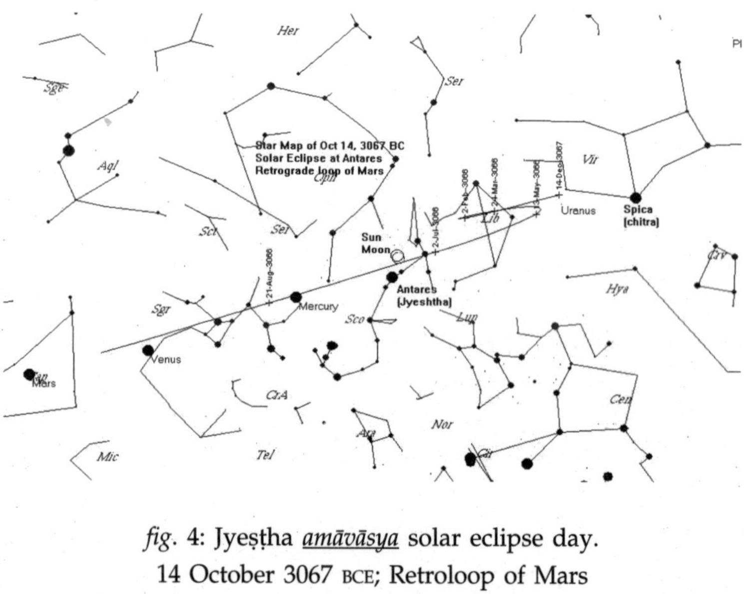

fig. 4: Jyeṣṭha <u>*amāvāsya*</u> solar eclipse day. 14 October 3067 BCE; Retroloop of Mars

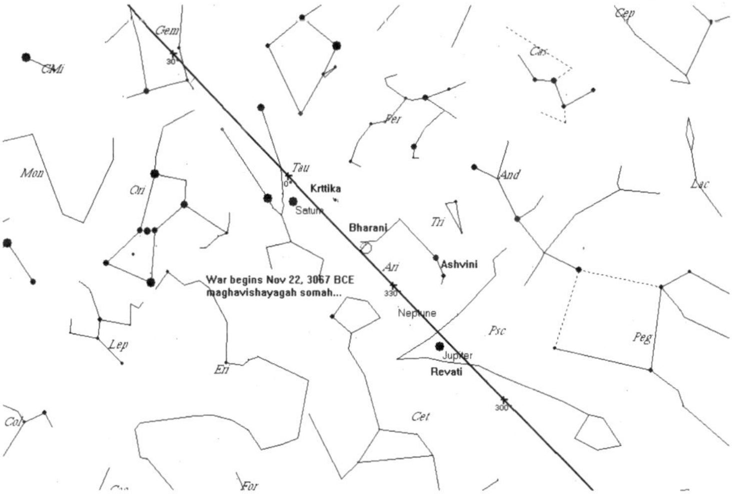

fig. 5: War begins 22 November, 3067 BCE. It is Bharaṇī day

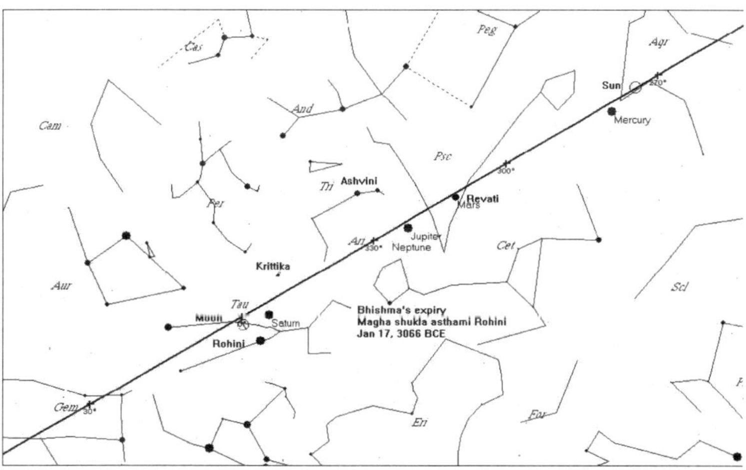

fig. 6: Bhīṣma's Expiry. Māgha *śukla aṣṭamī* Rohiṇi *nakṣatra*. 16 January 3066 BCE

consistency of the astronomical references reinforce conclusively the traditional belief that the war took place about 5,000 years ago, and that the astronomical references are not clever interpolations of some latter day astronomer.

At first sight, the date of 3067 BCE appears unbelievable. For, tradition has it that the war took place at the end of Dvāparayuga, and that Kaliyuga started in 3102 BCE. How can the war have taken place in 3067 BCE, which is 36 years after the start of the Kaliyuga? The author has discussed this and other issues that appear to conflict with different traditions regarding the date of the war, such as the Āryabhaṭṭa, Varāhamihira, and the Bhāgavata traditions. He has shown that when examined closely, there is no conflict because the epic says only that the war took place during the transition of Dvāpara and Kaliyugas. The transition itself is not sharp, but diffused. In fact, there is some evidence in the epic that Kali may have already started before the war, and that as long as Kṛṣṇa was on this earth, Kali could not have an influence.

9. Astronomy-Based Chronolgy of Ṛgveda

It has been well known that more than 100 years ago Jacobi and Tilak independently arrived at the conclusion that astronomical references in *Ṛgveda* can lead to a determination of the chronology of *Ṛgveda*. Although most scholars have ignored the high chronology for *Ṛgveda* arrived at by astronomical methods, interest has been revived by recent scholars such as Frawley, Elst, Rajaram and Kak, among others. It will be interesting to examine using Planetarium software this chronology of *Ṛgveda* based on astronomical methods in relation to the date of 3067 BCE for the Mahābhārata war.

10. Key References for the Astronomy based Chronology of Ṛgveda

Although there are a large number of references on the

astronomical method, we restrict our consideration to the works of Tilak (1893), Jacobi (1894), Dixit (1896), Sengupta (1947) and Frawley (1991) as being the most pertinent for purposes of this work: The astronomical references considered most pertinent are the legends of Ṛbhus, legend of Vṛṣākapi, the legend of Maṇḍūkas, the legend of Yama and his two dogs, the solar eclipse attributed to Sage Atri, and finally the occurrence of vernal equinox in Kṛttikā, Rohiṇī, Mṛgaśirā, Ārdrā, and Punarvasu.

10.1. THE LEGEND OF ṚBHUS

Ṛbhus occur in eleven *sūkta*s in *Ṛgveda*, I.20, I.110, I.161, I.164, IV.33-37. Ṛbhus are three in number, Ṛbhu, Vibhvan and Vāj and are the sons of Sudhanvan. They learnt many crafts under Tvaṣṭra, and constructed *ratha*s and other equipment for the *deva*s. By their hardwork the *deva*s were pleased and they were granted immortality.

> *saudhanvanā ṛbhavaḥ sūrácakṣasaḥ*
> *saṁvatsare samápṛcyanta dhītibhīḥ* — *ṚV* I.110.4

> The Ṛbhus, children of Sudhanvan, bright as suns, were in a year's course made associate with prayers (connected with the ceremonies appropriated to the different seasons of the year — Wilson)

The Ṛbhus represent the three seasons of the year (lunar year of 354 days) at the end of which they take rest for 12 days in the house of Āgohya (the unconcealable, the sun) before they start their work again in the New Year. They are awakened from their sleep and Vasta gives the information that they were awakened by the hound.

> *suṣupvāmsá ṛbhavastadápṛcchat āgóhya ka idam nó abūbudhat* |
> *ṣvānám bastobódhayitārám abravīt saṁvatsara idamadyā vyákhyata* ||
> — *ṚV* I.161.13

> R̥bhus, reposing in the solar orb, you inquire, "who awakens us, unconcealable sun to this office of sending rain?" Sun replies "the awakener is the Dog and in the year you again today light up this world".

This legend can be taken as referring to the time of commencement of the year with vernal equinox. The *śvāna* obviously refers to the Dog-star. Tilak (1893) regards this as referring to the equinox in Mr̥gaśiras (identified by him with

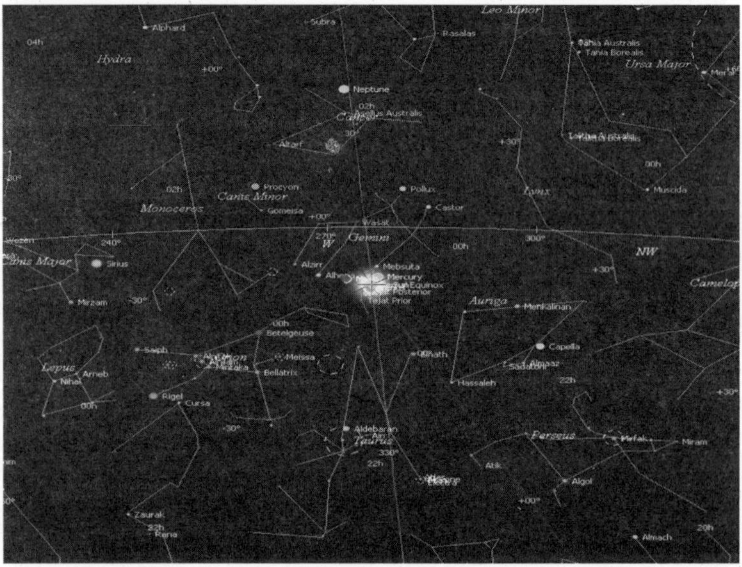

fig. 7: Vernal Equinox at α-Ori. 5000 BCE.
Note the passing of zero hour line of the coordinate
Right Ascension (RA) through Betelguese

the constellation Orion, which according to him also includes the Dog-star). He supported his interpretation with a large number of quotations from *R̥gveda* and other Vedic texts. The date corresponding to this event can be simulated. Taking the Orion to be represented by its brightest stars, Betelguese, α Ori, the vernal equinox occurring at α-Ori is shown in *fig*. 7. Tilak (1893) in his book *The Orion* first proposed the date of

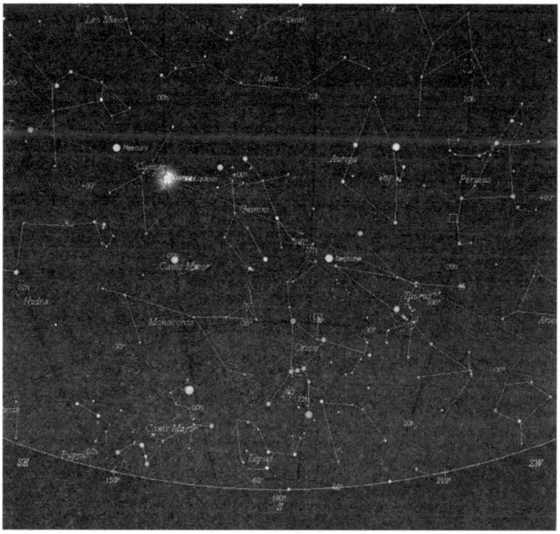

fig. 8: Vernal Equinox at Canis Major about 7000 BCE

4500 BCE, and then later on proposed the date of 5000 BCE. However, Sengupta interprets the R̥bhu legend as referring to the heliacal rising of Canis Major after the summer solstice. But this is not the correct interpretation either, as the beginning of the New Year was most likely at the vernal equinox. Therefore, our interpretation is that this reference is to the vernal equinox, with the Dog star at the vernal equinox and is illustrated in *fig.* 8.

10.2. THE LEGEND OF VR̥ṢĀKAPI

The legend appears in *R̥gveda* X.86 and is not an easy hymn to understand. Tilak (1893) gives a long verse by verse discussion of this hymn and concludes that the import of the legend can be understood by taking Vr̥ṣākapi to represent the sun at vernal equinox when the dog-star started the equinoctial year. Again Tilak interpreted this to mean vernal equinox occurring at Orion. However, it is obvious this also refers to the sameequinoctical year with the Dog-star and is illustrated by the *fig.* 8, displayed just above.

10.3. THE LEGEND OF MAṆḌŪKAS

The so-called "Frog Song", is the famous Maṇḍūka-Sūkta in *Ṛgveda*, VII.103. Jacobi finds in this *sūkta* a reference to the beginning of the year in the rainy season, which occurs after the summer solstice. According to Jacobi, the first rainy month was Bhādrapada, the full moon near the *nakṣatra* Proṣṭhapadā with the summer solstice occurring in the Uttarāphālguṇī *nakṣatra*. Jacobi finds support for his argument from the ritual of *upākaṇa* mentioned in the Dharma-sūtras and Gṛhya-sūtras.

As Law (1965) has pointed out, this hymn VII.103 (considered a late hymn by some scholars) should not be considered in isolation, but along with two previous hymns, VII.101 and 102. These three are prayers addressed to Parjanya for rain. *Nirukta* also indicates that this hymn is an invocation by Vasiṣṭha to Parjanya for rainfall. Law indicates that summer solstice in Uttarāphālguṇī also corresponds to vernal equinox in Mṛgaśiras.

Figs. 9 and 10 show the vernal equinox in Mṛgaśiras. This is based on the new identification of Mṛgaśiras with Beta-Tau rather than Lambda-Ori, as the former is closer to the Ecliptic and brighter. Zeta-Tau is the partner and the range of dates 4240-3820 BCE gives the time of the occurrence of this event. This is consistent with what Jacobi had proposed.

10.4. THE LEGEND OF YAMA AND HIS TWO DOGS

This legend occurs in *Ṛgveda* (X.14), in the following two verses:

> Pass by a secure path beyond the two spotted four-eyed dogs, the progeny of Saramā, and join the wise *pitṛ*s who rejoice fully with Yama.
>
> Entrust him, O King, to thy two dogs which are thy protectors, Yama, the four-eyed guardians of the road, renowned by man, and grant him prosperity and health.
>
> — Wilson's translation

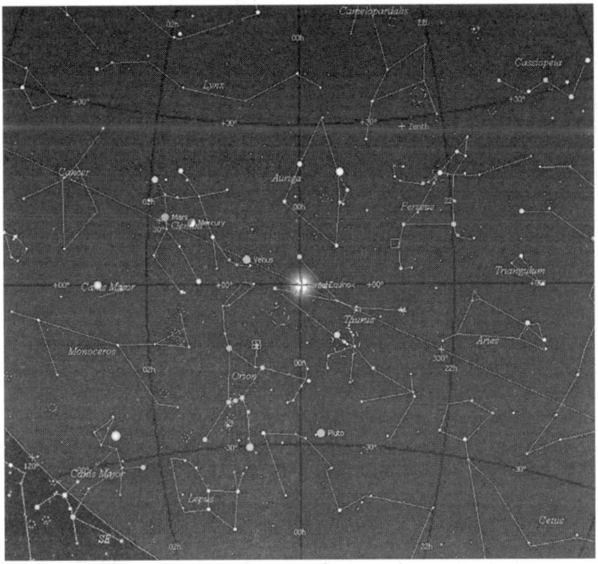

fig. 9: Vernal Equinox at Mr̥gaśira β-Tau about 3820 BCE

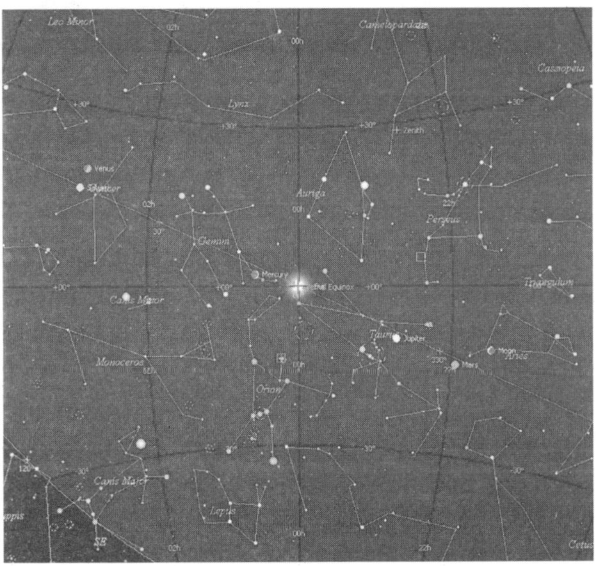

fig. 10: Vernal Equinox at Mr̥gaśira ζ-Tau, companion star about 4240 BCE

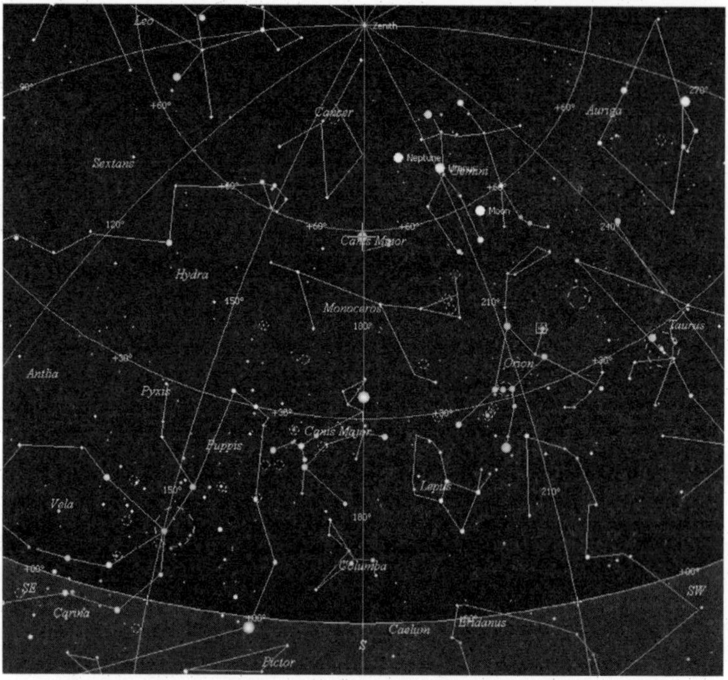

fig. 11: Two Dog-stars point to the South Pole 4350 BCE

The astronomical interpretation according to Sengupta, is that the two stars, α-Canis Minoris and α-Canis Majoris pointed to the south celestial pole. In other words, this referred to a time when the two stars crossed the meridian at the same time or, the two had the same right ascension. This event is represented in *fig*. 11. The date of 4350 BCE is again consistent with the range of dates given earlier.

10. 5 THE SOLAR ECLIPSE OBSERVED BY ATRI

A solar eclipse observed by Atri is described in *Ṛgveda* (V.40), and the first attempt to date it was made by Ludwig. Sengupta determines the date of this eclipse to be 26 July, 3928 BCE and regards this as also the date of Atri. *Fig*. 12 shows a sky map corresponding to this event. It may be noted that there are many places in *Ṛgveda* where reference is made to Atri, including the following: I.51.3, I.112.7, I.116.8, I.119.6, I.139.9, I.180.4, I.183.5, V. 73.6-7, VII. 68.5, VII.71.5, VIII.35.19, VIII.36.7, VIII.42.5, VIII.62.3-8, X.39.9, X.143.1-3, X.150.5. However, some caution must be exercised in using the data for eclipses for purposes of determining the dates. As has been discussed in detail by the author, in the planetarium software, the positions of the planets and the stars are computed using the latest astronomical theories and information available and they are highly reliable. However, there are uncertainties when it comes to determining eclipses on dates extrapolated to 4000 BCE. These uncertainties which may amount to about 15 minutes when extrapolated to dates around CE 1000, jump to more than 12 hours for the time of the occurrence of the eclipse when extrapolated to 3000 BCE, and even more when taken to 4000 BCE. The exact location of the eclipse and the exact time of

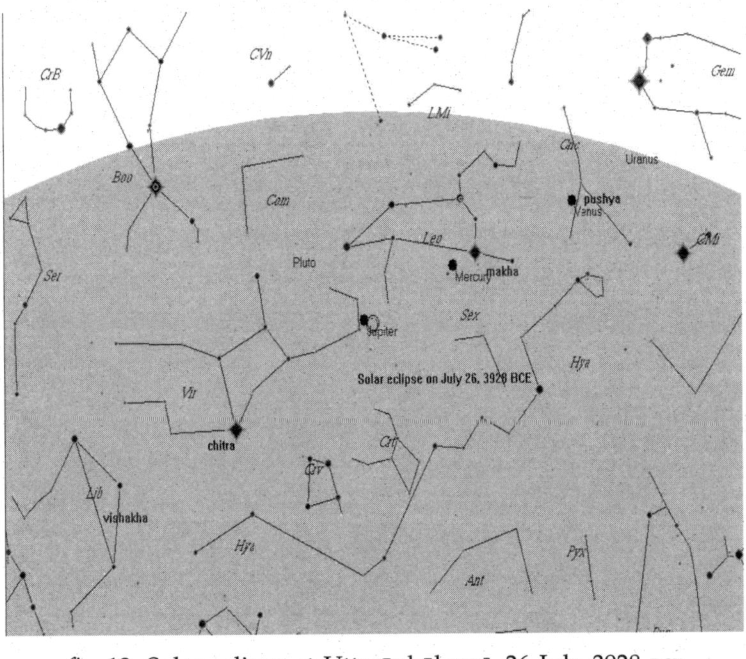

fig. 12: Solar eclipse at Uttarāphālgunī, 26 July 3928 BCE

visibility are uncertain, but the occurrence of the eclipse itself is certain. As a consequence, determining the date on the basis of eclipse data alone is risky. However, the eclipse data can be used as secondary information to confirm that it occurred on a particular date.

10. 6 EQUINOXES AT OTHER NAKṢATRAS

Frawley has also drawn attention to the fact that there are references in *R̥gveda* to astronomical events of equinoxes occurring at different *nakṣatra*s such as Punarvasu and Ārdrā. Thus there is an indication of the knowledge of vernal equinox occurring in various *nakṣatra*s, starting from Punarvasu

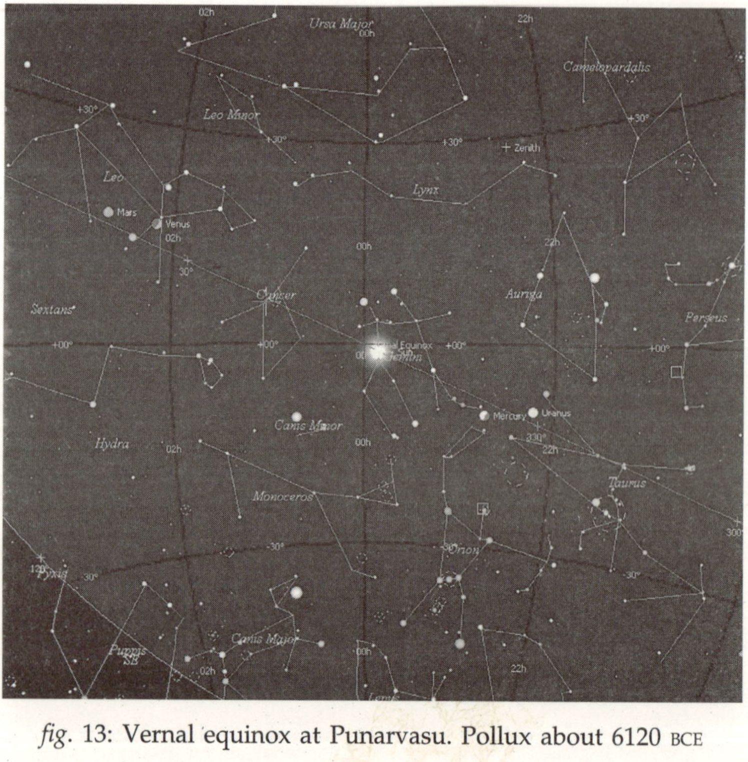

fig. 13: Vernal equinox at Punarvasu. Pollux about 6120 BCE

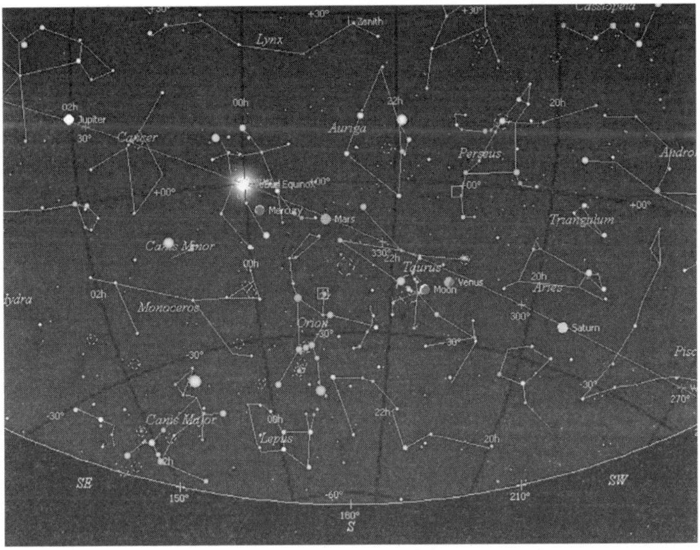

fig. 14: Equinox at Mṛgaśiras. Castor about 5740 BCE

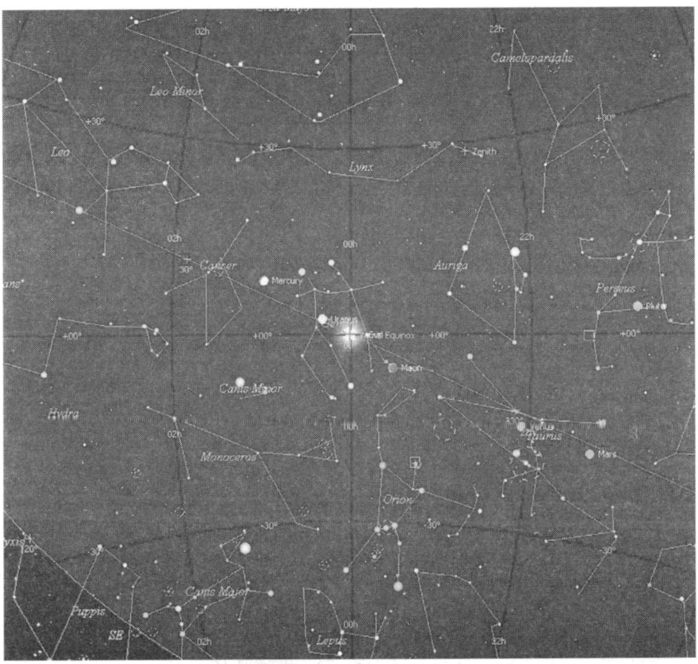

fig. 15: Vernal equinox at Ārdrā γ-Gem about 5440 BCE

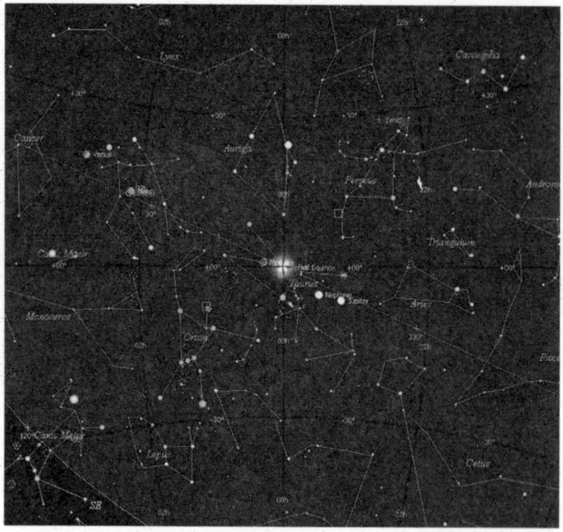

fig. 16: Vernal equinox at *Rohiṇī* α-Tau about 3220 BCE

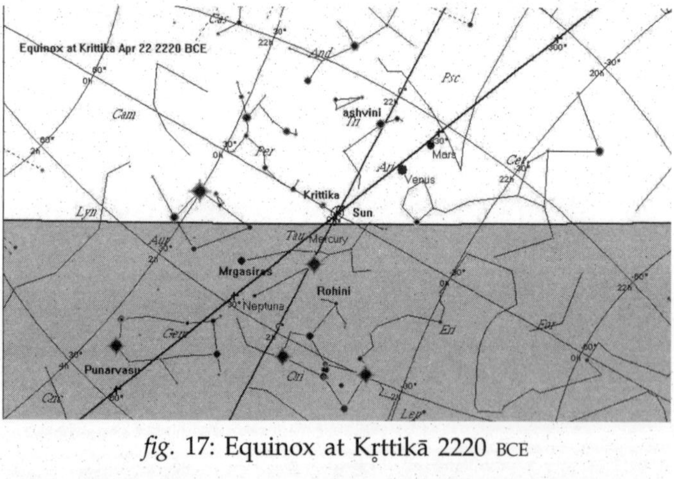

fig. 17: Equinox at Kṛttikā 2220 BCE

downwards all the way to Kṛttikā. This indicates an awareness of the phenomenon of precession and gives a chronology based on this from about 6000 BCE to about 3000 BCE. *Figs*. 13 through 17 show the occurrence of equinoxes at Punarvasu, Ārdrā, Mṛgaśiras, Rohiṇī, and Kṛttikā respectively.

11. Astronomical References in Other Vedic Texts

There are other astronomical data available in the brāhmaṇa texts. For example, *Śatapatha Brāhmaṇa* refers to Kṛttikās rising exactly in the East. As already mentioned, the date of the event referred to has been shown to be 2925 +/- 100 BCE, quite in agreement with Dikshit. Considering that this text is attributed to Yājñavalkya, a disciple of Vaiśaṁpāyana, who is an important narrator of the epic, the date of 3067 BCE for the war is consistent with the date of *Śatapatha Brāhmaṇa*. As already discussed, the author has shown (also on the basis of simulations using the planetarium software) that Lagadha's *VJ* should be dated to be about about 1800 BCE. The astronomy followed at the time of the Mahābhārata war is *VJ*, but is very much pre-Lagadha. The date of Lagadha's *VJ* is also consistent with the date of the war. It may be noted in passing that *Śatapatha Brāhmaṇa* mentions both Parīkṣit and Janamejaya. This is an independent check on the date of the war.

A passage in the *Pañcaviṁśa Brāhmaṇa* (XXV.15.3) connects Janamejaya with the *Sarpayāga* and has been referred to by Raychaudhuri (1923). A solar eclipse mentioned in this Brāhmaṇa text has been dated by Sengupta (1947) as occurring on 14 September 2451 BCE. *Fig*. 20 shows the star map for this day confirming the calculations of Sengupta. Winter solstice has been mentioned to occur at Pūrvaphālguṇī in *Kauṣītaki* and *Tāṇḍya Brāhmaṇa* texts also and Sengupta (1947) has calculated these dates to be 3521 BCE and 2934 BCE respectively. *Figs*. 21 and 22 illustrate the occurrence of winter solstice on these dates.

12. Summary and Conclusion

References to astronomical events in the Vedic texts as well as in the epic *Mahābhārata* have been re-examined with the help of planetarium software, which can project the view of the sky at any time and at any place. In this connection many of the misconceptions and misrepresentations regarding the state

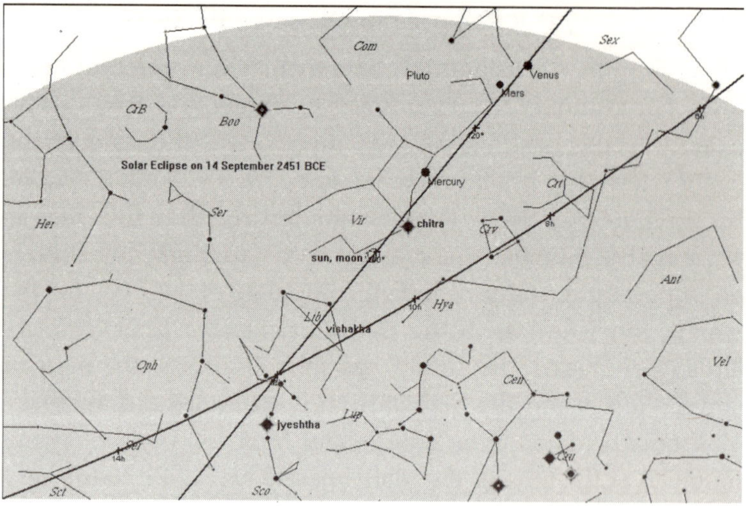

fig. 18: Solar Eclipse on 14 September 2451 BCE

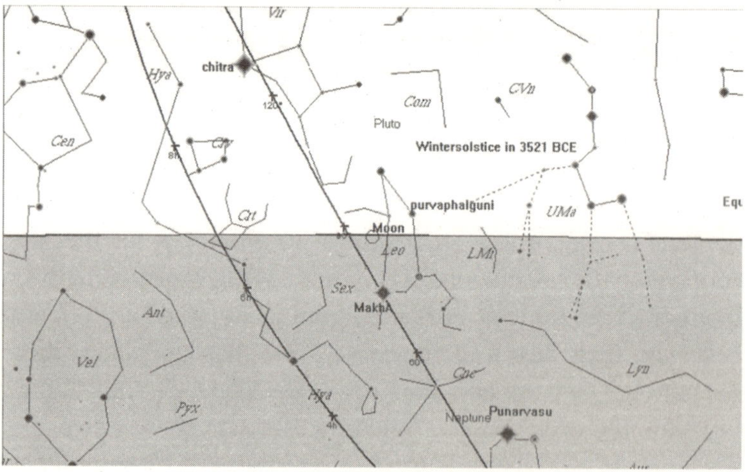

fig. 19: Winter solstice in 3521 BCE
occurs on full moon at Pūrvaphālguṇī

of astronomy in the Vedic times have been corrected. The simulations provide a reasonably consistent chronology of the *Ṛgveda*, other Vedic texts and the war epic *Mahābhārata*. The

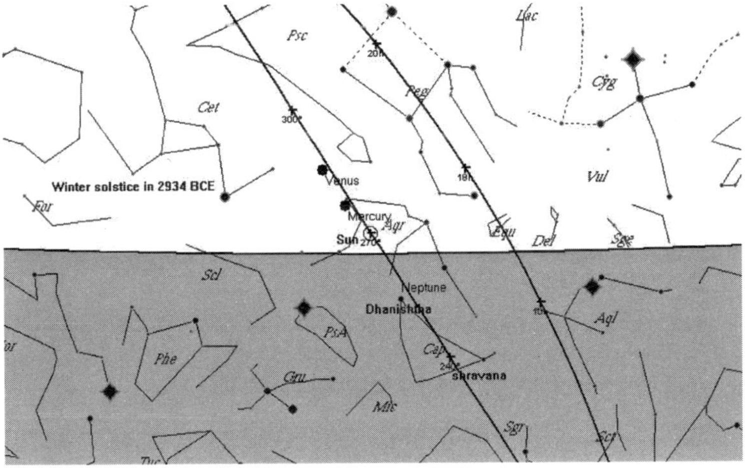

fig. 20: Winter solstice in 2934 BCE

dates derived from astronomical references span a range possibly from ~6000 BCE to about 2200 BCE. The references are derived from almost all the books of *Ṛgveda*. The dates for *Ṛgveda* are consistent with the date of Mahābhārata war based on astronomical references and verified by planetarium software. While some of the legends discussed may be understood in terms of non-astronomical interpretations as well, the astronomical ones can be considered plausible and serve as the basis for the high chronology. The author believes that the high chronology will bear the test of time.

List of Abbreviations

AP	*Atharvaveda Pariśiṣṭha*
MB	*Mahābhārata* Critical Edition
MNU	*Mahānārāyaṇopaniṣat*
RJ	*Ṛgjyotiṣa*
ŚB	*Śatapatha Brāhmaṇa*
VJ	*Vedāṅgajyotiṣa*

References

Achar, Narahari B.N., 1998a, "On the Vedic Origin of the Ancient Mathematical Astronomy of India", *Journal of Studies on Ancient India*, 1-2.

———, 1998b (2000), "Measurement of Time Using a Water Clock: An Interpretation of the Third Mantra of the Kāla Sūkta of Atharvaveda (XIX.53.3)", in Bhu Dev Sharma (ed), *New Perspectives on Vedic and Ancient Indian Civilization*, New York: World Association for Vedic Studies, pp. 157-65.

———, 2000a, "On the Astronomical Basis of the Date of Satapatha Brahmana: A re-examination of Dikshit's Theory", *Indian Journal of History of Science*, 35(1), pp. 1-19.

———, 2000b, "A Case for Revising the Date of Vedanga Jyotisa", *Indian Journal of History of Science*, 35.3, pp. 173-83.

———, 2000c, "On the Caitradi Scheme," *Indian Journal of History of Science*, 35.4 pp. 295-310.

———, 2002a, "In Search of *Nakṣatras* in *Ṛgveda*" in Bhu Dev Sharma (ed), *Contemporary Views on Indian Civilization*, New Delhi: World Association for Vedic Studies, pp. 361-70.

———, 2002b, "On the Identification of Vedic Nakṣatras", in Bhu Dev Sharma (ed), *Contemporary Views on Indian Civilization*, New Delhi: World Association for Vedic Studies, New, pp. 371-87.

———, 2004, "Date of the Mahābhārata War Based on Simulations Using Planetarium Software" in Kamath (ed.), *The Date of the Mahābhārata War Based on Astronomical Data* Bangalore, Mythic Society, pp. 65-115.

———, 2010, "The Mahābhārata War: Its Date on the Basis of Astronomical References" in Singh (ed.) *Origin of Indian Civilization*, New Delhi: DK Printworld.

Basham, A.L., 1953, *The Wonder That Was India*, New York: Grove Press Inc.

Bhat, Ramakrishna M., 1981, *Varāhamihira's Bṛhatsaṁhitā*, Part I, ed. with English translation, Delhi: Motilal Banarsidass.

Bose, D.M., S.N. Sen, B.V. Subbarayappa (1971) (eds.), *A Concise History of Science in India*, New Delhi.

Dikshit, S.B., 1895, "The Age of Śatapatha Brāmaṇa" *Indian Antiquary*, 24, pp. 245-46.

———, 1969, *Bhāratīya Jyotiṣa Śāstra*, Calcutta: Government of India Press.

Eggeling, J., 1963, *The Śatapatha Brāhmaṇa according to the Madhyandina School*, Delhi: Motilal Banarsidass, Part I, pp. 282-83.

Elst, Koenraad, 2007, *Asterisk in Bharopiyasthan*, New Delhi, Voice of India. David Frawley, 1991, *Gods, Sages and Kings*, Salt Lake City: Passage Press.

Gupta, S.P. & K.S. Ramachandran, 1976 (eds.), *Mahābhārata, Myth and Reality-Differing Views*, Delhi: Agam Prakashan.

Griffith, R.T.H. 1973, (New & Revised from the original 1889 edition), *The Hymns of the Ṛgveda*, Delhi: Motilal Banarsidass.

Iyengar, R.N., 2004, "Historicity of Celestial Observations of Mahābhārata", in Kamath (ed.), *The Date of the Mahābhārata War Based on Astronomical Data*, Bangalore: Mythic Society, pp. 150-86.

Jacobi, H.G., 1894, "On the Date of Ṛgveda", *Indian Antiquary*, 23, pp. 154-59 (translated from German by J. Morrison).

Kak, Subhash, 1994, *The Astronomical Code of the Ṛgveda*, New Delhi: Aditya Prakashan.

Kamath, S.U., 2004 (ed.), *The Date of the Mahābhārata War Based on Astronomical Data*, Bangalore: Mythic Society.

Kazanas, N., 2009, *Indo-Aryan Origins and Other Vedic Issues*, New Delhi: Aditya Prakashan.

Keith, A.B., 1919, *Ṛgveda Brāhmaṇas: The Aitareya and the Kauṣitaki Brāhmaṇa*s *of the Ṛgveda*, Delhi: Motilal Banarsidass.

Kielhorn, F., 1969, *Kleine Schriften*, Wiesbaden, Franz Steiner Verlag, GmbH.

Law, N.N., 1965, *Age of the Ṛgveda*, Calcutta: Firma K.L. Mukhyopadhyay.

Majumdar, R.C., H.C. Raychaudhuri, Kalikinkar Datta, 1978, *An Advanced History of India*, Madras: Macmillan India Pvt. Ltd.

Pingree, D., 1973, "The Mesopotamian Origin of Early Indian Mathematical Astronomy", *Journal for the History of Astronomy*, 4 (1) pp. 1-12.

Pingree, D. & P. Morissey, 1989, "On the Identification of the Yogatārās of the Indian Nakṣatras", *Journal for the History of Astronomy*, 20, pp. 99-119.

Rajaram, N.S. & D. Frawley, 1997, *Vedic Aryans and the Origins of Civilization: A Literary and Scientific Perspective*, New Delhi: Voice of India.

Ramachandran, V.G., 1998, "Date of Adi Sankara", in N. Mahalingam (ed.), *Ancient India*, Chennai, International Society for the Investigation of Ancient Civilization pp. 261-304.

Raychaudhuri, H.C., 1923, *Political History of Ancient India*, Calcutta: University of Calcutta, p. 10.

Saha, M.N. & A.C. Lahiri, 1955, *Report of the Calendar Reform Committee*, New Delhi: CSIR.

Sastry, T.S. Kuppanna, 1985, *Vedāṅga Jyotiṣa of Lagadha*, New Delhi: Indian National Science Academy.

Sathe, S., 1983, *Search for the Year of the Bharata War*, Hyderabad: Navabharati Publications.

Sengupta, P.C., 1947, *Ancient Indian Chronology*, Calcutta: University of Calcutta.

Sen, S.N., 1971, "Astronomy" in D.M. Bose, S.N. Sen, & B.V. Subbarayappa (eds.), *A Concise History of Science in India*, New Delhi: Indian National Science Academy, pp. 58-135.

Singh, Bal Ram, 2010, *Origin of Indian Civilization*, New Delhi: DK Printworld.

Sircar, D.C., 1969, "The Myth of the Great Bharata War", in *The Bharata War and the Puranic Geneologies*, University of Calcutta, pp. 11-27.

Talageri, S.G., 2008, *The R̥gveda and the Avesta: The Final Evidence*, New Delhi: Aditya Prakashan.

Tilak, B.G., 1893 (1984), *The Orion*, New Delhi: Cosmo Publications.

Vaidya, C.V., 1983, *The Mahābhārata: A Criticism*, New Delhi: Cosmo Publications, p. 80.

Vedavyas, E., 1986, *Astronomical Dating of the Mahābhārata War*, Delhi: Agam Kala Prakashan.

Venkatachelam, Kota, 1954, *The Plot in Indian Chronology*, Vijayavada, Arya Vijnana.

Wilson, H.H., 1850 (1977), *Rigveda Samhita*, New Delhi: Cosmo.

Winternitz, M., 1927, *A History of Indian Literature* (English translation, 1983-85), New Delhi: Motilaldass Banarsidass.

6

Oral Tradition in Indian Civilization

M.G. Prasad

Abstract

Vedas are at the foundation of Indian Civilization. It is known that for thousands of years till the present, Vedas are contributing to not only the culture of India but also to the global culture. The continuous transmission of the Vedas from ancient times to the present is enabled through oral tradition. In this oral tradition, the knowledge is carried on through Vedic chanting with precision in which the *guru* teaches the disciples at a very young age. This oral tradition is passed on from generation to generation. In 2003, the UNESCO proclaimed the Vedic chanting as an intangible cultural heritage of the world. In addition to Vedic chanting, the oral tradition has been instrumental and effective in India for teaching classical music, scriptures, poetic literature, folk music and folk tales. Thus oral tradition plays a very significant role in the Indian Civilization. This chapter presents various aspects of oral tradition that are contributing to Indian Civilization.

1. Introduction

The roots of Indian Civilization are traced back to the Vedas. The word Veda comes from the root *vid* which means "to know". The Vedas are a large collection of *mantra*s traditionally attributed to *ṛṣis*. A *mantra* is an utterance with intonations, which carries spiritual power. It is described as *mananāt trāṇanāt caiva*, which means "by repetition and contemplation the chanter is protected". A *ṛṣi* is one who has realized the Supreme Being through spiritual austerities and meditation and through blessings of the Supreme Being has obtained the deep insight into life and the cosmos.[1] Vedas are also called as Śruti, which means they were originally "heard" by *ṛṣis*. There have been a large number of *ṛṣis* in the history of Indian Civilization.[2] A *ṛṣi* is also known as *mantra-draṣṭā* meaning "the seer of *mantras*".

The enormous amount of Veda *mantras* has been classified as the four Vedas, namely — *Ṛgveda, Yajurveda, Sāmaveda* and *Atharvaveda*. The Vedas describe *dharma*, which refers to principles of nature that hold and protect all things. *Dharma* has many levels depending on the subject and contexts. It is for this reason Veda or Śruti is taken as the validating authoritative reference for any clarification regarding *dharma* to be followed as given by[3, 4]

dharmaṁ jijñāsānāṁ pramāṇaṁ paramaṁ śrutiḥ ।

The scriptures also refer to the Vedas as the breath of the Supreme Being. They are also called as *śabda* (the divine and transcendental sound) manifesting into *mantras*. They are like manuals, which are used in creation of this universe. Also the Vedas are beneficial to us like mother. In the words of Max Müller:

> In the history of the world, the Veda fills a gap which no literary work in any other language could fill. It carries us back to times of which we have no records anywhere and gives us the very words of generation of men of whom otherwise we could form but the vaguest *estimate by means of conjectures and inferences*.[5]

It is important to note that the *mantras* of the Vedas are associated with a triad. The triad consists of *ṛṣi* (seer), *chandas* (metre) and *devatā* (deity). The *ṛṣi* refers to the seer for whom the *mantra* was heard (or seen) by the blessings of Supreme Being. The *devatā* refers to the deity to whom the *mantra* is intended. It is to be noted that although many deities are referred, they are all manifestations of just one Supreme Being. The *chanda*s refer to the metre in which the *mantra* was cognized. The *mantra*s are generally prayers in poetic form. There are several types of metres and the commonly used seven types of metres are:[6]

Chandas	No. of Lines (pada)	Alphabets in Each pada	Total
Gāyatrī	3	8, 8, 8	24
Uṣṇik	3	8, 8, 12	28
Anuṣṭup	4	8, 8, 8, 8	32
Bṛhatī	4	8, 8, 8, 12	36
Paṅkti	5	8, 8, 8, 8, 8	40
Triṣṭup	4	11, 11, 11, 11	44
Jagatī	4	12, 12, 12, 12	48

These metres are found not only in the Veda *mantra*s but are also used in the enormous Sanskrit literature. The metre helps to memorize the *mantra*s and the poems.

The enormous development of literature in Indian Civilization is based on the Vedas. However, in addition to *chanda*s of the Vedas, there is a large number of works in Sanskrit language.[7, 8] The various scriptures in Sanskrit are composed in the form of *sūtra*s, which are short cryptic statements. Then there are historical epic works, namely the *Rāmāyaṇa* and the *Mahābhārata* composed as *śloka*, which generally refers to two lines in poetic form. It is to be noted that in spite of development of writing in Indian Civilization, the oral tradition has been effectively used from ancient times to present times. The oral tradition was not only used to transmit Veda *mantras* but also the scriptures, classical music, poetic works, folk music and folk tales.

2. Oral Traditions

2.1 VEDIC CHANTING

It is well known that Saṁskr̥tam, commonly known as Sanskrit language, has played a major role in Indian Civilization over thousands of years to present times. There has been interesting research into whether the origin of Sanskrit lies in India and also the refutation of the so-called Aryan Invasion Theory.[9, 10] The Vedic Sanskrit, also known as *chandas* (Saṁhitā), is slightly different from classical Sanskrit. Vedic Sanskrit is almost entirely religious. The Vedic Sanskrit has accents known as *svaras*. There are minor differences between the Vedic and classical Sanskrit in grammar, vocabulary and number of metres used in literature.[7] One can understand the meaning of Veda *mantras* using the knowledge of classical Sanskrit. Enormous literature in all fields of study in Vedic Hinduism exists in Sanskrit in addition to a large number of literary works.[7, 8, 11] Also, Sanskrit due to its well-structured grammar such as sage Pāṇini's grammar, has the suitability as a natural language.[12]

The beginning of oral tradition of the Vedas is referred[13] in *Śrīmad Bhāgavatam* as given by Maharṣi Vyāsa:

> In the beginning when the creator, four-headed Lord Brahmā, was focusing his mind on the Supreme Being Lord Nārāyaṇa, from whose navel he had risen, the *nāda* (a subtle transcendental sound) emanated from his *hr̥daya* (inner space of heart). This *nāda* that came out of his *hr̥daya* (inner space) consisted of three syllables (*A, U, Ṁ*), which merged and became the holy *praṇava* (*oṁ*). From this *praṇava* arose the alphabets of Sanskrit language and subsequently the

> four Vedas emerged from the four heads of Brahmā. Then Brahmā orally taught these Vedas to his sons, who were great sages. These sages orally passed them to their sons, who in turn continued this through the lineage.

Thus the tradition of transmitting the Vedas orally from the *guru* (master) to a *śiṣya* (disciple) has not only sustained over thousands of years but is continuing even in the present times at homes, temples, *āśrama*s and special schools for Vedic teaching known as *gurukulas*.[14, 15, 16] It is to be noted that this *guru-śiṣya sampradāya* (or master-disciple tradition) is an integral part of teaching-learning discipline, which has sustained the oral tradition through generations for thousands of years. In 2003, UNESCO proclaimed the oral tradition of the Vedic chanting as an intangible cultural heritage of the world. The proclamation is as below:

> . . . the verses of the Vedas were traditionally chanted during sacred rituals and recited daily in Vedic communities. The value of this tradition lies not only in the rich content of its oral literature but also in the ingenious techniques employed by brāhmaṇa priests in preserving the texts intact over thousands of years. To ensure that the sound of each word remains unaltered, practitioners are taught from childhood complex recitation techniques that are based on tonal accents, a unique manner of pronouncing each letter and specific speech combinations.
>
> — *UNESCO Proclamation 2003*
> *Intangible Cultural Heritage-ICH*

According to the *varṇa* system of India,[17] it is the essential duty of brāhmaṇas that they must learn as well as teach the Vedas through chanting. Also, the prerequisite to learn Vedic chanting is that the brāhmaṇa boys, at their age of eight years, have to go through *upanayana* (wearing a sacred thread) ritual. In this sacrament, they are initiated through the well-known *Gāyatrī Mantra*, and take a vow to learn the chanting of Veda *mantras* and study the Vedas. Then these young brāhmaṇa boys start learning Vedic chanting from a *guru*. It is noted that many times the father is himself the *guru*. At this young age of eight years, these boys are highly capable of learning and retaining the Veda *mantras*. The teaching procedure is that the *guru* chants one *mantra* with intonations first, and then the disciples need to chant it precisely the same way, twice. The *guru* corrects any mistakes till the chanting precisely follows the same as the *guru*'s chanting. Neither the *guru* nor the disciple uses any written text. The teaching and learning is on aural (oral) basis. Then, after the teaching session the disciples must practise repeatedly to properly memorize the chants. The master goes to the next line or segment only after the previously learnt portion is fully memorized. It is important to note that the memory is indispensable in oral tradition. Also, the disciples lead a disciplined life, which enhances the memorization and learning. Thus, the tender age with proper teaching and learning method along with a disciplined life plays a very important role in the success of oral tradition through Vedic chanting. The harmonious relationship between the master and the disciple is very important in oral transmission through Vedic chanting. A Vedic *mantra* noted below as invocation provides the common vision for both the master and the disciple.

> *oṁ saha nāvavatu, saha naubhunaktu, saha vīryaṁ karavāvahai* |
> *tejasvināvadhitamastu mā vidviṣāvahai, om śāntiḥ śāntiḥ śāntiḥ* ||

> May both of us be protected together, May both of us eat together, May both of us engage in noble and productive work together. May our study and understanding be brilliant. May we not hate each other. May there be Peace, Peace, Peace.

The success of oral tradition for transmission through Vedic chants from master to disciple over the generations is due to several important guidelines, namely: (1) phonetic guidelines, (2) simple to complex patterns of chanting and (3) chanting disciplines. It is important to note that knowledge and practice of precise chanting will also supplement the study of the Vedas.

2.1.1 PHONETIC GUIDELINES

The phonetic guidelines are critically important, as they are the rules of pronunciation for Vedic chanting. The science of phonetics clearly emphasizes the importance of error-free chanting. In *Nāradīya Śikṣā*, a treatise on phonetics, says:[18]

> If the Vedic text (chanting) employed in the sacrifice is defective in the accent (pitch) or sounds or used for the performance of the wrong rites, it does not yield the desired results.

The six parameters that control the precision in pronunciation are given according to a *mantra* in *Taittirīyopaniṣad* are: *varṇa* (alphabet), *svara* (accent or pitch), *mātrā* (duration), *balaṁ* (emphasis), *sāma* (uniformity) and *santānaha* (juxtaposition).[12, 19, 20]

Varṇa deals with the pronunciation of all Sanskrit sounds with the use of full mouth. The Sanskrit sounds based on the places of pronunciation with respect to mouth are classified as guttural (from the throat — *kaṇṭhya*), palatal (the tongue against the back of the palate — *tālávya*), retroflex (the tongue further forward on the palate — *mūrdhanya*), dental (the tongue against the back of the front teeth — *dantya*), Labial (the lips either closed or pursed — *auṣṭhya*) and nasal (through the nasal passages — *nāsikya*). Also the aspirated and unaspirated sounds play important role in pronunciation.

Svara refers to the three main tonal accents, namely *udātta, anudātta* and *svarita*. These three accents are acute, grave, and circumflex. In addition, two extended notes called *nigadha* and *prachaya* are used. The accents play a key role in Vedic chanting because change in accents results in not only the change in the meaning of *mantras* but also yield different results. There is an example given in *Taittirīya Saṁhitā*[3] as:

> Tvaṣṭā, who was not well disposed towards Indra, for some reason wanted a son capable of killing Indra so that he could settle old scores with Indra. So Tvaṣṭā performed *homa* (fire-sacrifice) chanting a *mantra*: *Indra śśatrur vardhasva*. When chanting it, the correct way was to utter "Indra" in even tone (i.e. without raising or lowering accent). In *śatru*, the *tru* should have been high, and similarly, *vardhasva* should have been high. If recited properly as above, it would mean "let Tvaṣṭā's son grow up to kill Indra". By the efficacy of the sound of the properly chanted *mantra* alone, Tvaṣṭā's son should have grown up and killed Indra. But Tvaṣṭā erred in pronunciation. That is, he raised the tone high in *dra* in Indra, the *śatru* was recited evenly and in *vardhasva* the *rdha* was lowered in tone instead of being raised. As a result, instead of "let Tvaṣṭā's son grow up to kill Indra" the meaning got topsy-turvy (reversed). Although the words and letters were not changed, due to the fault in intonation, the result was just contrary to what Tvaṣṭā wanted. In other words, Indra killed Tvaṣṭā's son. Thus the father Tvaṣṭā became responsible for the death of his son, Vṛtra, at the hands of Indra.

Mātrā refers to the length or duration of each vowel or consonant. The commonly used duration units are *hrasva*, *dīrgha*, *pluta* and *ardha mātrā*. The *hrasva* is taken as one unit of *mātrā* as equivalent to blinking eye five times or saying five syllables. The *dīrgha* is two *mātrā*. The *pluta* is three or four *mātrā*. *Ardha mātrā* is half a *mātrā*. The duration of chants are based on *mātrās*, which need to be precisely adhered to while chanting.

Balaṁ refers to the articulatory force of a syllable. The force (quantity of air) depends on the type of syllables, namely *alpa prāṇa* and *mahāprāṇa*. In *alpa prāṇa* syllables, no aspiration is required whereas in *mahāprāṇa* syllables, aspirations are required. The aspiration energy for *mahāprāṇa* syllables comes from the abdomen area. The sitting posture on a mat on the ground with straight back is required so that the posture enables proper breathing and thus proper energy required for articulation.

Sāma refers to continuity, proper speed and pleasantness in chanting. It is important to note that chanting has to be continuously smooth as the change of *svaras* occurs in the *mantras*. In collective chanting, it becomes important that each chanter maintains continuity in harmony so that the chanting from the group is continuous and all voices are in unison.

Santāna refers to the combination and juxtaposition. When compound letters are encountered, the proper pronunciation with correct *mantra* is required. *Santāna* also refers to proper punctuation. The stops taken for inhaling while chanting are critical for both the melody and meaning of the chants.

Thus all the above six parameters are equally important in chanting which can only be taught orally to a disciple by the master. The *Nāradīya Śikṣā,* like the other phonetic manuals, emphasizes severe penalties incurred by the chanter who fails to perform his task accurately, whether by mispronouncing the text, accenting it incorrectly, erring in either the length or the tonal quality of a syllable, failing to render the text with sufficient clarity or simply suffering any mental lapse.[19]

2.1.2 PATTERNS OF CHANTING

In order to maintain the oral tradition of Vedic chanting to be error-free and precise, eight types of variations of the three original patterns of the *mantras* have been developed by *ṛṣis*. In total there are eleven types of chanting patterns in which the first three, namely Saṁhitā, *pada* and *krama* are simple patterns, whereas the additional eight patterns, namely *jaṭā, mālā, śikhā, rekhā, dhvaja, daṇḍa, ratha* and *ghana* (bell) are complex in the ascending order.[3, 14] These names indicate the design of patterns, namely: braid, garland, topknot, row, flag, staff, chariot and bell respectively.[14] For example, in *jaṭā* (braid), as two strands of hair are made into one by entwining to form a tress. Similarly, by entwining two words of a *mantra*, the pattern of *jaṭā* comes into being. An entwining process that involves a reversal of the stems forms a garland of flowers (*mālā*). Similarly, a unit of two words is treated in precisely the same way as in the type of *mālā* known as *puṣpa mālā*. In the pattern of *śikhā* (topknot), a coiffure adopted especially by ascetics, the hair is bound and encircled around the top of the head, with the end of the strand left over after each encirclement. In this *śikhā* pattern, the basic *jaṭā* scheme is adopted, but one word is added to the end of each unit. Likewise, the other patterns are designed.[14] However it is important to note that all the six phonetic parameters discussed earlier have to be followed in the pattern that is chanted.

All these patterns are used in present times. However, more commonly found patterns especially in south India are, namely Saṁhitā (source), *pada* (words) *krama* (order), *jaṭā* (braid) and *ghana* (bell). These patterns are shown as below:

Name of Pattern	Pattern
Saṁhitā	*namaḥ Śivāya ca*

In the Saṁhitā *mantra* pattern above, let the numbers 1, 2 and 3 represent the three units namely, *namaḥ* (1) *śivāya* (2) and *ca* (3). The patterns look like:

It is very important to remember that all of the six phonetic parameters, namely *varṇa, svara, mātrā, balam, sāma* and *santānaḥ* depend on the pattern. It is seen that only through oral recitation can the master teach all these patterns to the disciples. The studies on sound and memory in oral traditions have shown that strong evidence exists for the important role of sound patterns in recalling and in a stable transmission of oral traditions.[21]

2.1.3 CHANTING DISCIPLINE

In addition to strictly following the phonetic guidelines, required repetition and memorization of various chanting patterns, the disciple should avoid certain undesirable chanting characteristics. These undesirable characteristics of Vedic chanting are given as,[3, 4]

Name of Pattern	Pattern
saṁhitā	1, 2, 3
pada	1; 2; 3
krama	12; 23
jaṭā	12 21 12; 23 32 23;
ghana	12 21 123 321 123;
	23 32 23;

gīti śīghrī śiraḥkampī tatha likhitapāṭakaḥ ।
ānarthājāñolpakanṭhaśca ṣadete pāṭhakādhamāḥ ॥

Which means that the one who has these six undesirable characteristics is not good in Vedic chanting. The six undesirable characteristics are: singing (instead of chanting), high speed in chanting, oscillating the head, reading from written script (instead of chanting from memory), not understanding the meaning of chants and a weak and shrill voice quality.

Likewise, the six desirable characteristics of Vedic chanting are given as,[3, 4]

mādhuryamakśaravyaktiḥ padacchedastu susvaraḥ ।
dhairyaṁ laya samarthaṁ ca śadete paṭhakāguṇāḥ ॥

Which means that one who has these six desirable characteristics is good in Vedic chanting. The six desirable characteristics are: pleasant chanting, full clarity in pronunciation, proper breaking of words, correctness in intonation, strength and steadiness in chanting and proper speed and continuity in chanting.

Thus the Vedic chants of all of the four Vedȧs, namely *Ṛgveda*, *Sāmaveda*, *Yajurveda* and *Atharvaveda* have been transmitted orally, preserving the original way from the generations after generations through precise memorization and efficient method through memory techniques. It is important to note that the oral transmission to the disciple begins at a very young age at which the capability of memory is very high. The aim of Vedic chanting is to instill an automatic and total command of the Vedic text that would rule out even the slightest possibility of error. Also the memorization was reinforced by additional methods such as *mudrās*, which are finger positions and motions (corresponding to the type of chants) that are essential in performance as they are for learning and remembering the *mantra*.[16, 19]

3. Ślokas and Sūtras

The Vedic literature in Sanskrit is predominately in poetic form as metrical verses and short aphorisms. These compositions also conformed to special requirements of an old literature, namely consciousness, memorability, predictability, rhythm, formulaic construction, suitability for oral delivery and appropriateness for teaching and learning. Because the Vedas themselves are in the form of verse, it seemed an obvious choice for Vedic literature, and from the Vedas the tendency spread into various fields of knowledge.[19]

One of the most dominating metres that are found in the Sanskrit literature is *anuṣṭup* metre. A *śloka* or a verse consists of two lines and each line (i.e. top and the bottom line) contains two parts. A *śloka* in *anuṣṭup* contains 16 syllables per line. Each part of the line contains 8 syllables. So a *śloka* in *anuṣṭup* metre contains 32 (8 × 4) syllables. The two epics *Rāmāyaṇa*, which has 24,000 verses, and the *Mahābhārata*, which has 100,000 verses, use mainly the *anuṣṭup* metre. It is said that Maharṣi Vālmīki, who composed the *Rāmāyaṇa* orally taught it to two young boys (brothers) who were sons of King Śrī Rāma. They in turn recited the entire *Rāmāyaṇa* in an assembly in the court of King Śrī Rāma. It is common to see that even at present times there exists oral tradition of teaching and learning chapters from the *Rāmāyaṇa* and the *Bhagavad-Gītā* (700 verses) of *Mahābhārata*. In addition there are *subhāṣitas*, which are verses of wisdom abundantly found in Sanskrit literature. It is also common to see very young boys and girls being orally taught these *subhāṣitas*, which they memorize and understand their meaning as they grow older in life.

The *sūtras* (formulaic statements) are commonly used in Sanskrit treatises. For example, the grammar treatise written by Maharṣi Pāṇini has about 4000 *sūtras*. In traditional teaching of the Pāṇini's grammar, the *sūtras* are taught orally for memorization so that they can later be recalled instantaneously from memory in the application of *sūtras* in the formulation of words.

4. Classical Music and Dance

The origin of classical music of India is from the Vedas. The chants of the *Sāmaveda* are more musical in particular, due to the extended *mātrās* i.e. durations of the three *svaras* of the Vedas. These three *svaras* (accents) of the Vedas, namely *udātta* (acute) to *anudātta* (grave) and *svarita* (circumflex) are related to the seven notes which are also called as *svaras* of music. The seven *svaras* in the classical music are *sā, re, gā, mā, pā, dhā, nī* and *sā*. It is interesting to note the correspondence between *svaras* of the Vedas and *svaras* of the classical music. In *Nāradīya Śikṣā*[18] the correspondence is given as the *svaras* *nī* and *gā* originate in *udātta*, while *re* and *dhā*, originate in *anudātta*. Then *sā, mā* and *pā* have their origin in the *svarita*. In addition to the relationship with the Vedas, the seven *svaras* (notes) of music are related to the sounds from animals. In *Nāradīya Śikṣā*,[18] it is given as the note *sā* is from a peacock, *re* is from a bull, *gā* is from a goat, *mā* is from a curlew, *pā* is from a cuckoo, *dhā* is from a horse and *nī* is from an elephant. Thus it is seen that music is related to Vedic chants and also to the sounds of nature. The origin of music in India is traced to divinity. The visual pictures of Lord Kṛṣṇa holding the musical instrument bamboo flute and Goddess Sarasvatī holding a musical instrument *vīṇā* indicates that music is not only for entertainment but also for the spiritual development. In the words of Yogī Śrīraṅga Sadguru:

> Music should become the bridge that takes the listeners from sensual level to the spiritual level of *ātman*.[1]

Given that the music tradition in India is also from the Vedic origin, the oral tradition is essentially used to transfer this art from generation to generation through face-to-face instruction from *guru* to *śiṣya* by demonstration and imitation. This oral tradition of music is referred as *paramparā* in Sanskrit language, which means that knowledge orally transferred well from one generation (master) to another generation (disciple). This is known as *guru-śiṣya paramparā*. In the book Euphony[22] well-known violinist L Subramanian says:

> Even today students are discouraged from singing and playing their instruments looking at the book with the musical notation. Rather they are expected to listen to the *guru*, repeat the lesson, memorize it and play (or sing) from memory. All the great performers have been products of the *guru-śiṣya paramparā*, still considered the most effective way to learn Indian music.

In north Indian music, the traditions are kept through what are known as *gharānās*. Every *gharānā* would specialize in one or the other specific feature of classical music.[23] The master to disciple oral tradition essentially keeps the *gharānā* tradition intact.

In classical music also like the oral tradition of Vedic chanting, the disciples will be of very young-age girls and boys. The seven notes or *svara*s are taught in simple to complex patterns at various speeds in increasing order. For example, the three orders are shown below.[24]

> ***Simple type***
> *sā ri gā mā pā dhā nī sā*
> *sā nī dhā pā mā gā re sā*
>
> ***Jumping Type***
> *Sa Ri Sa Ga Ri Ma Ga Ri*
> *Sa Ri Ga Ma Pa Dha Ni Sa*
> *Sa Ni Sa Dha Ni Pa Dha Ni*
> *Sa Ni Dha Pa Ma Ga Ri Sa*
>
> ***Linked type***
> *Sa Sa Ri Ri Ga Ga Ma Ma*
> *Pa Pa Dha Dha Ni Ni Sa Sa*
> *Sa Sa Ni Ni Dha Dha Pa Pa*
> *Ma Ma Ga Ga Ri Ri Sa Sa*

Thus, it is seen that the various features of Indian classical music such as delicate nuances, ornamentations, and microtones influence the rendering of *rāga*s. It is due to these reasons the oral tradition is the most efficient method for the *guru* to teach the disciple. In the words of George Ruckert:[25]

> The *guru* taught the music directly through oral repetition: hear, repeat, practise, repeat, hear again and practise. A literature of *rāga* and *tāla* was accumulated slowly along with the technical abilities to be executed with greater refinement and discernment of ear, and the student was continually required to prove that he or she was ready for the next step.

It is interesting to note that the Sanskrit word *saṅgīta* is used to refer music. However the Sanskrit word *saṅgīta* actually refers to vocal music, instrumental music and dance. The ancient classical dance of India is called Bharata Nāṭyam. The origin of Bharata Nāṭyam is also from the Vedas. The Bharata Ṛṣi says[26] that he was inspired by the Lord to formulate the *Nāṭyaveda* or Veda of dance as a composite of the well-known four Vedas. The composition by Bharata Ṛṣi was based on text of recitals from the *Ṛgveda*, the music element from the *Sāmaveda*, the histrionic and gestural representation from *Yajurveda* and the sentiments from the *Atharvaveda*. In dance the disciple has to learn to sing music also, so that coordination between music, movements and storytelling sequence can be coordinated. The art of classical dance such as Bharata Nāṭyam is also transferred from the *guru* to *śiṣya* in a combined oral and visual tradition. The disciples start at a very young age to learn this classical performing art of dance.

5. Folk Music and Folk Tales

Folk music of India is traced back to the ancient Indian civilization and culture. In the words of poet Laureate, Rabindranath Tagore:

> Folk songs enable us to understand the mind and heart of the common people. A unity in the people's thought can be seen through rural folk songs from different villages of India.[27]

The folk songs in ancient Indian villages were composed and sung which were then orally transmitted to the next group of people. The themes of the folk songs were day-to-day things of village life and celebrations. As an example a farmer says in a Kannada folk song:[27]

> *mādeva ninahortu nanyāra nambilla* |
>
> *nā māduvenemba alavilla mallayya* |
> *nee nadeso nanna saruvella* ||

> O Lord Śiva, I have not believed in any one other than you.
> I do not feel that I am the doer. O the capable one, you make it happen.

Thus the folk songs deal with all facets of life. The oral tradition of folk music performance is still practised[28] such as the tales of well-known King Bhartṛhari of Ujjain and King Gopichand of Bengal through oral traditional performances in Ghatiyali, Rajasthan.

Similar to oral tradition of folk songs and music is the oral tradition of folk tales in India. In the words of noted author A.K. Ramanujan:

> Anyone studying the culture of India needs to study not only its written classic but its oral traditions of which folklore is an important part. Folklore prevails childhoods, families and communities as symbolic language of the non-literature parts of the people and the culture.[29]

However, the folk tales through oral tradition would have changes in the choice of words and language but the essence of the story would continue from generation to generation. The oral tradition plays important role not only in folk tales but also in religious moral stories.[30] In Indian context the oral tradition of tales goes back to stories from Upaniṣads and other ancient literature not only in Sanskrit but also in all regional languages and dialects. In the words of A.K. Ramanujan:

> Indeed, one way of defining verbal folklore for India is to say it is the literature of the dialects, those mother tongues of village, street, kitchen, tribal hut and wayside tea shop. This is the wide base of the Indian Pyramid on which all other Indian literature rest.[29]

6. Conclusion

Thus it is seen that oral tradition has a significant role in the Indian Civilization. The oral tradition through *guru-śiṣya paramparā* is responsible for sustaining Vedic chanting, scriptures, classical music and dance and folk music and tales from ancient times to the present times. In reference to chants and music in ancient India, it is noted by Guy Beck:

> the Hindu experience of scripture has been oral (aural) from the beginning with a strong emphasis on maintaining of purity of transmission by means of disciplined memorization.[31]

The key elements that are responsible for the sustenance of oral tradition is that it begins at a very young age of disciples, who have a high capacity to memorize. Also, the fact that the Vedas are revered, because they deal with knowledge of life and the cosmos in addition to the Veda *mantras* being the manifestation of the spiritual and transcendental sound.[32, 33] The Vedas, as an authoritative validating reference sustained through oral tradition, form the basis of the Vedic civilization and culture.[34] The Vedic civilization and culture formed the foundation for the development of the cultural history of India.[35]

Even in present times it can be seen that the Hindu rituals and religious occasions in temples[36] provide opportunities on a continuous basis for the oral recitation of the Vedic chants and music. It is always preferred that even in present times the Vedic chanting and classical music are learnt directly from *guru* so that the various phonetic guidelines can be demonstrated properly by the *guru*. This is due to the principle that a book cannot replace the *guru* who is a life force, in transmitting properly the Vedic chanting and music with all details to the disciple. Thus the intangible heritage of oral tradition of Vedic chanting, in addition to its own significance, is the foundation of all other oral traditions of music, dance and folklore. It is interesting to note that the modern research in neuroscience and cognitive sciences indicates that there is compelling evidence suggesting that brain's response to music is innate and has strong biological roots.[37] The efficiency of oral learning and remembering the chants, which are of musical nature at a very young age, is very high. Thus the ancient Vedic civilization seems to have successfully used this approach for sustaining the oral tradition of Vedic chanting, music, scriptures and story-telling. This intangible cultural heritage of oral tradition continues to play an important role in maintaining the continuity of Indian civilization from the ancient times to present times.

Acknowledgements

The author is grateful to Yogī His Holiness Śrīraṅkga Sadguru and Yogī His Holiness Śrī Raṅga Priya Swami of Aṣṭāṅga Yoga Vijñāna Mandiram for their inspiration and guidance. Also, the author is grateful to his teachers Vidwan R.S. Srinivasa Murthy, Vidwan R.K. Srikanta Kumara Swamy and Vidwan Putta Narasimha Shastry for teaching him the Vedic chanting through oral tradition.

References

1. Sriranga Sadguru, 1983-2009 (20 vols), *Amaravani: Lectures on Sanatana Dharma*, Mysore: Astanga Yoga Vijnana Mandiram.
2. Shrikant Prasoon, 2009, *Rishis and Rishikas: The Earliest Exponents of Hinduism*, Delhi: Pustak Mahal.
3. Sri Chandrasekharendra Saraswati, 1988, *The Vedas*, Mumbai: Bharatiya Vidya Bhavan and Sudakshina Trust.
4. P.S. Rameshvaravadhani, chief editor, 1997, *Krishna Yajurveda*, Bangalore: Jyoti Samskritika Pratishthana.
5. Max Müller, 2005, *India: What can it Teach us?*, New Delhi: Rupa and Co.
6. V. Gyanshruti and R. Vidyananda, 2006, *YAJNA: A Comprehensive Survey*, Bihar: Yoga Publications Trust.
7. Gaurinath Sastri, 1998, *A Concise History of Classical Sanskrit Literature*, Delhi: Motilal Banarsidass.
8. T.K. Ramachandra Aiyar, 1998, *A Short History of Sanskrit Literature*, Palghat: R.S. Vadhayar and Sons.

9. Angela Marcantonio, 2011, *The Origin of Indian Civilization: Critical Analysis of the Contribution of Linguistics*, Dartmouth: Proceedings of the Conference on the Origin of Indian Civilization, The Center for Indic Studies, the University of Massachusetts at Dartmouth.
10. N. Kazanas, 2006, *Indo-Aryan indigenism and the Aryan Invasion Theory Arguments (refuted)*, Athens: Omilos Meleton Institute.
11. M.G. Prasad, 2010, *Multi-Faceted Vedic Hinduism*, New York: Foundation for the Advancement of Arts and Sciences from India.
12. Girish Nath Jha, 2004 (vol. 4), *The System of Panini*, www. Language India.com
13. Howard Crosthwaite, 2007, *The Art of Vedic Chanting*, Canada: Trafford Publishing.
14. Wayne Howard, 1986, *Veda Recitation in Varanasi*, Delhi: Motilal Banarsidass.
15. Frits Staal, 2008, *Discovering the Vedas*, New Delhi: Penguin Books, India.
16. R. Bharathadri, (Director), 2003, DVD, *Oral Tradition of Vedas*, New Delhi: Indira Gandhi National Centre for the Arts.
17. M.G. Prasad, 2011, *The Vedic Perspectives of Varna System*, Conference on Varna, Jati and Kula, World Association of Vedic Studies, New Jersey.
18. Usha R. Bhise (ed. and tr.), 1986, *Naradiya Siksha*, Poona: Bhandarkar Oriental Research Institute.
19. Lewis Rowell, 1992, *Music and Musical Thought in Early India*, Chicago: The University of Chicago Press.
20. Swami Gambhirananda (2 vols.), 1957, *Eight Upaniṣads*, Himalayas: Advaita Ashrama.
21. David C. Rubin, 1995, *Memory in Oral Traditions*, New York: The Oxford University Press.
22. L. Subramanian and Viji Subramanian 1995, *Euphony: Indian Classical Music*, New Delhi: Affiliated East-West Press Private Ltd.
23. Richa Varma, 2010, *Indian Music: Gateway to Salvation*, Delhi: Sasta Sahitya Mandal.
24. Text Book Committee, 2005, *Carnatic Music (Junior Grade)*, Bangalore: Directorate of Text Publications.

25. George E. Ruckert, 2004, *Music in North India*, New York: The Oxford University Press.
26. A Board of Scholars, *The Natya Sastra*, Delhi: Sri Satguru Publications.
27. B.S. Gaddagimatha, 1969, *Kannada Folk Songs (Kannada Janapada Geetegalu*, Dharwar: Karnataka University.
28. Ann Grodzins Gold (tr.), 1992, *A Carnival of Parting*, Berkeley: University of California Press.
29. A.K. Ramanujan, 1991, *Folk Tales from India*, New York: Pantheon Books.
30. Megan McKenna, 2004, *Keepers of the Story: Oral Traditions in Religion*, New York: Sealaury Books.
31. Guy L. Beck (ed.), 2010, *Sacred Sound, Experiencing Music in World Religions*, New Delhi: Motilal Banarsidass.
32. Guy L. Beck, *Sonic Theology*, 1993, South Carolina: The University of South Carolina Press.
33. M.G. Prasad, 2009, *Vedic Perspectives on Acoustics*, Workshop on Exploring Vedic Sciences organized by the Center for Indic Studies, The University of Massachusetts at Dartmouth.
34. Kenneth Chandler, 2011, *Origins of Vedic Civilization*, Chapters from Book in Progress, www.scribd.com
35. A.L. Basham (ed.), 1985, *A Cultural History of India*, Delhi: Oxford University Press.
36. Jennifer Peace, 2005, Sound Rituals: A comparative Study of Chanting and Communal identity in a Hindu Temple and Christian Abbey (Ph. D Thesis), California: The University of California at Berkeley.
37. David A. Sousa, 2006, *How the Brain Learns*, California: Corwin Press; Sage Publications Company.

7

Dialectics of Power and Civilization

Knowledge Centred Indian Civilization

R.P. Singh

Abstract

A discourse on civilization in the present millennium is different from all occasions. We have advanced scientific knowledge with technology which is the most capable and sophisticated, the fifth generation microsoft with knowledge and information; but do we have wisdom to make use of all these on civilization achievements? One of the features of human history has been that people, resources, ideas, consciousness and above all civilizations move from one place to another, and in the era of globalization these are moving all too fast and getting transformed gradually. The basic question arises: what exactly is that basic feature of Indian Civilization through which it can be identified even after so many upheavals and transformations? The answer is: it is the knowledge centred civilization which has two basic features, namely: (1) it has the feature of colossal continuum of contact, conflict and confluence; (2) there is plurality of approaches to thought constructions on reality. Continuity and plurality are dialectically operating in Indian Civilization and it is with reference to power that it becomes hierarchical.

The philosophico-religious quests and cultural-civilization achievements of India have been of colossal continuum of power in terms of contact, conflict and confluence. We instinctively suspect attempts to homogenize a civilization and culture and impose a single identity on it, for we are acutely aware that every civilization and culture is internally plural and differentiated. And we remain equally sceptical of all attempts to present it as one whose origins lie within itself, as self-generating and *sui generis*, for we feel persuaded that all civilizations are born out of interaction with and absorb the influences of others and are shaped by wider economic, political, technological, linguistic and other forces. This undercuts the very basis of Afro-centrism, Euro-centrism, Indo-centrism, Sino-centrism and other kinds of centrisms, all of which isolate the history of the culture concerned from that of others and credits its achievements to its own genius.

On Civilization

A discourse on civilization in the present millennium is different from all occasions. We have advanced scientific knowledge with technology which is the most capable and sophisticated, the fifth generation microsoft with knowledge and information; but do we have wisdom to make use of all these on civilization achievements? One of the features of human history has been that people, resources, ideas, consciousness and above all civilizations move from one place to another and in the era of globalization these are moving all too fast and getting transformed gradually. The basic question arises: what exactly is that basic feature of Indian Civilization through which it can be identified even after so many upheavals and transformations? The answer is: it is the knowledge centered civilization which has two basic features, namely: (1) it has the feature of colossal continuum of contact, conflict and confluence; (2) there is plurality of approaches to thought constructions on reality. Continuity and plurality are dialectically operating in Indian Civilization and it is with reference to power that it becomes hierarchical.

On Power and Civilization

The relationship between power and civilization is a top-down model that conceives of power as a monolithic force imposed by dominant social/cultural/civilization groups. Power is in terms of various articulations of force circulating throughout the social-civilization bodies and shaping people's knowledge/understandings of themselves and their relations to the world in which they act. Power is force, not a substance — a force that is fluid and productive, and not merely coercive. Power cannot be conceived except in terms of its relations, relations that range from the microphysical to the global and that can be traced in terms of the strategies, techniques and practices within which such relations are enacted. The power-civilization nexus becomes evident if we take culture as the horizon of people's body (of knowledge/power) and we come across multiple horizons. One definitely faces the problem of contact, conflict and confluence of cultural horizons. This situation will inevitably transform each nation, the people who now hold power, and those whose labour creates all values.

Indian Civilization

The philosophico-religious quests and cultural-civilization achievements of India have been of colossal continuum of power in terms of contact, conflict and confluence. We instinctively suspect attempts to homogenize a civilization and culture and impose a single identity on it, for we are acutely aware that every civilization and culture is internally plural and differentiated. And we remain equally sceptical of all attempts to present it as one whose origins lie within itself, as self-generating and *sui generis*, for we feel persuaded that all civilizations are born out of interaction with and absorb the influences of others and are shaped by wider economic, political, technological, linguistic and other forces. This undercuts the very basis of Afro-centrism, Euro-centrism, Indo-centrism, Sino-centrism and other kinds of centrisms, all of which isolate the history of the culture concerned from that of others and credits its achievements to its own genius. Likewise, Indian Civilization and culture came in contact with Jewish religion, Christianity, Zoroastrianism and Islam in the pre-independent India. In the post-colonial and independent India, we came in contact with Tibetan Buddhism in a big way and most recently, we came in contact with the Bahai's Faith. There have been conflicts regarding the fundamental beliefs, practices, myths and rituals. But there is no conflict so far as the notion of Absolute is concerned. It is confluence, which has prevailed and sustained all through the ages. Different religions have all preserved their identities, maintained their rituals, propagated their beliefs and value systems and cherished their culture. Not only that the northern Bhārata came in contact with the Greeks, the Mongols and the Persians, but the southern Bhārata was also in greater contact with Egypt, Syria, Palestine, Babylonia as well as Persia, long before the Persian or Achaemenian imperialism extended their empire into India in the days of Cyrus (558-530 BCE.). King Solomon of Palestine and his ally king of Syria sent Phoenician sailors to trade with India and their contacts were mostly with the south. The flourishing spice trade was an avenue for many contacts between the southern Indians and their trade partners in the Middle East. I do not wish to impress this fact that our contact with others was based on trade alone. That is of course one aspect but not all that is the case. These are stronger philosophico-religious and civilizational-cultural factors too. We should not forget the fact that Zoroastrian community came to Gujarat coast much before the Christian era and that Jewish community had migrated to Bombay and Kerala when their faith was shattered by the Roman tyranny. Christianity also came to southern

India in 54 BCE. with St. Thomas. During Middle Ages Islam and Sūfism came to India under certain historical conditions which includes feudal expansionism. But the contact with other cultures did not stop there. In the post-independent India, Tibetan Buddhism came to India as big diaspora. And few decades back Bahai's Faith has also found a respectable place on our soil. In a nutshell, we can say that all the religions of the world emerged in Asia and all Asian religions can be found at one place, i.e. Bhāratavarṣa.

About Hinduism it can be said that it is not a religion like Zoroastrianism, Christianity and Islam. It is rather a kind of *Sanātan Dharma*, or "perennial duty". By its origin and development, it has a collection of thoughts that encompass all aspects of not only human existence but also of the existence of plants, insects, animals, rivers, mountains, moon, sun, etc. including the climates, seasons and everything. It is essentially **cosmo-centric** as against anthropocentric of European thinking. The very fact that Hindus worship an entire pantheon of gods and goddesses means that the faith is an all-inclusive one. There is always room for dissent and digression and the freedom of choice. In fact, the Vedas and the Upaniṣads do not preach a particular religion, nor do they spell out a list of do's and don'ts. The *Ṛgveda* says that *āno bhadraḥ kṛtavo yantu viśvataḥ* (let noble thoughts come to us from everywhere).

Power Asymmetry

It may be pointed out that a dominant civilization explains macro outcomes by aggregating a large set of civilization concepts which are under domination. The individual civilization preferences and plans are explained by dominant civilization background. While useful for several purposes, the weakness of this model lies in its simplistic treatment of civilization and disregard of power. The quest for recognition by other civilizations is the driving force towards power. The *locus classicus* for this type of recognition is Hegel's master-slave dialectics,[1] later reinterpreted by Alexandre Kojve.[2] Moreover, the cognitive, connotative and normative aspects of civilizations, the conventions should not be treated solely as given. Actors use them purposively, by breaking, reinterpreting or using them as a weapon against adversaries. There is historical evidence to the use of military-economic-technological-linguistic superiority to suppress/subordinate the adversaries. Beneath the façade of civilizations, there is an underlying power asymmetry. It is this kind of perspective that has not come out comprehensively in the composition of the volume *Origin of Indian Civilization.*[3] In what follows, I would like to develop the salient features of the book along with my critical assessment of it in the light of dialectics of power and civilization. The book is a compilation of papers presented in the Fourth Annual Indic Conference held at University of Massachusetts, Dartmouth, USA, 23-25 June 2006, in which the participants included historians, philosophers, astronomers, archaeologists, geneticists, linguists, and mathematicians. It was the first open meeting in which "there were sparks of disagreements on the usual fault lines of political entrenchment of disciplinary scholarship". However, progress was made to the extent that scholars from different fields were able to learn and appreciate perspectives of disciplines other than their own.

On Origin of Indian Civilization

The range of historical/archaeological, astronomical, scientific, political and genetic theorizing in the volume *Origin of Indian Civilization* is extraordinary. It deals mostly with the theme related to the myth of Aryan invasion. As many as six articles out of the nine have been devoted to this issue. This shows the seriousness of the issue but such an allocation of emphasis on this issue is also likely to detract us from the fullness of the concern of the multifaceted aspects of Indian Civilization. In addition, the volume has tried to raise astronomical calculations concerning the Mahābhārata war and has sought to achieve a thoroughgoing synthesis from the historical point of view. It is not easy to assess the contributions of the volume, whose professional competence extends from history to genetics and from both these to astronomy, by way of the more recondite sources of Indian scientific heritage. Besides the rich notes, statistical references, maps, etc., there is intense bibliography for further reading.

The subject is well chosen. We have for long needed a whole book on it. It is one of the most sensitive academic issues in India and needs to be debated and discussed with indigenous approach and ability. However, as the editor contends that "the origin of Indian Civilization has been marred with conflicting debate on whether it has largely indigenous origin or it has largely been influenced by outside invasion or migration". This question has significant political, cultural, and historical impact, both in India and globally. Such debates have spilled in American school textbook adoption process, which can significantly affect classroom learning, especially for Indian American Children.[4]

The volume on *Origin of Indian Civilization* deals with different areas of study, including the philosophy of Myth and History of the Aryans under cultural and civilization foundations. Indian Civilization, considered as the only living ancient civilization, as the editor (Bal Ram Singh) opines, has remained fancy for scholars, travellers, businessmen, rulers, and seekers of truth for millennia. And, this level of broad interest in people throughout the history has obviously attracted controversies of all kinds, including debate about the Indian Civilization's origin itself. In what follows, I wish to furnish a critical review of *Origin of Indian Civilization* along with certain annotations, quotations and summations that might be relevant to the limited end of the 2006 conference.

The context in which the symposium was held in 2006 has been to challenge the Euro-centric bias on Indian Civilization. Scholars overwhelmingly concluded that Indian Civilization and its human population is indigenous and hence "completely debunking the Aryan Invasion Theory".[5] India's civilization has had a long existence that is documented in a huge amount and variety of literature, its scientific advancements over the centuries, its continuing cultural practices and preservation of art and music. This volume comprises papers that explore various aspects relating to the ancient origin of the Indian Civilization.

Scholars have presented diverse perspectives to delve into the contention and controversies that surround questions such as the one concerning the origin of the Aryans. The papers examine the events that gave rise to the Aryan Invasion Theory and debunk the theory as a myth and present evidence and arguments supporting the theory that the *R̥gveda* was composed in its bulk in the fourth millennium BCE. An effort focuses on the problem of identifying the earliest region of the Aryan homeland, including that of identifying its epic centre (referring to the cultural horizon of epics like the *Rāmāyaṇa* and the *Mahābhārata*) in India. Incorporating the latest research in history, archaeology, philosophy, genetics, and other disciplines, the papers explain the origin and evolution of the idea of the ancient South Asian cities. Quoting from the epic literature, Narahari Achar, a physicist from the University of Memphis, clearly showed with astronomical analysis that the "Mahābhārata war" took place in 3067 BCE, thus poking a major hole in the outside Aryan origin of the Vedic people.[6] Peter A. Underhill analyses patterns of Y-chromosome diversity in the contemporary South Asian gene pool to throw light on migrations of modern humans within south-west Asia.[7] Accompanied by maps and other illustrations, the volume will interest scholars from a range of disciplines who are keen to study the origin and evolution of Indian Civilization and culture.

How ancient is the Vedic civilization can be understood with the description of Dwārkā which was built on land reclaimed from the sea. Boulders have been found under the fortified city walls, showing that it was the result of land reclamation. The *Mahābhārata* also mentions that Kṛṣṇa warned the residents of Dwārkā that the city would be reclaimed by the sea. The discovery of a seal engraved with a three-headed animal at the Dwārkā site corroborates a reference made in the *Mahābhārata* that such a seal was given to the city. Seven nearby islands described in the *Mahābhārata* have also been discovered. Since archaeological research shows that the city was submerged around 1600 BCE, this would date the *Mahābhārata* at least before 1600 BCE. Again, this is a minimum time. Pottery found at the site, inscribed with the script of the Indus Valley Civilization, has been established by thermo-luminescent tests to be about 3530 years old. The *Mahābhārata* was written toward the end of the classical Vedic period. This again marks the minimum date of the *Ṛgveda*, and should not be construed as a fixed date. Frawley[8] and Rajaram,[9] as well as many others, now put the date of the "Mahābhārata war" at about 3,000 BCE.

The *Ṛgveda* has been dated to 1500 BCE by those who use linguistics to claim its origin as Aryans coming out of Central Asia and Europe. The archaeologist B.B. Lal and the scientist and historian N.S. Rajaram disagreed with the position of linguists, in particular Witzel who claimed literary and linguistic evidence for the non- Indian origin of the Vedic civilization.[10]

Comprehensive population genetics data along with archaeological and astronomical evidence presented in *Origin of Indian Civilization* shows that the original people and culture within the Indian subcontinent may even be a likely pool for the genetic, linguistic, and cultural origin of most of the rest of the world, particularly Europe and Asia. Leading evidences come from population genetics, which was presented by two leading researchers in the field, V.K. Kashyap and Peter Underhill. Their results generally contradict the notion of Aryan invasion/migration theory for the origin of Indian Civilization.

Critique of Origin of Indian Civilization

Notwithstanding the merit of the above-mentioned book, I would like to point out that there is wide spread confusion in the composition of the book regarding myth, history, philosophy, science, astronomy, etc. One is required to clarify these terms in order to make one's position exact and precise. For instance, the dividing line of myth and history is very thin and at times quite uncertain. A myth could be a community-forming narrative on "big questions": origins of the universe, human beings, their good, etc. It involves a calendar of celebrations (cycles in nature and in the community). It requires priesthood. But history requires "datability", "locatability" and causality. And philosophy could be systematic inquiry, by way of logos and dialectic, from what is better known to what is less known on "big questions", and then from general principles to particular conclusions. It involves a "way of life". Likewise, science could be a systematic, theoretical and experimental inquiry into the principles and operations of nature.

The use of philosophical examples has certain advantages. Undoubtedly, philosophy is a way of life and offers more nuanced and complex descriptions of social life that are difficult to capture through ordinary political and economic categories. Philosophy is claimed to be an unusually obstinate attempt to think clearly. Stated or unstated, knowingly or unknowingly, philosophers are obsessed with having thought in a certain way and followed a definite method. Emancipation from one method and therefore adopting a different method has led to the emergence of different philosophical schools and individuals. Philosophy is conceived parochially on an international scale. It is a subject that means different things to different continents, different countries, different universities and different minds. There is no one philosopher.[11] In India, the methods used by the Vedic seers and followed by the Upaniṣadic sages involve several operative terms; such as dialogue, hermeneutic, dialectic, plurality, questioning as an enquiring act, deferring, analogies, synthesis, metaphors/ aphorisms, paradoxes, etc. It has even involved such terms as mysticism and monologue. Likewise in the Greek tradition, we have dialogue, dialectic, anti-foundationalism, scepticism, hermeneutics, followed by phenomenology, analytic trend, critical rationalism, polylogue, deconstruction, plurality, etc. These methods are used to understand the problems concerning the nature of Reality (natural, conceptual and social) and the place of man in that reality viewed from a definite perspective. In fact the ontological, epistemological and ethical doctrines become explicit with the help of the method that a philosopher adopts.

As a matter of fact, the ancient world was finite in terms of its socio-economic conditions, scientific development, historical and cultural products. The modern world is infinite in terms of ideology, scientific and technological development, logo-centrism, foundationalism, essentialism, and teleology, unified world-order, rationality, conceptions of morality and justice, etc. The postmodern world has again shrunk into finite propositions in terms of anti-foundationalism, anti-essentialism and anti-teleology, fragmentation, irrationality and plurality of ethnic identities, linguistic identities, etc. In the ancient world beginning from sixth century BCE, the Indians, the Chinese, the Greeks lived without much contact with one another and in that sense there was pluralism. But each culture regarded its principles to be universally valid. The *ṛta* of the Vedas, the Platonic *Forms*, the *Tao* of the Chinese all claimed to be universal. Without their knowing it, they agreed that, as in the cosmos, so in the human order *yathā piṇḍe, tathā brahmaṇḍe* (as in the womb so in the cosmos). Or, as Socrates used to say to Phaedrus: "My dear Phaedrus, we live in cosmos, not chaos". Today the world is one; the Greeks, the Indians, the Europeans or the Americans mingle in academia and in the marketplace. Modern technology has played the most important role in bringing the people to have dialogue with one another and come close to one another by means of hermeneutics.

Dialectics is theory-loaded and elevated concepts. The pre-theoretical surrogate of these concepts can be found in the dialogues of the Upaniṣads as well as in Socrates (*c.* 470-399 BCE), whose doctrine features in the works by Plato (*c.* 428-348 BCE). I shall expound and examine the nature and status of a dialogue and bring out its stimulating characteristics that could have helped the emergence and growth of other aspects like hermeneutics, dialectics, etc. To substantiate the points, let me take up some of the important dialogues.

A **dialogue** is a process of conversation, argumentation and mutual supplementation of ideas between two individuals. With dialogue, a method has evolved in which the encounters with other thinkers are essential. It is just opposed to a monologue, which can formulate nothing but a dogma. The ideas I formulate to defend my standpoint must confront with other approaches, must give expression to other thinkers *as others*, and not as possible elements of a system in which I can recognize my own thought. Other thinkers must be permitted to speak as others on the same subject. I am and remain only a participant. We come across such instances of dialogue in the Upaniṣads. Here the totality of moments of participation comes to be on a specific subject. Two or more than two thinkers exchange their ideas through argumentation with the aim of the *search for truth.* It is the search for truth that provides food for thought and thus thinking is stimulated. In Plato's *Theaetetus,* for instance, in discussing the question of the nature of knowledge, Theaetetus advances an ostensive definition: he claims that sciences, such as Geometry, Astronomy, Harmony and Calculation, are knowledge. And the dialogue goes on. Socrates is often portrayed as seeking definitions of particular excellence: courage in the *Laches*, soundness of mind in the *Charmides*, piety in the *Euthyphro* or excellence in general in the *Meno*. The only method which is followed here is dialogue. Professing perplexity in the process of dialogue, Socrates goads another person into offering an account of an excellence, but refuses to be satisfied with examples, insisting on a general characterization that can be used to tell whether something is, indeed, an example of that excellence. When an account is offered, Socrates presses the other party with questions requiring a "yes" or "no" answer, and by means of inferences drawn from the statements to which the other party is committed, Socrates drives him into contradiction. Another definition may be tried, or occasionally the other party may be given a chance to change his answer to one of Socrates' questions. In either case another contradiction results and the dialogue eventually ends with the participants in the same state of perplexity as Socrates.

In a dialogue it is the view of the other *as the other* or the *contradiction* which is the operative term. But a dialogue is possible only when both the speakers maintain a fundamental consensus, i.e. both the speakers "(a) speak and (b) listen, (c) aim at truth, (d) understand each other's language, (e) understand each other's way of thinking (f) and do not live in two worlds whose contents totally differ."[12] These elements prepare a meeting ground for a dialogue to be possible. As a speaker, I am successful when my words elicit a response. Total silence or applause interrupts or ends my speaking. The listener who assimilates what I have said can produce an answer, which can stimulate me in return. My listener becomes speaker and vice versa. Master and pupil exchange places. In

Socrates' dialogues we thus find two characteristic features, namely consensus and contradiction. These are the two operative terms for the possibility and development of ideas under the method of dialogue. Absolute consensus is nothing but a dogma. Absolute contradiction leads us nowhere. It is only under certain degree of consensus that certain amount of contradiction is entertained and thinking is thus stimulated.

Dialogue has been used to raise, discuss and to resolve/ dissolve not only the metaphysical and epistemological issues but also the ethical issues, the ethical dilemmas concerning civilizations and cultures and the ethical preferences. Since the method of dialogue is at the centre of Upaniṣadic ethics, it will be quite fruitful to explain the operative terms of the dialogues in the Upaniṣads. Dialectic has been used in almost all the dialogues available in the Upaniṣads. Dialectic has been operating at two levels: It is a mode of argumentation to bring out a contradiction in the views of the other party. This process is generally known as the *pūrva pakṣa* (earlier position), the *khaṇḍana* (its rejection) and finally the *uttara pakṣa* (the latter position). It resolves/dissolves/sublates the contradictions at higher levels.

Consciousness is at the centre of metaphysics, knowledge, mysticism, hermeneutics and morality. It is on the basis of consciousness alone that the Upaniṣads present a synthesis of these five aspects. Metaphysics without ethical backbone might only result in pure abstraction inasmuch as a mystic without ethical-hermeneutical orientation might be a hideous creature who is a blot on the spiritual evolution of man. In the same way hermeneutics without metaphysics and mysticism will be unintelligible and without any goals. It would therefore be totally fruitless to develop the metaphysical problems reached in the Upaniṣads without the final mystical realization in the Upaniṣads. We can just illustrate it by furnishing an instance of dialogue. The *Kaṭha Upaniṣad* utilizes an ancient story from the

Ṛgveda about a father who gives his son Naciketā to death (Yama). This brings in some of the highest teachings of mystical spirituality, helping us to realize why the Upaniṣads are referred to as the "end of the Vedas" in the double sense of completing the Vedic scripture and in explaining the ultimate goals.

To substantiate this position, we come across several dialogues in the Upaniṣads among peoples, such as Satyakāma and his mother Jābālā in *Chāndogya,* Prajāpati and his sons in *Bṛhadāraṇyaka,* Yama and Naciketā, Ghora Aṅgirasa and Kṛṣṇa in *Chāndogya,* Nārada and Sanatkumāra in *Chāndogya,* Prajāpati, Indra and Virocana in *Chāndogya,* Śvetaketu and Uddālaka in *Chāndogya,* Āruṇi and Śvetaketu in *Chāndogya,* Yājñavalkya, Maitreyī and Kātyāyanī in *Bṛhadāraṇyaka.* Various issues have been scrutinized according to the necessities of the discussions. The Vedic *ṛṣis* expressed their vision of the Absolute or the Ultimate Reality in the form of hymns, evoking responses at the varying levels of self-realization, worshipful devotion or ritual sacrifices. The Upaniṣadic saints tried to impart the knowledge of the Absolute to his pupil through the method of a dialogue. An example of this is found in the *Bṛhadāraṇyaka Upaniṣad* in the dialogue between the Sage Yājñavalkya and his wife Maitreyī, who asks him question about the way to realize the Absolute or the ultimate Truth. As the dialogue proceeds, Yājñavalkya convinces her that it is the *ātman* or self that should be known, and when this knowledge is achieved, everything in the Universe is known, because there lies an identity between *ātman* (self) and *Brahman* (the Ultimate Reality). The five *mahāvākyas* or great teachings (literally, Great Sentences), express this vision from different Upaniṣads in the following:

1. *Prajñānam brahma,* "Consciousness is *Brahman*" (*Aitareya Upaniṣad,* III.1.3); *aham brahmāsmi* "I am *Brahman*" (*Bṛhadāraṇyaka Upaniṣad,* IV.3.23),

2. *Aham eva idam sarvo 'smi* "I indeed am this whole Universe" (*Chāndogya Upaniṣad*, III.10-15).
3. *Tattvamasi* "That Thou art" (*Chāndogya Upaniṣad*, VI.8.7).
4. *Ayam ātma brahma* "This *Ātman* is *Brahman*" (*Chāndogya Upaniṣad*, III.10-14; *Taittirīya Upaniṣad*, I.5; *Bṛhadāraṇyaka Upaniṣad*, II.5.19).
5. *Sarvam khalu idam brahma* "Everything is *Brahman*" (*Muṇḍaka Upaniṣad*, III.13.1.; *Chāndogya Upaniṣad*, III.14.1).

The *mahāvākyas*, in brief, are the different paths for the realization of the Absolute. The statement *prajñānam brahma* directs the seeker to meditate on the *cittasvarūpa* (Pure Consciousness form) of *Brahman*, leading to the merger of the individual consciousness in the Universal and the attainment of *mukti* (liberation from worldly bondage), and the state of Supreme Bliss (*paramānanda*). *Aham brahmāsmi* is an endeavour to make the pupil engage in deep meditation to realize the Absolute. In the *tattvamasi* the teacher is trying to make his pupil realize that his innate Being is part of the Absolute. *Ayam ātma brahman* also accomplishes the same thing.

In dialogue, there is an aspect of plurality. The Vedic exhortation is *ekam sat viprāḥ bahudhā vadanti* (Reality is one, wise people explain it differently). This has been the fundamental act of philosophizing in India. The Reality admits of alternative approaches in terms of thought constructions and linguistic expressions. It is pluralistic in its expression. Pluralism has been expressed in many ways in the later development of Indian philosophical systems, such as in the Vedānta philosophy, where we go from one to many, or in Vallabha Vedānta, we go from many to one. In Sāṁkhya and Nyāya-Vaiśeṣika systems we go from many to many, and in Buddhism we go from nothing, i.e. *svabhāva śūnya*, to many.

This has got its reflection in the initial characteristics of Indian society which is diverse, liberal, democratic and pluralistic in regulating and restructuring the morals, ethos and values. The pluralistic nature of Indian society is manifested in various ethnic identities, community structures, linguistic identities, different nationalities, languages and so on. In search of our local identities, we have to go into the details of our tradition. Indian tradition could be divided into two kinds, namely: the Brāhmanical tradition and the *Śramaṇa* tradition. The former is the textual, the written, the intellectual tradition or the *Śāstrīya paramparā*, consisting of the Dharmaśāstras, *puruṣārthas*, *āśramas*, etc. The latter is the folk tradition, the tradition of the people or the *lokaparamparā*. Fortunately, both the traditions are equally strong. However, it is the folk tradition that has a stronger social basis. It consists of three pillars: family, community and the economy, around which idioms, symbols, proverbs, riddles and *sūtras* developed. This was the corpus of knowledge.

We need to have **dialectical dialogue**, which can incorporate dialogue on the one hand, and the dialectic on the other. Dialectical dialogue is deeply rooted in the plurality of human existence in terms of their identities, ethnicities, cultures and civilizations. From a pluralist perspective the good society cherishes the diversity of human solidarity, community, a sense of rootedness, selflessness, deep and self-effacing humility, contentment and encourages a creative dialogue between its different cultures and their moral visions. Such a society not only respects its members' rights to their culture and increases their range of choices, but also cultivates their powers of self-criticism, self-determination, imagination, intellectual and moral sympathy, and contributes to their development and well-being. For Indian minds, I will humbly recommend to go to the Upaniṣads. There is no other way of detoxifying ourselves from the fumes of Enlightenment Rationality, because the western way is not the only way of thinking and experiencing. Let us as Indians emerge ourselves in our own rich Indian Heritage, especially before its breaking up into Buddhism, Jainism and Hinduism for example, the Sāṁkhya-Yoga heritage, common to all three traditions — the great philosophical perspective that undergrads all Upaniṣadic, Vedic, Buddhist, or Jaina thought and experience. Keep your painfully acquired critical rationality from Kant and Hegel, but do get not tyrannized by it. Stay critical, but do not reject out of hand what seems strange at first. Expose yourself without hesitation to a system of thought and experience, which has endured for millennia and awarded us with freedom, autonomy and sovereignty.

To bring this article to a close, we can say that dialogue along with other perspectives will incorporate, absorb all contradictions, oppositions and differences between one civilization and another, and will try to transcend and sublate them, so that it becomes all-inclusive and can evolve a global culture. *One's* identity (linguistic, ethnic, cultural, civilization, etc.) could be identified and shaped only by means of a dialogue through its exposure to, and experience of the *other's* identity of the same, or the neighbouring culture/civilization. An identity is therefore identical within differences depending on the power asymmetry. This is the principle of ten dialectics known as the unity and the struggle of opposites. The being of an identity is being-with and being-in-contrast-with-other identities in the power nexus. Dialectics of power and civilization will address the problems not in abstraction, but in terms of the social nexus, spatio-temporal frame, earthly existence, historical and actual life of the humanity. It is hermeneutic in its comprehension, dialectical in its presentation and pluralistic in its manifestation, so that one civilization theme can participate with that of the other, of the East and the West, Indian and Ionian, Oriental and Occidental. Such a discourse is not merely instrumental but also emancipatory at the same time.[11]

References

1. G.W.F. Hegel, 1979, *Phenomenology of Spirit,* tr. A.V. Miller, Oxford: Clarendon Press, pp. 111-19.
2. Alexander Kojeve, 1991, *Introduction to the Reading of Hegel,* London: Basic Books Inc. Publishers.
3. Bal Ram Singh (ed.), 2010, *Origin of Indian Civilization,* Dartmouth, Massachusetts, USA: Center for Indic Studies, & New Delhi: D.K. Printworld.
4. Bal Ram Singh (ed.), 2010, *Origin of Indian Civilization,* Dartmouth, Massachusetts, USA: Center for Indic Studies, & New Delhi: D.K. Printworld., p. vi.
5. B.B. Lal, "An Ostrich: Like Attitude is Perpetuating the Aryan Invasion Myth", in *Origin of Indian Civilization . . .,* etc. pp. 29-35.
6. B.N. Narahari Achar, "The Mahābhārata War . . ., etc.", *Origin of Indian Civilization . . .,* etc. pp. 204-50.
7. Peter A. Underhill, "Patterns of Y-Chromosome Diversity . . . etc." *Origin of Indian Civilization . . .,* etc., pp. 253-81.
8. D. Frawley, 2001, *The Ṛgveda and the History of India,* New Delhi: Aditya Prakashan.
9. N.S. Rajaram, "The Aryan Myth in Perspective . . . etc." in *Origin of Indian Civilization,* etc. pp. 163-78.
10. M. Witzel, 1995, 1997, *Early Sanskritization: Origin and Development of the Kuru State,* EJVS vol. 1. Also in B. Kölver (ed.), *Recht, Staat und Verwaltung im klassischen Indien. The State, the Law, and Administration in Classical India,* München, R. Oldenbourg, p. 27-52.
11. J.O. Wisdom, 1995, *Philosophy and Its Place in Our Culture.* London: Garden & Beach Science Publishers, pp. 1-2.
12. A.T. Paperzak, 1986, *System and History in Philosophy,* State University of New York Press, p. 84.

7. Dinner at Ayurshree restaurant — Pt Ramsamooj, Dr Shaffer, Dr Kazanas

8. Dinner at Ayurshree restaurant — students of Prof. Bal Ram Singh

8

South Asian Archaeology
Late Prehistoric Cultural Continuity or Discontinuity

Jim G. Shaffer
Diane A. Lichtenstein

Abstract

For two centuries, scholars concentrating on ancient South Asian studies have described an Indo-European/Aryan migration/invasion from the Northwest into South Asia to explain the formation of historic Indian Civilization. The conflating of language, people/culture, "race" required to maintain this "myth of the Aryan invasion" (Poliakov 1974) continues, perhaps, as the eminent social anthropologist Edmund R. Leach (1990: 237) so cogently notes, due to the academic prestige at stake. For example, the distinguished scholar Colin Renfrew (1987), failing to identify archaeological evidence for such an Indo-Aryan migration in the European post-Neolithic periods, argues instead for an earlier Indo-European/Aryan human migration associated with the spread of food production economies from Anatolia. In doing so, he ignores critical archaeological data from Southwest Asia (Lamberg-Karlovsky 1988) and South Asia (Shaffer 1990). The South Asian archaeological data reviewed here does not support either Renfrew's position or any version of the migration/invasion hypothesis describing a Western population movement into South Asia in the prehistoric periods. Rather the physical distribution of prehistoric sites and artefacts, stratigraphic data, radiometric dates, and geological data describing the prehistoric/proto-historic environment can account, in large measure, for the Vedic oral tradition describing a cultural discontinuity of what was an indigenous, regional population movement into the Indo-Gangetic region, referred to here as the "Haṛappan Diaspora" (Shaffer and Lichtenstein 2005).

Terminology and Chronology

The last fifty years of archaeological research has revealed an unanticipated record of cultural synchronic and diachronic diversity in the North-western South Asia. Traditional interpretative schemes (i.e., Wheeler 1963) were inadequate for reflecting the complexity of the cultural dynamics revealed by this research. A more flexible scheme incorporating these emerging cultural dynamics has been proposed (Shaffer 1992), and successfully applied to the archaeological record (e.g., Kenoyer 1998; Coningham 2009); however, earlier archaeological categories persist and continue to be utilized in summary discussions (e.g., Possehl 2002; Wright 2010), and primary field reports such as those cited here. To distinguish prehistoric culture groups and chronological categories, terminology already used in published archaeological surveys and other reports, are retained here, with one exception. These prehistoric ethnic and chronological categories have acquired a degree of consensual definition among South Asian archaeological scholars (Shaffer 1992; Possehl 2002). The named exception of cultural category is that of Early Haṛappan, which is used here rather than the label of "pre-Haṛappan" used, in one cited source (Joshi et al. 1984). Early Haṛappan is consistent with other authors' descriptive terminology for this early time period (e.g., Possehl 2002: 29). The cultural/chronological categories used in this discussion are given in *fig*. 1.

These categories subsume archaeological data of specific time and place to build broader comparative cultural and chronological units, descriptive of the regional human settlement patterns within a broader Indo-Gangetic Cultural Tradition (Shaffer 1993). Human settlements, established via archaeological survey and excavation (when possible) are classified as being occupied during a specific time period based on material culture remains (especially pottery) found on the soil surface. Given the chronological boundaries of the cited categories above, without excavations, it is not possible to

Hakra	3800-3200 BCE
Early Haṛappan	3200-2600/2500 BCE
Haṛappan	2500-1900 BCE
Late Haṛappan	1900-1300/1100 BCE
Painted Grey Ware	1300/1100-500 BCE

fig. 1: Cultural/Chronological Categories

precisely determine a settlement's chronological duration. Thus, the number of human settlements, to which the data refer, may be somewhat overrepresented for any named category. For example, the Early Haṛappan category incorporates locally diverse archaeological units (Regionalization Era — Shaffer 1992: 444-48), such as Koṭ Dījī, Amri, Sothi-Siswal, and Rāvī (Kenoyer and Meadow 2000), that preceded and contributed to the Haṛappan phenomenon formation. However, some Koṭ Dījī, and other Regionalization Era units, settlements persisted longer and were contemporary with the Haṛappan. Therefore, a limited number of Early Haṛappan settlements may have been contemporary with the Haṛappan. Indeed, archaeological diversity, "Domains"

(Possehl 2002: 6-7), within the Haṛappan category itself (Integration Era — Shaffer 1992: 448-50) have been defined; and a cultural diversity based on a common Haṛappan heritage proposed for the Late Haṛappan (Localization Era — Shaffer 1992: 450-52). Future archaeological research focused on the Haṛappan phenomena may establish even more refined interpretative cultural group and chronological categories. For now, the cultural/chronological categories named above are adequate to present the general pattern of human settlement dynamics presented here.

Regional Survey Data (fig. 2)

The Cholistan survey (Mughal 1997) represents a very significant regional data base for understanding ancient settlement dynamics. The survey area was a specifically defined track along the dry Ghaggar-Hakra/Sarasvatī River covering 13,524 km^2 (Mughal 1997: 27-28). Located in a very arid, eastern region of the central Indus River Valley, its physical characteristics enabled identification of numerous (370) archaeological sites including camp sites (pastoral nomads?), specialized industrial sites, cemeteries and settlements (only sites with permanent habitation areas — settlements — are discussed below), encompassing the entire spectrum of cultural/chronological categories studied here (**Note**: Hakra and Painted Grey Ware (PGW) categories are identified only in Mughal's study). Areas west and south (Sindh) of Cholistan have experienced, over time, more extensive alluvial deposition in areas which combined with modern extensive industrial, commercial and agricultural development have limited the possibility of survey results comparable to that of Cholistan. Moreover, archaeological data indicates Cholistan was a region of intense cultural activity between the fourth and second millennium BCE; and, the Ghaggar-Hakra/Sarasvatī River was culturally very important in early Vedic traditions. Therefore, the Cholistan data is

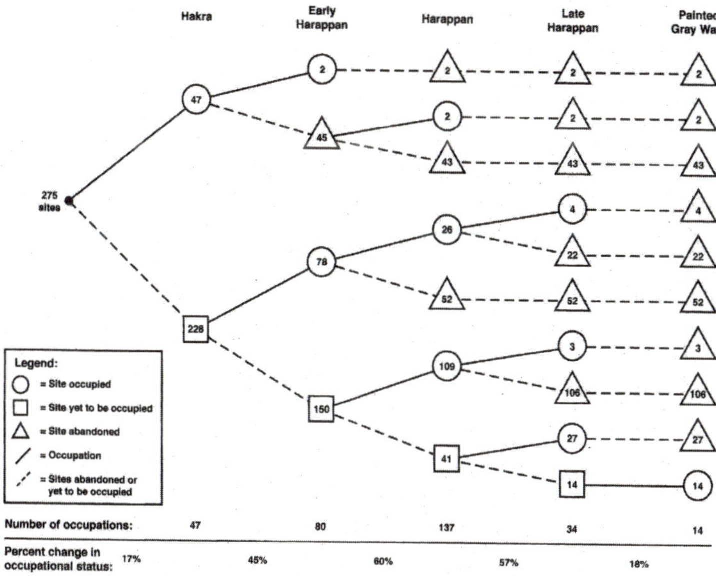

fig. 2: Cholistan and Sindh

assumed here to reflect cultural processes affecting the entire central Indus Valley during the period discussed here.

Presently, available archaeological survey data for Sindh (Flam 1981, 1993, 1999; Possehl 1999) have focused on Early Haṛappan-Haṛappan cultural relationships. Consequently, Late Haṛappan designations in this data may be underrepresented. None the less, Sindh settlement pattern dynamics are similar to those of Cholistan (for specific discussions see Shaffer and Lichtenstein 1999, 2005). Together, these data provide a comparable north-south parallel to the Eastern Site Regional Data presented below.

Hakra settlements (here in Cholistan only) represent the first 47 settlements. During the Early Haṛappan the number of settlements increased to 80, including 78 new settlements (98 per cent of the total), while 45 (96 per cent) Hakra settlements were abandoned. Thus, 98 per cent of the Early

Haṛappan settlements changed their settlement status (new + abandoned settlements). During the Haṛappan period, 109 new settlements were established (80 per cent of all Haṛappan settlements), 26 Early Haṛappan settlements continued to be occupied (19 per cent of Haṛappan settlements); 2 previous abandoned Early Haṛappan settlements were reoccupied (1.5 per cent of Haṛappan settlements); 54 previously abandoned Early Haṛappan settlements remained abandoned. Thus, 71 per cent of the settlements changed their occupation status between the Early Haṛappan and Haṛappan. Only 27 Late Haṛappan settlements were new settlements (79 per cent of total Late Haṛappan settlements); 7 previous Haṛappan settlements continued to be occupied into the Late Haṛappan (21 per cent of Late Haṛappan settlements), whereas 130 Haṛappan sites were abandoned in the Late Haṛappan (95 per cent of Haṛappan settlements). Thus, 157 settlements (60 per cent) changed their occupation status between the Haṛappan and Late Haṛappan. In Cholistan, all Late Haṛappan sites were abandoned, and 14 new PGW sites were established, a 100 per cent change in settlement occupation status.

The above settlement history of the Cholistan-Sindh regions suggests a significant degree of Indus River Valley sedentary settlement mobility. Certainly, a degree of internal population dynamics occurred, but the high percentage (82 per cent excluding the PGW) of sedentary populations changing their settlement status cannot be attributed solely to this factor. This fluidity in settlement pattern essentially mirrors the variety of ecological problems discussed below; especially, but not exclusively, a capturing of the Ghaggar-Hakra/Sarasvatī River drainage by the Yamunā/Gaṅgā River System. There is no archaeological evidence of a foreign, Western human intrusion, nor is there evidence of a Western movement out of the Indus Valley. Rather, evidence suggests a major population displacement took place to the East between the late third and late second millennium BCE, i.e. a "Haṛappan Diaspora".

Eastern Sites (fig. 3)

Data discussed here are based on surveys published by Joshi, Bala and Ram (1984). Aerial coverage is that of the "eastern Punjabi Plain" in the north (the Indian states of Punjab, Haryana and adjacent districts in neighbouring states), and Gujurat in the south. In evaluating these data, it must be remembered that the total geographic area studied is significantly larger than Cholistan and Sindh. For example, the Cholistan survey covered 13,524 km^2, while the surveyed area (based on total district sizes) in Haryana State was 30,432 km^2, an area 2.25 times larger than Cholistan. Despite the larger research area (consequently a greater possibility of more

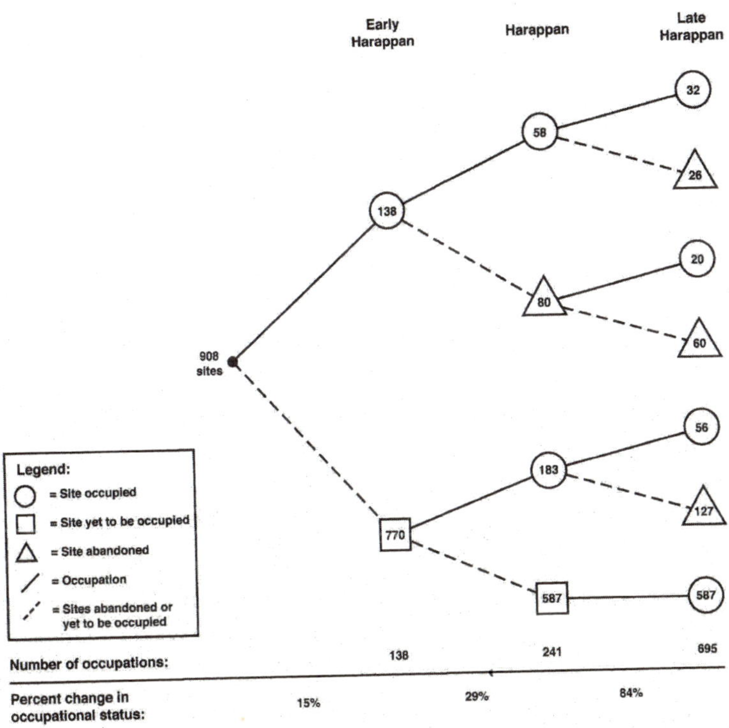

fig. 3: Eastern Sites (Eastern Punjab and Gujarat)

settlements identified), the ancient settlement pattern dynamics indicates that the difference in aerial dimensions does not affect the cultural patterns defined below (see Settlement Density discussion below). Another problematic issue is the absence of Hakra settlements in this region. It seems possible at least some Hakra settlements were identified as Early Haṛappan. However, the position here is that this does not significantly modify Early through Late Haṛappan settlement patterns discussed below. Similarly, absence of PGW settlement identification by Joshi et al. (1984) is unfortunate, since the presence of numerous PGW settlements in the eastern Punjabi Plain is well documented. None the less, absence of PGW site identification does not diminish the importance of changes in settlement patterns between the Early through Late Haṛappan periods.

Early Haṛappan settlements represent the first 138 settlements recorded. During the later Haṛappan period, the number of settlements increases to 241, including 183 new settlements (76 per cent of all Haṛappan settlements), while 80 Early Haṛappan settlements were abandoned (58 per cent of Early Haṛappan settlements), and 58 continued to be occupied (42 per cent of Early Haṛappan settlements). Thus, 82 per cent of the settlements changed their occupation status between the Early Haṛappan and Haṛappan. During the Late Haṛappan, a total of 587 new settlements were established (85 per cent of the 695 Late Haṛappan settlements); 88 Haṛappan settlements continued to be occupied into the Late Haṛappan (37 per cent of previous settlements); 153 Haṛappan settlements were abandoned in the Late Haṛappan period (64 per cent of previous settlements), and 20 (25 per cent) of the previously abandoned Haṛappan settlements were reoccupied. Thus, 82 per cent of the settlements changed their occupation status in the Late Haṛappan period, with 587 (63 per cent) of these being new settlements. The average change in settlement occupation status was 82 per cent between the Early and Late Haṛappan periods, and the increase in number of settlements was 557, or 404 per cent.

Settlement Stability

An additional settlement dynamics revealed by survey data is the absence of site occupational stability. In the West only 4 (1.5 per cent) of the 275 sites were continuously occupied from Early Haṛappan to Late Haṛappan periods. None were continuously occupied through all five periods. In the East only 32 (3.5 per cent) of the 908 sites were occupied from Early through Late Haṛappan periods. Only 36 sites (3.0 per cent) in the 1,183 site samples remained continuously occupied for three consecutive occupational periods. Likewise, when sites were abandoned they remained abandoned. In the West only 2 (0.7 per cent) abandoned sites were reoccupied, between Early Haṛappan and Haṛappan periods, of the total 275 sites in the sample. In the East only 20 (2.2 per cent) abandoned sites were reoccupied of the total 908 sites in the sample, between Haṛappan and Late Haṛappan periods. Only 22 (1.9 per cent) of the 1,183 sites were reoccupied after abandonment. These factors indicate a directional movement from the West to the East with little indication of a shifting back and forth.

Settlement Density (figs. 4 and 5)

A limited study of the settlement density index (number of settlements per thousand square kilometres per period) for the western (Cholistan) and eastern (Haryana) regions is presented to compensate for the different area dimensions surveyed. Mughal (1997: 27-28) specifically defined the surveyed area along the dry Ghaggar-Hakra/Sarasvatī River channel in Cholistan which covered 13,524 km^2. Surveyed areas in Haryana were not as precisely defined (Joshi et al. 1984). Therefore, only the total areas (km^2) of districts surveyed are used for comparison. The Haryana surveys were selected for comparison with Cholistan because of its central location in the eastern Punjabi Plain; presence of a contemporary, comparable identifiable ecology. Early through Late Haṛappan period settlements; and, surveyed district geographic areas allow grouping into two units, Haryana Group A and B, that compare in total area to surveyed areas of Cholistan (see *figs.* 4 and 5). It should be repeated that Hakra and PGW settlements were not identified by Joshi et al. (1984) in the eastern region. However, PGW settlements have, however, been extensively recorded for this region; and, the stratigraphic interlocking of PGW and Late Haṛappan periods at Bhagawānpurā, and other sites, is critical for understanding the cultural continuity discussed here (e.g., Suraj Bhan, 1975; Suraj Bhan and Shaffer

Cholistan - Surveyed Area: 13,524 km²

Category	Number of Settlements	Number of Settlements: km²	Change
Hakra	47	1.287.7	
			-77.8km² (-27 per cent)
Early Haṛappan	37	1:365.5	
			+202.6 km² (+55.4 per cent)
Haṛappan	83	1:162.9	
			-320.1 km² (-197 per cent)
Late Haṛappan	28	1:483.0	
			- 483.0 km² (-100 per cent)
Painted Grey Ware	14	1:966.0	

Haryana Group A - Surveyed Area: 15, 492 km² (15 per cent larger than Cholistan)

Category	Number of Settlements	Number of Settlements: km²	Change
Early Haṛappan	64	1:242	
			-462 km² (-191 per cent)
Haṛappan	22	1:704	
			+637 km² (+951 per cent)
Late Haṛappan	232	1:67	

Districts: Bhiwani, Jind, Karnal, Kurukshetra, Rohtak

Haryana Group B - Surveyed Area: 14,940 km² (11 per cent larger than Cholistan)

Category	Number of Settlements	Number of Settlements: km²	Change
Early Haṛappan	41	1:364	
			-286 km² (-79 per cent)
Haṛappan	23	1:650	
			+430 km² (+195 per cent)
Late Haṛappan	68	1:220	

Districts: Ambala, Bhiwani, Gurgaon, Hissar, Mahendragarh

fig. 4: Settlement Density

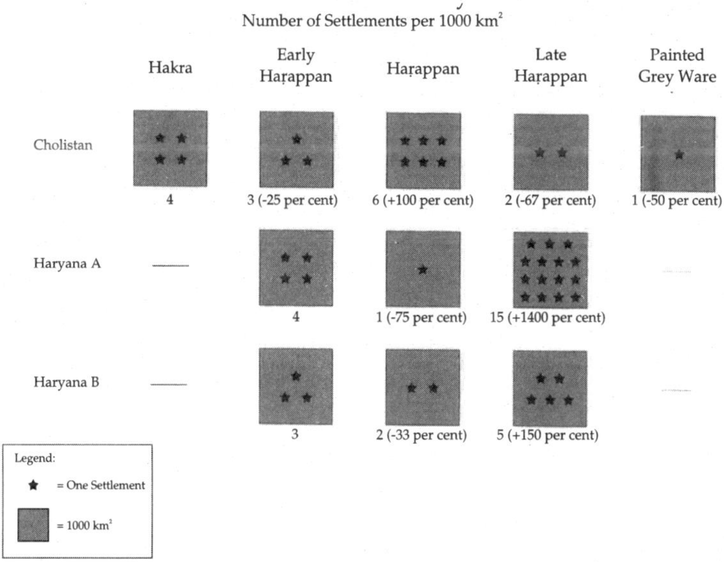

fig. 5: Settlement Density

1978; Lal 1984; Chakrabarti and Saini 2009; Thakran 2000; see also Shaffer and Lichtenstein 1999: 252-53, 2005: 89-91). Therefore, the discussion below is limited to the Early through Late Haṛappan period site densities.

Early Haṛappan settlement densities for Cholistan and Haryana Groups A and B are essentially similar, indicating a comparable settlement dynamic. Between the Early Haṛappan and Haṛappan periods, the number of settlements in Cholistan increased by 55 per cent and settlement density by 125 per cent. This increase is attributed, in part, to an influx of Haṛappan groups from outside Cholistan, and an increase in sites larger than 10 ha, including Ganwerīwālā (82 ha) an urban centre. The Haryana settlement pattern is different. In Haryana, the number of settlements declined between Early Haṛappan and Haṛappan periods (Group A = 66 per cent; B = 44 per cent), as did settlement densities (Group A = 191 per cent; B = 79 per cent). Although published data are not available, it is suggested here these changes reflect a shift of indigenous and incoming populations to larger (20+ ha) population centres such as Banawālī and Rākhī Gaṛhī in Haryana Group B. Likewise, several large settlements have been identified in Bhatinda district, eastern Punjab State (Joshi et al. 1984: 513-14). In contrast, the shifts in settlement dynamics between Haṛappan and Late Haṛappan are dramatic for both regions. In Cholistan, the number of Late Haṛappan settlements declines by 66 per cent, and the settlement density by a striking 197 per cent to 1:483 km^2, the lowest in the sequence excluding PGW settlements. Furthermore, all Late Haṛappan settlements were abandoned and not reoccupied. In Haryana, by contrast, the number of settlements increases dramatically (Group A = 955 per cent; B = 196 per cent) and settlement density equally so (Group A = 951 per cent; B = 195 per cent), the highest settlement density for the entire sequence. Available settlement density data indicate that between the Haṛappan and Late Haṛappan periods, a significant population increase occurred in the eastern Punjabi plain, which cannot be attributed solely to indigenous, regional population growth. Population increases of such magnitude can reflect significant numbers of people coming from throughout the Indus Valley region, and not exclusively from Cholistan, during the second millennium BCE — a human diaspora.

The Painted Grey Ware Complex

The magnitude of the number of sites involved in the eastward diaspora indicates that more social groups were involved than just those located in the Sarasvatī River drainage. The rarity (absence?) of second millennium BCE sites throughout Baluchistan (Possehl 2006) suggests that the diaspora incorporated social groups which belonged to the Baluchistan Tradition (Shaffer 1992). This suggests that the causes for this encompassing population displacement were diverse and widespread. Dispersal, and subsequent interactions between the Baluchistan and Indo-Gangetic Tradition social groups, in part, were responsible for Localization Era developments and the PGW cultural complex.

The PGW cultural complex was defined at Hastināpur (Lal 1954-55, 2002; Tripathi 1976) as the second occupation following an Ochre Coloured Pottery (OCP) occupation, which is Late Haṛappan/Localization Era Phase group, and the PGW occupation at Hastināpur was succeeded by a Northern Black Polished Ware (NBPW) occupation, which was followed by subsequent Early Historic cultural occupations. At Hastināpur, each occupation was separated by a stratigraphic discontinuity, suggesting chronological gaps between each occupation. The PGW cultural occupation stratigraphic position, together with the first C-14 dates of the site, dates, the seemingly abrupt appearance of the distinctive PGW pottery style, presence of iron artefacts, and a geographical distribution of these traits limited to the Yamunā-Gangetic region were used to establish an early archaeological interpretation of the PGW complex as representing the early Indo-Aryan invasions (e.g., Time-Life, eds. 1994: 63-68). However, recent research has raised serious questions about this particular interpretation of the PGW cultural complex.

Excavations at Bhagwānpurā, Nagar, Kaṭhpalon, and Dadheri (see Chakrabarti and Saini 2009; Lal 1984; and Singh 2005 for discussion) demonstrated that PGW and Late Haṛappan cultural remains were found in the same stratigraphic levels and were thus chronologically contemporaneous. PGW and Late Haṛappan phenomena are not separated by significant chronological discontinuities. Consequently, the traditionally proposed cultural continuity linking PGW with Early Historic period occupations must be extended to include the Late Haṛappan as well. The association of early iron artefacts, an essential component of the intrusive Aryan "invasion package", with the PGW cultural context, suggested their identification as Indo-Aryans. However, recent research (see Shaffer 1984; Chakrabarti 1992; Agrawal 2002 for discussion) indicates that iron technology was an indigenous South Asian development, dating to at least the early second millennium BCE. Unfortunately, the very limited excavated area of PGW occupations hinders discussion of other cultural attributes (e.g., architecture, subsistence, trade, burials). With the exception of the distinctive grey ware pottery, there are no cultural traits documented for the PGW complex which are significantly different from those used to define the Late Haṛappan culture.

PGW potteries, both red and grey wares, are distinctive from other ceramics. Very little quantitative and analytical studies of PGW potteries have been done; thus, observations noted here are tentative. The few studies of this stylistic pottery complex have focused on the grey wares, which, perhaps, are less than 20 per cent of the total pottery remains. The equally distinct undecorated red wares represent the majority of ceramics in this stylistic complex and, except for some descriptive discussions, remain essentially unstudied. Among the decorated PGW potteries grey wares (i.e., that pottery with painted widely spaced, simple geometric motifs) examples are limited (20 per cent?), yet they are used as the type artefact to describe this complex. Certainly, these widely spaced, painted geometric decorations on grey wares represent a marked contrast to the extensive, chronological sequence of elaborate, decorative painted motifs (geometric, zoomorphic and floral motifs) found on the red wares of the Indo-Gangetic and Baluchistan Traditions. However, some limited production of a range of decorated grey wares extends back into the third millennium BCE in both the Indo-Gangetic and Baluchistan Traditions (i.e., Dales and Kenoyer 1986; Wright 1984). The Indo-Gangetic and Baluchistan Traditions' decorated grey wares have painted motifs (black or red) that are stylistically comparable to the complex range of painted motifs found on the redwares of those Traditions. During the late third millennium BCE, these greywares emerge as one of the most unique, technologically sophisticated potteries in the ancient world — Faiz Muhammad Grey Ware (Wright 1984, 1995, 2010: 60, 69, 74). The best studied sequence for this pottery type is Mehrgarh Periods V-VII (Wright 1984), but it has been recorded also for several Baluchistan Tradition sites. Faiz Muhammad Grey Ware also occurs as an intrusive pottery type in south eastern Afghanistan sites, and as far west as Shahr-i Sokhta in south-eastern Iran. Faiz Muhammad Grey Ware is distinguished by its complex method of manufacture, distinctive vessel forms, and style of painted (black or red) geometric, zoomorphic and floral decorations. Unfortunately, only a few C-14 dates are available for the Faiz Muhammad Grey Ware pottery. At Mehrgaṛh (Jarrige et al. 1995: 556), only two dates are available: Period VI = 2470 BCE; Period VII = 1923 BCE; the few additional dates from sites where Faiz Muhammad Grey Wares are intrusive (Shaffer 1992) also suggest a last half of the third to early second millennium BCE date for the pottery. In other words, Faiz Muhammad Grey Ware was contemporary with, not exclusively prior to, the Haṛappan cultural phenomena.

My own personal analysis of Faiz Muhammad Grey Wares (Shaffer 1978)) and PGW (Suraj Bhan and Shaffer 1978) potteries indicate Faiz Muhammad Grey Wares were the technological predecessor of PGW pottery in the Yamunā-Gaṅgā region. We both suggest that the Faiz Muhammad Grey Ware technology was transferred to the Yamunā-Gaṅgā region as a direct, and indirect result, of the eastward population cultural diaspora noted above. The differences in vessel forms found in PGW potteries may reflect a variety of yet-to-be-determined cultural and economic influences affecting late second millennium BCE social groups in the Yamunā-Gaṅgā area. More problematic is the disappearance, after three millennia, of the extensive variety of geometric, zoomorphic and floral motifs in the PGW pottery, together with its continued absence in later Early Historic Period sites, where NBPW become characteristic.

The precise cultural meaning of Red Ware painted motifs (and vessel forms?) in these earlier Indo-Gangetic and Baluchistan Traditions remains unknown. Yet, the persistence of these complex motifs, in various stylistic combinations over three millennia, in various ecological areas, and across social/ethnic boundaries argues for their cross-cultural importance. The issue is why were these complex cultural symbols (the painted motifs of Indo-Gangetic and Baluchistan Traditions Red wares and Grey wares) were replaced by a technologically sophisticated Grey Ware decorated with painted, widely spaced, simple geometric motifs, which in turn was replaced by an equally technologically sophisticated NBPW pottery which lacked painted decoration and characterizes the Early Historic Period. A similar archaeological situation was defined in ancient Mesopotamia by Nissen (1988: 62-63) during the ceramic transition from the Late Ubaid period, with its largely insignificant painted pottery decorations, to the Uruk period, with no or almost no painted pottery decorations. Nissen attributed these changes to significant changes in socio-economic production and distribution systems associated with emergence of stratified societies and the early state. We propose here that an analogous example is reflected in the Late Haṛappan-PGW-NBPW pottery transitions. The ceramic changes and distribution of PGW potteries reflect a fundamental transition in the social and economic structure of Indo-Ganagetic Tradition societies. Previous local cultural identities, in part reflected by local ceramic styles/symbols, were, for the first time, being replaced by more centralized political and religious organizations with their own more public symbolic representations, i.e. temples and palaces. The local symbolic identities of the late Haṛappan diaspora were subsumed by a new centralized, stratified organization incorporating the emergence of the ancient Early Historic period "state". The first well-defined examples of temples and palaces in the archaeological and historical records note this cultural change. Public architecture was replacing pottery in the archaeological record as the cultural identifier of cultural complexity. While somewhat analogous to the ancient Mesopotamian state example, the ancient South Asian state had its own unique cultural/economic/political structure which is considered elsewhere (i.e., Maisels 2010 for discussion).

Discussion

Beginning in the third millennium BCE, the population shift eastward from the Indus Valley, i.e. the Haṛappan Diaspora, included several of the Indus Valley Tradition's cultural groups (Shaffer and Lichtenstein 1989, 1995). In general, this was a gradual process spanning two millennia, but it was also one marked by episodes of more intense activity, especially in the mid-second millennium BCE, the Late Haṛappan period. Agriculturalists, pastoralists and urban dwellers were involved, all attempting to reconcile their existing cultural patterns with certain changing social, economic and ecological conditions they were encountering. Since 1979, archaeological data has helped to interpret contact between and among groups of the western and eastern geographic areas of South Asia (Possehl and Kennedy 1979). This is a cultural contact of social groups within the Indus Valley Tradition with social groups within a Decco-Gangetic Tradition (Shaffer, in press).

The Decco-Gangetic Tradition, which occupied this eastern geographic area, had an extensive chronological and archaeological record paralleling, to some extent, that of the Indus Valley Tradition. Certainly, by the third millennium

BCE, this Decco-Gangetic Tradition consisted of groups of foragers and sophisticated food producers with their well-developed craft industries. Archaeologically, they are represented by the Mālwā-Jorwe, Dāimābād, Chopanī Māṇḍo, Pāṇḍu Rājār Ḍhibi, and "Southern Neolithic" complexes, to cite a few (see Chakrabarti 1999 for discussion). Some of these groups had been in contact with those comprising the Indus Valley Tradition for an extended period. Such contact involved at least the exchange of some organic and non-organic materials (e.g., minerals, semiprecious stones), an exchange which may have been intensifying by the Late Haṛappan period. Indeed, some important aspects of the Decco-Gangetic Tradition, such as various food technologies and certain domesticated animal and plant species (Fuller 2006), often attributed to Indus Valley Tradition contacts, may have been indigenously developed in the eastern areas. The Decco-Gangetic Tradition, however, never experienced an Integration Era, nor are urban centres, writing or public architecture of this era known until the Early Historic period. Therefore, social groups comparable to those in the Indus Valley Tradition, occupied an underpopulated, ecologically similar land-space in which the Haṛappan Diaspora could take place — and did.

Still, there is the question of why a Diaspora took place. There is no archaeological evidence for intrusive cultural factors being responsible. Current data indicate severe ecological changes were responsible. There is a scholarly debate about the possibility of extended periods of inadequate monsoon rainfall for the periods discussed here. Given the location of the Indus Valley on the north-western fringe of the south-western monsoon pattern, possibilities of significant moisture shortages of varying duration always exist (Wright 2010: 25-44 for discussion). Such rainfall shortages might be compensated for by various human technologies (Possehl 2002: 64-65). A more critical ecological development involved mountainous tectonic activity, which significantly altered drainage patterns of important Indus River tributaries. Specifically, over the second millennium BCE, waters feeding the Sarasvatī River and associated rivers were diverted eastwards into the Gangetic River system. Consequently, in Cholistan, a densely populated area, the major perennial river supplying sufficient moisture for surplus food production disappeared by the first millennium BCE, a situation also significant for the Sindh region. These climate and geological changes altered permanently this region's ability to sustain intense agricultural and pastoral production throughout this period (see Damino 2010). In consequence, a cultural adaptation to these changing geological and climatic conditions was relocation, the "Haṛappan Diaspora" described here.

The Diaspora may have facilitated a shift in agricultural production with emphasis on a winter (*rabī*) and summer (*kharīf*) cropping system, which may have increased the importance of rice and millet crops (Weber and Belcher 2003). This, perhaps, altered labour demands and organization, changed land tenure concepts, while concomitantly increasing surplus production to support these modifications. Cattle pastoralism possibly declined in economic importance, due to changes in pasturage resources while, at the same time, cattle continued to retain their cultural significance. Area sources of materials critical for craft activities were perhaps altered and/or access routes for known sources changed. These developments redefined where Haṛappan urban centres were located, with the possibility that some Late Haṛappan centres may be found in the lowest archaeological levels of Early Historic urban area sites. Particularly important would have been the concomitant restructuring of social, political and economic relationships affecting interactions between the Indus Valley/Indo-Gangetic and Decco-Gangetic Traditions social groups.

Between the mid-second and mid-first millennium BCE, a significant degree of social and economic restructuring took place within the indigenous cultural traditions of the Greater Indus and Ganges River valleys. This restructuring combined the existing cultural traits, moulding them to meet the altered social, economic and ecological conditions encountered in these eastern regions. South Asian scholars have a valid point in noting socio-cultural links between Haṛappan cultural phenomena and comparable traits of the Early Historic Period in South Asia (i.e., Lal 2005, 2009). The archaeological evidence does not indicate that a significant cultural discontinuity separates the Haṛappan past from the Early Historic period. There is no convincing evidence for an Aryan invasion that "re-invigorated a stagnant Late Haṛappan culture", as proposed by Piggott (1950) and Wheeler (1968), or Fairservis' (1975) "Vedic night" separating the Late Haṛappan form the Early Historic periods in the mid-second millennium BCE archaeological record.

In the absence of any historical, verifiable documentation, it is difficult archaeologically to distinguish migration (invasion) from various types of stimulus diffusion (Adams, Van Gerven, and Levy 1978). Cultural anthropology has repeatedly demonstrated that ideas, objects, technologies, styles, and languages can disperse independently of human movement, via a form(s) of stimulus diffusion. Consequently, lacking verifiable historical records, it is difficult to take any trait, or complex of traits (including language), and determine that a distribution reflects human physical migration rather than stimulus diffusion. Archaeology has been able to document human migrations where it has been able to document regionally based site distribution changes — the culturally and chronologically contemporary abandonment of sites in one area and the establishment of new sites in another ecologically and/or culturally compatible area. This is what the "Haṛappan Diaspora" explains here.

The "Haṛappan Diaspora" is the only major population displacement documented for the mid-second millennium BCE, the "traditionally accepted date" of the Indo-Aryan migration into South Asia. There is no evidence of a population movement from the north-west regions outside South Asia into the Indus Valley at this time (nor is there evidence of a migration westwards from South Asia). The population movement indicated in the Vedas is essentially the Haṛappan Diaspora. Differences in material cultural items and social behaviours described in the Vedas, but absent in the Late Haṛappan period, may reflect later embellishments of an oral tradition, facilitating its correlation with later period cultural self-descriptions of cultural beginnings.

Indeed, the description by many contemporary scholars of a migrating/invading Aryan social group from a "homeland" somewhere northwest of South Asia is equivalent to an example of Anderson's (2006) "imagined communities" — a community of the past which is imagined, created, to justify a present identity. The "Indo-Aryan/European imagined community" was created by late nineteenth- and twentieth-century philological and historical scholars to justify their contemporary "colonial, racial and ethnocentric" world view paradigms (Figueira 2002 for South Asia discussion). By the mid-twentieth century, there emerged the discipline of archaeology's scientific and verifiable chronological techniques, associated with a greatly expanded archaeological data set for the South Asian region. It is necessary to develop new interpretative paradigms incorporating data revealed by the archaeological record to help document the complexities of South Asian cultural traditions. The geological and climate data pertaining to South Asia's prehistoric period, and the archaeological data of South Asian prehistoric settlement changes, document the link between the prehistoric and early historic periods in the South Asian cultural tradition.

Afterthoughts

Archaeological research of the past thirty/forty years has witnessed considerable activity focused on the origins and nature of Haṛappan culture. The Mehrgaṛh excavations opened new vistas into the indigenous origin of South Asian food production, and its role in the foundation of the Haṛappan and other contemporary social variations to be found. Recent research at Moheṅjo-Dāṛo by Dales and later the German team, Dales and Kenoyer at Haṛappā and Bisht at Dholāvīrā, have added new dimensions to our understanding of the Haṛappan culture. Unfortunately, the same cannot be said for research into the Late Haṛappan period. Perhaps this is a reflection of Marshall's and Mackay's description of it as "degenerate", conquered by Aryans (as the British did India), and of no real consequence to what came after. Kenoyer's detailed excavations of the Late Haṛappan occupations at Haṛappa are an important and exciting development in this respect. Likewise, Shinde's excavations at Farmana may illustrate the interactions between Indus Valley and Decco-Gangetic Traditions proposed here. Still, a vast number of Late Haṛappan and PGW sites on the Indian Punjabi Plain, we fear, have been lost to economic development and with that critically important information for understanding the proposed cultural "restructuring" that took place. Equally important are the early occupations awaiting exposure at known large/urban Early Historic sites (e.g., Kauśāmbī and Mathurā). We sincerely hope that future research will focus as much effort on this part of the sequence as it has on the earlier phases before it disappears.

References

Adams, William Y., P. Dennis van Gerven, and Richard S. Levy, 1978, "The Retreat from Migrationism", *Review of Anthropology* 7: 483-532.

Agrawal, D.P. 2002, "Archaeometallurgical Studies in India: A Review", in *Indian Archaeology in Retrospect*, vol. III, *Archaeology and Interactive Disciplines:*, ed. S. Settar and Ravi Korisettar, New Delhi: Manohar and ICHR, pp. 423-42.

Anderson, Benedict, 2006, *Imagined Communities*, 2nd edn., New York: Verso (1st edn. 1983).

Chakrabarti, Dilip K., 1992, *The Early Use of Iron in India*, Bombay: Oxford University Press.

———, 1999, *India: An Archaeological History*, New Delhi: Oxford University Press.

Chakrabarti, Dilip K. and Sukhdev Saini, 2009, *The Problem of the Sarasvati River and Notes on the Archaeological Geography of Haryana and Indian Punjab*, New Delhi: Aryan Books International.

Coningham, Robin, 2009, "South Asia: From Early Villages to Buddhism", in *The Human Past*, 2nd edn., ed. Chris Scarre, London: Thames and Hudson, pp. 518-51 (1st edn. 2005).

Dales, George F. and J. Mark Kenoyer, 1986, *Excavations at Mohenjo-Daro, Pakistan*, Philadelphia: The University Museum, University of Pennsylvania.

Danino, Michael, 2010, *The Lost River: On the Trail of the Sarasvati*, New Delhi: Penguin Books.

Fairservis, Walter A., 1975, *The Roots of Ancient India*, 2nd edn., Chicago: University of Chicago Press (1st edn. 1971).

Figueira, Dorothy M., 2002, *Aryans, Jews, Brahmins: Theorizing Authority through Myths of Identity*, Albany, NY: State University of New York Press.

Flam, Louis, 1981, "The Palaeogeography and Prehistoric Settlement Patterns in Sindh, Pakistan (*ca*. 4000-2000 BCE)", PhD dissertation, South Asia Regional Studies, University of Pennsylvania, PA.

———, 1993, "Fluvial Geomorphology of the Lower Indus Basin (Sindh, Pakistan) and the Indus Civilization", in *Himalaya to the Sea*, ed. J.F. Schroder, New York: Routledge, pp. 265-326.

———, 1999, "Ecology and Population Mobility in the Prehistoric Settlement of the Lower Indus Valley, Sindh, Pakistan", in *The Indus River: Biodiversity-Resource-Humankind*, ed. A. Meadows and P. Meadows, Oxford: Oxford University Press, pp. 313-23.

Fuller, Dorian Q., 2006, "Agricultural Origins and Frontiers in South Asia: A Working Hypothesis", *Journal of World Prehistory* 20: 1-86.

Jarrige, Catherine, Jean-Francois Jarrige, Richard H. Meadow, and Gonzaaque Quivron, eds., 1995, *Mehrgarh: Field Reports 1974-1985, From Neolithic Times to the Indus Civilization*, Karachi: The Department of Culture and Tourism, Government of Sindh.

Joshi, J.P., M. Bala, and J. Ram, 1984, "The Indus Civilization: Reconsidering on the Basis of Distribution Maps", in *Frontiers of the Indus Civilization*, ed. B.B. Lal and S.P. Gupta, New Delhi: Books and Books, pp. 511-31.

Kenoyer, Jonathan M., 1998, *Ancient Cities of the Indus Valley Civilization*, Karachi: Oxford University Press.

Kenoyer, Jonathan M. and Richard M. Meadow, 2000, "The Ravi Phase: A New Cultural Manifestation at Harappa", in *South Asian Archaeology 1997*, ed. M. Taddei and G. De Marco, Rome: Instituto Italiano per l'Africa el'Oriente, pp. 55-76.

Lal, B.B., 1954-55, "Excavations at Hastinapura and Other Excavations, 1950-52", *Ancient India* 10-11: 4-151.

———, 2002, "Historicity of the Mahabharata and the Ramayana: What has Archaeology to Say in the Matter?", in *Indian Archaeology in Retrospect*, vol. IV, *Archaeology and Historiography: History, Theory and Method*, ed. S. Settar and Ravi Korisettar, New Delhi: Manohar and ICHR, pp. 29-70.

———, 2005, *The Homeland of the Aryans: Evidence of Ṛgvedic Flora, Fauna and Archaeology*, New Delhi: Aryan Books International.

———, 2009, *How Deep are the Roots of Indian Civilization?: Archaeology Answers*, New Delhi: Aryan Books International.

Lal, Makkhan, 1984, *Settlement History and Rise of Civilization in Ganga-Yamuna Doab (from 1500 BCE to 300 CE)*, Delhi: Orient Book Distributors.

Leach, Edmund R., 1990, "Aryan Invasions Over Four Millennia", in *Culture Through Time: Anthropological Approaches*, ed. E. Ohnuki-Tierney, Stanford, CA: Stanford University Press, pp. 227-45.

Lamberg-Karlovsky, C.C., 1988, "Indo-Europeans: A Near Eastern Perspective", *Quarterly Review of Archeology* 9: 1, 8-10.

Maisels, Charles, 2010, *The Archaeology of Politics and Power: Where,*

When and Why the First States Formed, Oxford: Oxbow Books.

Mughal, Mohammad Rafique, 1997, *Ancient Cholistan: Archaeology and Architecture*, Karachi: Ferozsons (Pvt.) Ltd.

Piggott, Stuart, 1950, *Prehistoric India*, Middlesex: Penguin Books.

Poliakov, Leon, 1974, *The Aryan Myth: A History of Racist and Nationalist Ideas in Europe*, New York: Basic Books.

Possehl, Gregory L., 1999, *Indus Age: The Beginning*, New Delhi: Oxford and IBH Publishing Company.

———, 2002, *The Indus Civilization: A Contemporary Perspective*, Walnut Creek, CA: AltaMira Press, a division of Rowan and Littlefield Publishers, Inc.

———, 2006, "Transformation of the Haṛappan Civilization", in *Early Haṛappans and Indus-Sarasvati Civilization*, vol. 1, ed. D.P. Sharma and Madhuri Sharma, New Delhi: Kaveri Books, pp. 210-36.

Possehl, Gregory L. and Kenneth A.R. Kennedy, 1979, "Hunter-gather/Agriculturalist Exchange in Prehistory: An Indian Example", *Current Anthropology* 20(3): 592-93.

Renfrew, Colin, 1987, *Archaeology and Language: The Puzzle of Indo-European Origins*, New York: Cambridge University Press.

Shaffer, Jim G., 1978, *Prehistoric Baluchistan (With Excavation Report on Said Qala Tepe)*, Delhi: B.R. Publishing Corp.

———, 1990, "Review of Language and Archaeology: The Puzzle of Indo-European Origins by Colin Renfrew", *Ethnohistory* 37: 354-56.

———, 1992, "Indus Valley, Baluchistan and the Helmand Traditions: Neolithic Through Bronze Age", in *Chronologies in Old World Archaeology*, ed. R.W. Ehrich, Chicago, IL: University of Chicago Press, vol. I, pp. 441-64, vol. II, pp. 425-46.

———, 1993, "Reurbanization: The Eastern Punjab and Beyond", *Urban Form and Meaning in South Asia: The Shaping of Cities from Prehistoric to Precolonial Times*, ed. H. Spodek and D.M. Srinivasan, Washington D.C.: National Gallery of Art, pp. 53-67.

Shaffer, Jim G. and Diane A. Lichtenstein, 1989, "Ethnicity and Change in the Indus Valley Cultural Tradition", in *Old Problems and New Perspectives in the Archaeology of South Asia*, ed. J. Mark Kenoyer, University of Wisconsin, Madison, WI: Wisconsin Archaeological Report No. 2, pp. 117-26.

———, 1995, "The Concepts of Cultural Tradition and Paleoethnicity in South Asian Archaeology", in *The Indo-Aryans of Ancient South Asia: Language, Material Culture and Ethnicity*, ed. George Erdosy, Berlin: Walter de Gruyter, pp. 126-54.

———, 1999, "Migration, Philology and South Asian Archaeology", in *Aryan and Non-Aryan in South Asia: Evidence, Interpretation and Ideology*, ed. J. Bronkhurst and M.M. Deshpande, Harvard Oriental Series, Opera Minora, vol. 3. Cambridge, MA: Department of Sanskrit and Indian Studies, Harvard University, pp. 239-60.

———, 2005, "South Asia Archaeology and the Myth of Indo-Aryan Invasions", in *The Indo-Aryan Controversy: Evidence and Inference in Indian History*, ed. E.F. Bryant and L.L. Patton, New York: Routledge, pp. 75-104.

Singh, Pushp L., 2005, *Settlement Pattern in Northern India (Circa 600 BCE – Circa CE 300)*, Delhi: Agam Kala Prakashan.

Suraj Bhan, 1975, *Excavations at Mitathal (1968) and Other Explorations in the Sutlej-Yamuna Divide*, Kurukshetra: Kurukshetra University Press.

Suraj Bhan and Jim G. Shaffer, 1978, "New Discoveries in Northern Haryana", *Man and Environment*, 2: 59-68.

Time-Life Books (eds.), 1994, *Ancient India: Land of Mystery*, Alexandra, VA: Time-Life Books.

Thakran, R.C., 2000, *Dynamics of Settlement Archaeology* (Haryana). New Delhi: Gyan Publishing House.

Tripathi, Vibha, 1976, *The Painted Grey Ware: An Iron Age Culture of Northern India*, Delhi: Concept Publishing Co.

Weber, Steven A. and William R. Belcher (eds.), 2003, *Indus Ethnobiology: New Perspectives from the Field*, Lanham, MD: Lexington Books.

Wheeler, Sir Mortimer, 1968, *The Indus Civilization*, 3rd edn., London: Cambridge University Press (1st edn. 1953).

Wright, Rita P., 1984, "Technology, Style and Craft Specialization: Patterns of Interaction and Exchange on the Indo-Iranian Boderlands Third Millennium BCE", PhD. Diss., Harvard University and University Microfilms.

———, 1995, "Fine Ware Traditions at Mehrgarh", in *Mehrgarh: Field Reports 1974-1985 from Neolithic Times to the Indus Civilization*, ed. C. Jarrige et al., Karachi: The Department of

Culture and Tourism, Government of Sindh, pp. 662-71.

———, 2010, *The Ancient Indus: Urbanism, Economy and Society*, New York: Cambridge University Press.

9

The Origin of the Indic Languages
The Indo-European Model

James Clackson

Abstract

This paper presents the basic assumptions underlying the hypothesis that the Indic languages belong to the Indo-European language family, whose other members include Latin, Greek, Hittite, Persian and many of the major European languages. However, it is argued that this model of language relationship on its own can tell us very little, if anything, about the homeland or society of the original speakers of the language, ancestral to the Indo-European family.

Introduction

THE Indo-European (IE) model of language relationship has held the field in language science and language study for the last 200 years. But it is right to say that this model should be questioned and examined critically by scholars, rather than accepted without comments. In this paper, I shall set out the basic assumptions on which the grouping of languages into the IE model rests. I shall then look more closely at two critical treatments of the IE model, and I shall try to show how these supposed criticisms can be met by a more careful distinction of what can be achieved through the reconstruction of a parent language. As I shall demonstrate at the end of the paper, similar misconceptions of the nature of reconstructed "Proto-

IE", which underlie the critical treatments of the model, also feature in the overly positivist attempts to tally linguistics with archaeology (as in a recent book by David Anthony).

Language Change and the IE Model

The grouping of languages into the IE family rests on the following assumptions. First, the primary form of language is spoken language. Written language is primarily (although not exclusively) a representation of spoken language, and is a production particular to particular moments in time and reliant on cultural factors. Every human being can speak, but not everyone has command of a written language, and numerous spoken languages do not have, or never have had a written form. Spoken languages have a number of features which distinguish them from written languages, one of which is of especial importance, and constitute our second assumption: all spoken languages change over time. Change may be exhibited in every area of language. Sometimes, change can be obvious to speakers, such as changes in the pronunciation of sounds (such as the tendency in British English to pronounce the interdental fricative represented by the spelling *th* in words such as *think*, as a labiovelar fricative, represented by the letter *f*, leading to a prevalence of utterances such as "I *fink*"). Change in vocabulary is also easily recognized by speakers, who become aware when words such as *sad* or *mouse* develop different senses. It is less easy to spot changes in the structures underlying spoken language, for example, changes in syntax and phonology, the rules of the language through which speakers construct well-formed words and sentences. Languages, which do not or which do not appear to change over time (such as Sanskrit), are in some way artificial, preserved forms of language, either kept isolated from change through their documentation in written form or their learned use in culturally-specific environments.

These two assumptions have, as a corollary, a third

essential assumption that no spoken human language has continued unchanged over a long time period (except when artificially supported through writing or some other means). Furthermore, we are able to document the change in spoken languages, through comparison of various stages of surviving written language texts. It is clear from the documentary record that when languages change, they also may develop into entities which are labelled as different languages. Thus, the Romance languages, which are now known by the names of French, Italian, Spanish, Portuguese, etc. can be derived back from forms of spoken Latin (see Ostler 2007 for an accessible account of the history of the Romance languages). Note, however, that since the definition of what constitutes a single language is often based on political or cultural factors as much as linguistic factors, it is possible for a language to change into a number of different varieties which are not recognized as separate languages, although they may be as far removed from each other as two varieties accorded the status of different languages. Portuguese and Galician are both as far removed from Spanish as each other, but Portuguese is generally recognized as a different language whereas Galician is not widely so recognized since Galicia is not an independent sovereign state, but an autonomous community within Spain.

From these core assumptions about the nature of spoken language, we, therefore, arrive at a notion of historical relationship between different spoken languages. (A note on terminology: languages which derive from a common ancestor are described as being related to each other and related languages are said to constitute a genetic family of languages.) Currently, there is no alternative scientific hypothesis to describe the diversity of human languages than through a model which includes processes of change and language relationship. Language evolution is thus generally seen as in some way analogous to the process of evolution in the biological sciences (Croft 2000, Ritt 2004), and this comparison is already made in Chapter XIII of Darwin's Origin of Species (Darwin 1869: 501-2).

Related languages inevitably share similarities, but since linguistic change may operate at different rates and may affect different areas of the language, it is impossible to say precisely what commonalities will be found between two related languages. Certainly, there will usually be a large overlap in the area of basic vocabulary and of the structural properties of the language. Languages in the Romance family share a large amount of common words and grammar, but not everything has changed in the same way. Standard French and Italian share the same words for "brother" and "sister", words which derive from Latin *frater* and *soror* respectively, but in Spanish, the words have been replaced by different lexemes — *hermano* and *hermana*. All of the Romance languages except French share the property that personal pronouns are not obligatory with verbs, so the word for "it rains" is *piove* in Italian, *llueve* in Spanish but *il pleut* (with obligatory pronoun *il*) in French.

Similarities between languages may therefore arise through a genetic connection between languages. But similarities might also arise by chance or through periods of linguistic contact. Linguistic contact is the term which linguists use to cover a range of different situations in which language users may have control over more than one language. A simple example is a case where a bilingual speaker is brought up using two languages, but the label also extends to situations where an individual or a section of society has control of a learned written language alongside their spoken idiom (as French or Italian speakers may have control over the Latin language). Prolonged or intense linguistic contact may result in words or structures from one language becoming incorporated into the other. Most frequently, the result of contact is the incorporation of non-native vocabulary items into a language, but there are also documented cases of the borrowing of syntactic and even morphological features from one language to another.

So if two given languages are similar, how is it possible to tell whether the similarity has arisen because of a shared genetic history or through borrowing, or just through chance? The answer is the same as in other sciences and social sciences, through hypothesis formation and testing. It is possible to construct either a hypothesis that a given language, or group of languages, belongs to the IE language family (for example), or a hypothesis that the similarity between languages arises out of a prehistoric contact situation. Such hypotheses can be tested by other scholars working in the field, and the results analysed to see if they match the hypothesis or not. Within the history of linguistics, many different such hypotheses have been formed at different times and some hypotheses have been shown to be less effective at explaining linguistic evidence than others. For example, the Armenian language was originally hypothesized to belong to the Iranian branch of languages. However, an alternative hypothesis has been put by Heinrich Hübschmann in 1878, which sees Armenian as an independent branch of the IE, but with a great deal of influence by contact from the Iranian languages. This hypothesis is now universally accepted, since it takes better account of the diversity of linguistic evidence in Armenian. Similarities between the Lydian and Lycian languages and the IE languages were hypothesized to be due to chance, until new data shedding light on the earlier history of the Anatolian branch of IE emerged, after which Lydian and Lycian were hypothesizsed to be IE languages, a hypothesis which still holds sway. Hypotheses may also be formed about prehistoric language contact, as well as language relationship. Thus, for example, Martin Bernal (Bernal 2006) has argued that there

9. Dr James Clackson presenting his paper

has been extensive contact between Greek and the Ancient Egyptian languages; the linguists Jay Jasanoff and Alan Nussbaum have argued strongly that this hypothesis is not supported by the evidence (Jasanoff and Nussbaum 1996), and Bernal's theory has not found general acceptance. Sometimes, several alternative hypotheses have been put forward for the language affiliations of a single language and the question may still be open. Thus, for example, the Etruscan language has frequently been hypothesized to be an IE language or to have undergone heavy contact with early IE languages (see Wallace 2008: 215-18 for discussion and bibliography) but so far neither of these hypotheses has been generally accepted by scholars. Hypotheses of larger family groups, encompassing IE and other language families, have also been proposed, but these hypotheses have not yet been generally accepted (see Clackson 2007: 20-25 for examples and discussion).

Criticisms of the IE Model I: Linguistic Artefacts

As with any other scientific endeavour, it is possible that the motives for hypothesis formation in linguistics and language relationship may have originated within a discourse which is framed by a particular political or cultural agenda. Thus, in the case of IE language relationships, it is possible to make the argument that the creation of a hypothesis relating the languages of northern India to those of Europe was initially created and promulgated by nineteenth-century scholars in order to promote agendas of colonialism or racism (see Bryant 2001, Bryant and Patton (eds.) 2005 and Thapar 2008 for discussion of the construction and use of labels such as "Āryan" in the history of India). Bernal has similarly argued that the Semitic and African influence on the Greek language was downplayed if not deliberately sabotaged in the nineteenth century under the influence of an anti-Semitic and anti-African racial theory (Bernal 1987, 1991 and 2001, see also Berlinerblau 1999 on the wider controversy Bernal's work caused). It is worth remembering that no scholarship exists in a vacuum, and contemporary cultural and political influences may affect scholarship in ways unrecognized by the practitioners themselves. However, we must be wary of not jumping to conclusions based on what the proponents of scientific theories thought or might have thought at the time of their making, but examine the theories in the light of the evidence and the robustness of the hypothesis under scrutiny. A suitable analogy might be given to Darwinian evolutionary theory. There is no doubt that many of the early proponents of Darwinianism, such as Frederick Galton, used the theory to underpin racist ideas and to propose unsavoury eugenic practices. We may abhor these views, but this does not mean that we should reject Darwinian evolution.

Recently, Angela Marcantonio has subjected the IE model to a critical assessment in a number of papers, including one in Marcantonio (ed. 2009). I shall not take issue with her paper in detail here, but state one area where we are in agreement. She states, amongst other criticisms, that linguistic reconstructions are artefacts of the mechanism of reconstruction. In this, I am in agreement: linguistic reconstructions are artefacts of the method, inasmuch as they are results of the operation of the comparative method, rather than "naturally occurring" linguistic forms. Indeed, I think recognizing this fact helps us understand a lot about the nature of linguistic reconstruction. It will help discuss an individual reconstruction to illustrate the point, and I shall make reference to the reconstructed Proto-Indo-European (PIE) verb form **b^hereti* "he or she carries" (note that IE reconstructions are usually preceded by an asterisk "*" in order to indicate that they are not observed in any attested language). This form is necessarily an artefact. It is not a recording of an actual word of the spoken language which lies behind the IE language family. It is a result of comparison of the IE languages, in particular individual verb forms in IE languages such as the following: Sanskrit *bharati*, Avestan *baraiti*, Latin *fert*, Greek *pherei*, Armenian *berê*, English *bears*, Old Irish *berid*, Phrygian *beret* (see Rix et al. 2002: 76 for a full listing of forms).

The reconstructed item is different from a recorded term of a language in a number of ways. First, there is no certain phonetic reality of the reconstructed form. We are able to reconstruct (largely) the minimal distinctive units of sound of IE (i.e. the phonemes) but we can never know with absolute certainty the phonetic realization of these phonemes. Second, we have no context for this linguistic form — we know the semantic meaning is something which has enough commonality to be able to develop into words meaning "carry" in daughter languages, but we don't know when a speaker would have used this word of another word of similar semantic scope. Would a pregnant woman use it of carrying a child, for example, a use which is found for this verb across many IE languages? In many languages the same term is used for "carry" and "be pregnant" and derivatives from this root often develop meanings associated with pregnancy in different languages. However, we can never be sure this is not a later widening of the original meaning (as the word "carry" in modern English has widened its meaning from "transport in a cart" and can also be used of pregnant women). Third, we do not know whether this linguistic artefact was necessarily used at the same period of time as other linguistic re-constructions of IE. Unlike a "real" language, our reconstructed proto-language is not limited to a single point in time, but it is an amalgam of reconstructions which may correspond to actual spoken features of different chronological eras.

It is useful to stress this distinction between the hypothetical reconstructed "language", which is the result of comparison of forms in the daughter languages, and the unattested spoken language from which we presume all the daughter languages in a family. Linguists can (and should) distinguish the two entities more carefully than is sometimes the case. In the IE language, for example, we might contrast "reconstructed PIE" with "the spoken IE parent language". Reconstructed PIE is the compilation of linguistic artefacts, of the types which has been criticized in Marcantonio (2009). It is an academic construct which does not have an existence at a particular time and place (other than in academic discourse), and is unlike a real language in that it has never been a spoken language. Indeed, it is not clear that it would be possible to speak reconstructed PIE, since the reconstruction is incomplete: we do not have the whole of the language system. For instance, as mentioned above, reconstructed phonemes do not have a clear correlation with phonetic reality in the way that phonemes of living languages do; we may know a reconstructed phonology, but not the phonetic detail. Furthermore, the reconstructed language cannot be associated with any particular time or place in prehistory (and may indeed contain elements belonging properly to a large geographical and temporal span).

The relationship between the reconstructed proto-language and the actual spoken parent language is not straightforward. It is probable that reconstructed features of the proto-language correlate closely to features which were present in the spoken language. In the case of the verb-form *b^hereti* reconstructed above, for example, Indo-Europeanists can be fairly confident that this corresponds closely to an actual sequence of three open syllables (with three phonemically distinct onsets and two phonemically distinct vowels) in the spoken parent language and that this sequence was a well-formed verb in the spoken language. But that does not mean that *b^hereti* is a word of the spoken IE parent language; rather it is an abstraction and imperfect attempt to represent a spoken word in the parent language.

The relationship between reconstructed forms and the spoken parent language is further complicated by the nature of most descriptions of attested languages (including under that heading both languages still spoken and recordable today, and languages no longer spoken but known from written records). Linguistic descriptions of attested languages are also abstractions, both from actual utterances of speakers and also from speakers' internalized knowledge of their language. Furthermore, most linguistic descriptions largely elide variations in speech communities and across small stretches of time. A single feature in language may be variously described depending on the level of abstraction which the linguist desires or which is demanded by the linguistic framework. Linguists may, therefore, employ extremely abstract representation of attested languages (for an extreme example, see Sidney Allen's representation of word-forms in the North West Caucasian language Abaza, such as *ygʸyzdmlrətxd* "he couldn't make them give it back to her" for a sequence which is pronounced [*jigi:zdimḷritʰəxd*], and which he theorizes could be written without even giving any full vowels at all: *ygʸyzdmlrtxd* [Allen 1956: 171]).

Representations of linguistic forms of attested languages consequently appear to be similar to the reconstructions of proto-languages (and indeed reconstructed forms are sometimes criticized for their outlandish appearance). Owing to this similarity, it is tempting, but misleading, to see reconstructions as in some way equivalent to linguistic representations of actual spoken language. True, both abstractions will correspond in some way to forms in spoken language, but forms such as Abaza *ygʸyzdmlrtxd* can be mapped directly onto an actual or potential Abaza utterance. We don't have the information to map a form such as **bʰereti* directly onto an IE utterance, and we certainly are unable to local the form in time or space (as we can with the Abaza word).

One metaphor which might help to express the distinction is a simple one: linguistic representations of real languages are like drawings of animals or plants made from life. The depiction of a cat or a caterpillar in a biology textbook is usually to some extent an idealized depiction, although it probably has its basis in an actual animal seen by the artist. The textbook drawing corresponds to the creature, but it is not the same as it.

To follow this metaphor through reconstructed linguistic forms are like the depictions of posited evolutionary ancestors of the cat family or butterfly larvae. As such they have no direct correspondence to an attested creature and cannot have the same degree of accuracy as the drawing of a member of a still existent species would have. Indeed, one only has to look at some nineteenth-century representations of extinct fauna and flora to see some of the potential hazards of attempting to depict palaeontological reconstructions in this way. However, pointing out the flaws or uncertainties of the depiction of the reconstructed animal is not in itself sufficient to dismiss the theory of the ancestor of a biological family. Linguistic depictions (as the example from Abaza makes clear) can be far more abstract than the graphic representation of a biological specimen and the linguistic reconstructions themselves consequently are yet further removed from what may actually have been spoken.

To summarize, linguistic reconstructions are certainly artefacts of the comparative method, and this means that they must be treated differently from linguistic data which are arrived at through the study of attested languages. The nature of linguistic reconstructions has certain important ramifications. In particular, there is a further problem which arises when comparing groups of reconstructed word-forms within an individual proto-language. Since none of the reconstructed forms has a fixed location in time and space, it is possible to make the mistake of setting one form alongside another, when in fact they correlate to spoken forms which were only ever in existence hundreds of years or miles apart (I shall show an example of this sort of comparison in the discussion of wheeled vehicles at the end of this paper). Again, it may be helpful here to employ a metaphor to aid the understanding. In this case, the most helpful metaphor is that of a "constellation" (first used by Eichner 1988). Constellations of stars in the night sky, such as *The Plough* or *Orion*, make sense to the observer as points on a sphere of a fixed radius around the earth. We see the constellations as two-dimensional dot-to-dot pictures on a curved plane. But, in fact, the stars are not all equidistant from the earth; some lie much further away than others. Constellations are an illusion and have no existence in reality. In the same way, some apparent groupings of words or indeed, grouping of parts of an individual work, in reconstructed PIE may only be a distortion of our viewpoint, and the result of the method employed.

Indo-Europeanists have various methods to avoid this sort of distortion of the picture of a reconstructed language. One method is to deny that individual reconstructions of the form *$*b^hereti$* have any validity in our picture of the reconstructed proto-language. True enough, something corresponding to this may have been attested in the spoken parent language, but we cannot be sure at what stage the form came into being, or even whether it was not first formed independently in separate daughter languages after the loss of mutual comprehensibility across the IE speech community. Instead, we could further hedge our bets by saying that *$*b^hereti$* corresponds to a *potential* formation of spoken IE, but we don't know for sure whether speakers actually availed themselves of the formation (we might compare an English formation such as *textable*, which has been a potential feature of the English language ever since "text" was first used as verb (in 1599 according to the *Oxford English*

Dictionary) but which has only come into use very recently with the advent of text-messaging to mean "in a situation where text-messages can be sent and received"). Through this reasoning, all we can reconstruct for IE are roots and some rules of word-formation. Thus, in the case of **bʰereti* we can reconstruct only a root **bʰer-*, a verbal suffix **-e/o-*, a personal ending **-ti*, and a rule that enables the formation of a verbal stem **bʰere-*. Without any support from other information, we cannot be sure that a potential form actually occurred at any time before it surfaces in one or more of the daughter language (Schlerath 1987).

This argument introduces a yet more abstract notion into linguistic reconstruction — the root. Roots can also be classed as linguistic artefacts, since although in some languages speakers may be aware of connections between derived forms which share the same underlying lexical roots, many speakers are not. Speakers of English, for example, are unlikely to be aware of any close connection between *loud* and *listen*. However, historically both these words derive from the same IE root **k´lew(s)- "hear"*. The connection may have been more apparent to speakers of Old English, who may have understood a connection between *hlyst* "sense of hearing" and *hlûd* "loud", and probably even clearer at more remote stages of the language. Roots are necessarily abstractions even from living languages and they become yet more removed when further refracted by the process of reconstruction. The distance of lexical roots from spoken forms of language, compounded with the necessary degree of uncertainty which surrounds any reconstruction (in any scientific field), leads to a high degree of abstraction. It may, therefore, appear reasonable to the non-specialist to deny the enterprise altogether. Roots may appear to be convenient methods for Indo-Europeanists to increase their stock of inherited material. However, the reconstruction of IE roots is not a conspiracy between linguists unaware of the pitfalls of circularity in reconstruction. Rather, in essence, it is no more than an admission of the Indo-Europeanist of the inadequacy of our reconstructed forms to approach closely the actual spoken parent language.

In summary to this section, I think some criticisms of IE reconstructions do not fully appreciate the degree of abstraction in which these reconstructions are made. One possible criticism, for example, of reconstructed IE is that there are only a small number of reconstructed items of the type of **bʰereti*, and most of the reconstructed roots in a comparative dictionary of IE do not show the same single form and meaning across a number of daughter languages. Of course, if there were more such reconstructions, life would be simpler (and there would not be so much for comparative Indo-Europeanists to do). But, unfortunately, the linguistic evidence available to us has not been so conducive to these results. However, this is not necessarily a weakness in the endeavour of Indo-Europeanists to reconstruct the language. As we have already seen, some scholars do not believe that attempting to reconstruct full-fledged word forms of IE is achievable or even desirable (any more than palaeo-biologists now spend a lot of time attempting to reconstruct the colours or patterning of fur on the evolutionary ancestor of the cat family). Given the available information comparative linguists do the best they can.

Criticisms of the IE Model II: Nikolay Trubetzkoy

The crux of the matter comes back, I think, to the points mentioned at the beginning of this paper. If there are similarities between the IE languages which cannot all be ascribed to chance, then how do we explain the similarities between these languages? If we are not to attribute the similarities to divine or alien intervention, or some other non-scientific explanation, then it is clear that the only alternative model to explain the similarity is through reckoning a scenario of prehistoric borrowing and language contact. In this section of my paper, I shall discuss briefly the only other serious challenge to the IE model and one which has often been supposed to theorize prehistoric borrowing and contact, that of Nikolay Trubetzkoy.

Trubetzkoy was one of the greatest linguists of the first half of the twentieth century and a founding father of modern studies on phonology. Leaving his native Russia after the Revolution, he eventually took up a place as Professor of Slavic Philology in the University of Vienna in 1922, where he stayed until his early death from a heart attack in 1938. His death was undoubtedly linked to the persecution and intimidation he suffered at the hands of the Nazis after the Anschluss in 1938; Trubetzkoy had been critical of Hitler's racialist theories and actions. This historical background is not irrelevant to Trubetzkoy's critical attitude towards IE, and indeed gives a further illustration of the contingency of scholarly ideas to their political and social framework.

In a famous article (Trubetzkoy 1939, the draft of a lecture given in 1936, which was published posthumously and unrevised in the Danish journal *Acta Linguistica*), Trubetzkoy stated that it was not possible to isolate a series of lexical and morphological elements which were present in all IE languages and absent from all non-IE languages. Instead, he proposed that a language could be classed as IE on the basis of the presence of the following six structural features: (i) absence of vowel harmony in IE languages (as exists in Turkic languages); (ii) absence of any restriction on which consonants could stand at the beginning of a word; (iii) possibility of deriving new words through prefixation (e.g. English *unkind*, derived from *kind*); (iv) use of vocalic alternations within the lexical stem in morphology (e.g. English *ride, rode, ridden*); (v) use of alternations of consonants within morphology (e.g. English plural morpheme has form /s/ in *cats* but /z/ in *dogs*); (vi) the subject of a transitive verb has the same form as the subject of an intransitive verb.

If one were to take Trubetzkoy's paper at face value, it would mean that a language could become IE if it adopted these structural features. It would also mean that as languages lost these structural features, they would cease to be IE. Thus, for example, modern Indic languages which show ergative structures, so that the subject of a transitive verb is not always the same as the subject of an intransitive verb, could no longer be classed as IE (see the same criticism made already by Allen (1953: 92)). Trubetzkoy's paper on IE has been widely criticized. As many scholars have pointed out, as a checklist for arriving at the same grouping of languages as the genetic method of grouping IE languages, Trubetzkoy's structural features are neither necessary nor sufficient. Yet, I believe that criticisms of Trubetzkoy on these grounds fail to understand the point of his paper. His main goal, in my view, was to highlight the divergence between the results of the comparative method and the spoken parent language of the IE language family and, in particular, the attempts by scholars (especially German scholars of the 1930s) to associate specific archaeological cultures and ethnic types (races) with the IEs. Trubetzkoy was particularly critical of scholars who sought to answer such questions as "what type of pottery was associated with the IEs?" (1939: 83). Trubetzkoy highlighted the inadequacies of attempts to reconstruct IE along the lines of a real language through stressing the divergences of the lexical and morphological material of IE. The (identification of structural features was a way to look again at how languages were grouped, but not a denial of the genetic grouping indeed in the paper Trubetzkoy continues to assume the existence of "ursprünglich Indogermanisch" (1983: 88)). Trubetzkoy was, I believe, attempting to show that this was not the only way to group languages in the world, and working towards a programme which eliminated the factor of time from comparative study of languages (see Allen 1953 for more developed and sophisticated arguments along the same lines as those attempted by Trubetzkoy).

(Mis)uses of the IE Model: Anthony

Unfortunately, the confusion between the results of the comparative method and a real language still persists today. Scholars nowadays usually do not talk in terms of race or pottery, but there is still much discussion of IE culture and homeland and origin. Of course, the existence of a language implies speakers, and it is natural to ask where the speakers of IE came from and when they existed. But, in addressing these questions, we must remember that the IE hypothesis is entirely a linguistic hypothesis and we must be careful to see what results we can gain from linguistics alone. In order to do this, I will consider in this section of the paper the most recent substantial work which attempts to tie the linguistic reconstruction of PIE with archaeological evidence, David Anthony's *The Horse, the Wheel and Language*, published in 2007. Anthony is very keen to marry linguistic evidence with archaeology. Indeed, he tries to integrate linguistic evidence into archaeology, making the provocative statement "[T]o an archaeologist it [reconstructed PIE] is more valuable than a roomful of potsherds" (2007: 86). Before highlighting the pitfalls of some of Anthony's work, I will sketch out briefly his model of prehistory, which will be relevant for the later discussion.

Anthony uses as the base for his archaeological model one of the recently constructed family trees of IE, arrived at partly through the use of computer modelling programmes originally developed for constructing cladograms in biological evolution. As can be seen from *fig.* 9. 1, this family tree shows that two branches of the family split off early. Both of these branches have died out and no longer have any speakers. The first, Anatolian, the branch which comprises Hittite, Luwian, Lycian

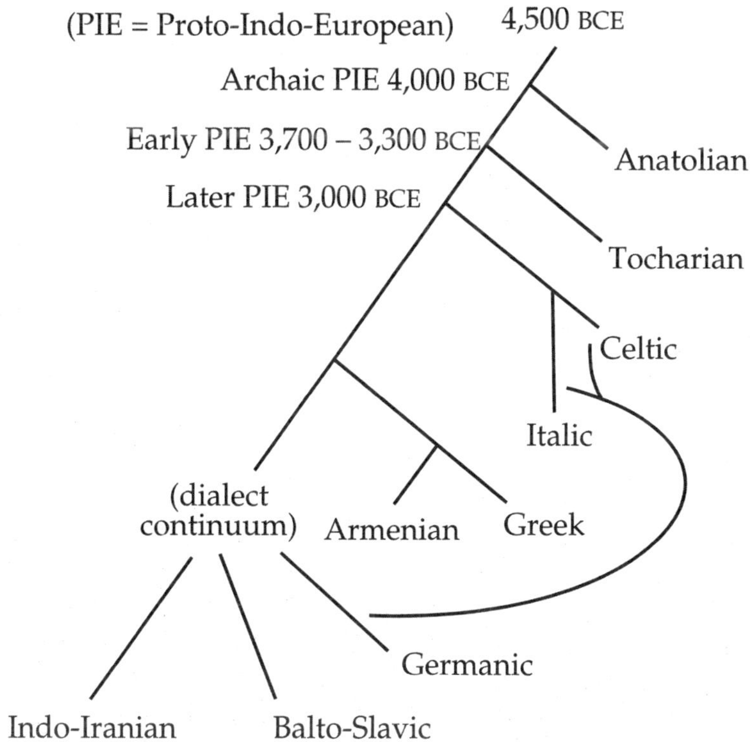

fig. 9.1. A tree-model of the IE family, taken from Figure 3.2 of Anthony (2007:37)

and some other ancient languages spoken in Anatolia, is also our earliest attested IE language, since we have texts in Hittite from the early second millennium BCE. The second — Tocharian — is known from texts discovered at the beginning of the century in Chinese Turkestan.

Anthony's family tree also includes dates for the early splits of PIE. These dates, it should be stressed, are not supported by any objective linguistic evidence at all. Indeed, although Anthony mentions that the dates are supported by research on rates of language change, the most recent attempt to date the splits of PIE through estimates based on the speed of vocabulary replacement have proved controversial and come up with different dates to the ones given by Anthony here (see Gray and Atkinson 2003). Rather, the dates on Anthony's tree are pretty much linguistic "best guesses"; linguists look at how far apart languages descended from Latin are, for example, and estimate from that how far apart they think that makes IE languages.

Another factor in the dating is also the reconstruction of datable items in the material culture, such as terminology for wool and weaving, "secondary products" and wheels, etc. Anthony fits the putative dating of the IE languages into an extended model for the expansion of IE speakers around the area north of the Black and Caspian Seas. It was here that he thinks horses were domesticated, first for food and, then towards the end of the fifth millennium, to be ridden. The notion that anyone rode on horseback this early, surprising to most archaeologists, is supported by archaeological evidence of wear on horses' teeth, most probably caused by bits made from rope or leather (unfortunately this evidence comes from Kazakhstan and is not currently paralleled from the Pontic-Caspian region). Anthony proposes that the domestication of the horse helped the steppe peoples to take advantage of a significant climate change around the turn of the fourth millennium, and to spread as far as the Balkans. This led to a split of the original population: one group, who would later be manifested as speakers of Anatolian variants of IE, Hittite, Luwian, Lycian, etc. moved early into Asia Minor. Only at the end of the third millennium does a single cultural type appear across the IE steppe regions, and this is facilitated by the development of wagon transport.

Anthony sees the spread of the IE speakers throughout Europe in the period 3100-2100 BCE not through conquest or steppe warriors mounted on horseback, but more generally through a series of frontier interactions with peoples on the frontier opting in to the IE cultural way of life — what he calls "franchizing", attracted by the feasting, social alliances, and the social status involved with riding and breeding horses. This theory allows him to avoid the mass migration theory of some of the earlier scholars; although he does believe that there were small movements of peoples, he can use franchizing to explain how other peoples were drawn into the IE orbit.

For the Indo-Iranian side, Anthony follows recent work which does associate the rapid spread of the Indo-Iranian family in central Asia, Iran and north India to military prowess and military advantage — particularly the horse-drawn chariot which seems to originate north of the Caucuses around 2100-1800 BCE. He assumes that a group of steppe-dwellers, who spoke an IE variety (the variety which was later to develop to the Indic and Iranian languages), adopt the horse-drawn chariot. The military superiority associated with the chariot allows them to invade Iran and then to penetrate into the Indian subcontinent. The speakers of Indo-Iranian languages, according to Anthony, are specifically associated with central Asian settlements and burials which can be linked to descriptions in the oral poetry of the early Sanskrit hymns.

Much of the linguistic support for this theory rests on the reconstructed vocabulary which Anthony uses to link "IE expansion" with chariots and also with horses. Some of this vocabulary is famous and much discussed, such as the terms relating to the wheel. In the list below (Table 9.1). I list some of these vocabulary items. For PIE, Anthony follows many other scholars in suggesting that it is possible to reconstruct at least two words for wheel (some Indo-Europeanists would reconstruct three or more). Both words are preserved across the IE branches, and curiously both refer in some languages to "wheel" and in others to "chariot". Thus, the first word on the list, **k^{w}ek^{w}lo-*, means wheel in Sanskrit, sometimes in Greek and in English, and in other languages (Tocharian) means "chariot"; the second word means chariot in Sanskrit, but wheel in the western languages. The shift in meaning from "wheel" to "wheeled vehicle, set of wheels" is not unusual or particularly noteworthy: "wheels" can mean a car in English. But it is worth saying that having two different words for wheel, both attested across different IE languages, is a little problematic. In other cases of shared vocabulary, we more usually find a single word which is attested across different languages, but replaced in some by new formations. Thus, the original word for "hand", *$*g^{h}$'es-r-*, seems to be retained in Hittite, Greek, Tocharian, Albanian and Armenian, but is replaced by new words in different parts of the IE world, such as *manus* in Latin and terms related to *hand* in the Germanic languages (see Wodtko et al. 2008: 170). Why then do we have two wheel words? Anthony speculates, as others have done, that there were two different types of wheel (2007: 63; it seems however unlikely that one of these words refers to the spoked wheel, since this seems to be a late third millennium innovation). Note also that I have included in Table 9.1 three other words which Anthony does not include in his discussion but which should be mentioned in the context of wheeled transport. The first is the word for "horse", the second is the very widespread word for "yoke" and the third is the word for the "hub" of a wheel. Anthony is quite scrupulous in not mentioning these words since he allows that none of them need apply to chariots which were probably not originally drawn by horse — yokes can be used for ploughs and the hub word also applies to the boss of a shield.

Fig. 9.2 depicts Anthony's attempt to represent the survival of the wagon terminology in different branches of IE by constructing diagrams. Thus, we appear to have the full chariot in Indic and Iranian, but just pieces in the other branches (note that the Tocharian languages, as far as I know, only show

***Table* 9.1: List of terms relating to wheeled transport in IE languages** (expanded from Anthony 2007).

*$k^w ek^w lo$- "wheel"	Sanskrit *cakrá-*, Greek *kúklos* "circle", Tocharian B *kokale* "wagon", Old Norse *hvel*, Old English *hweohl*, etc.
**rot(H)o-* "wheel"	Old Irish *roth* m., Old High German *rad*, Lithuanian *ratas*, *$roteh_2$- in Latin *rota*, *$roth_2o$- in Sanskrit *rátha-* "chariot".
*h_2eks- "axle"	Sanskrit *áksa-*, Greek *áksōn*, Latin *axis*, Old English *eax*, Old High German *ahsa*, Old Church Slavonic *osĭ*.
*h_2iHs-eh_2- "thill" (i.e. pole between chariot and yoke)	Hittite *hissa-* "pole", Sanskrit *īṣā-* "shaft", Avestan, Greek *oiāks, oiēks* "rudder", Old English *ar* "oar", Russian *vojë* "shaft".
*$weg^{h\prime}$- "drive, carry"	Sanskrit *vahati*, Latin *ueho*, Lithuanian *vežù*, Welsh *amwain*, Old Norse *vega*, Greek (dialectal) *wékhō*, Church Slavonic *vesti*.
"wagon" / "cart" / "chariot" (derived from *$weg^{h\prime}$-)	Sanskrit *vāhana-*, Greek *ókhos*, Latin *uehiculum*, English *wagon, wain*, Old High German *wagan*, Old Irish *fen*, Lithuanian *vežimas*, Church Slavonic *vozŭ*.
*$h_1ek'wo$- "horse"	Sanskrit *áśva-*, Luwian *asu-*, Lycian *esbe*, Greek *híppos*, Latin *equus*, Old Irish *ech*, Old English *eoh*, Tocharian A *yuk*.
**yugom* "yoke"	Hittite *iukan*, Sanskrit *yugá-*, Greek *zdugón*, Latin *iugum*, Welsh *iau*, Old Church Slavonic *igo*, English *yoke*, etc.
*h_3neb^h- "hub"	Sanskrit *nábhya-*, Old High German *naba*, Old Prussian *nabis*, Armenian *aniw* "wheel".

definitely one of the wheel words, rather than the whole set as depicted).

In my view, Anthony's confidence in these linguistic reconstructions is misplaced. In essence, he makes the mistake of confusing the results of linguistic reconstruction with actual words in a spoken language. I have already discussed above the abstraction inherent in the comparative method, and I have already touched on the problem of the attribution of meaning

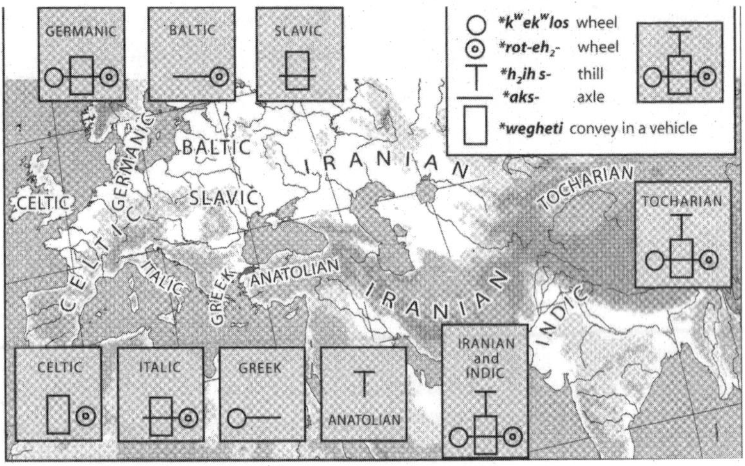

fig. 9.2: Sketch of the geographic distribution of IE wagon terms, reproduced from Anthony (2007: 64).

to a reconstructed word. This is much more problematic than the association of meaning with a lexical item in an attested spoken language. Take the case of the word $*h_2iHs\text{-}eh_2$-. Does this really mean "thill" and not "pole" or similar? If we examine again its meaning in the IE languages, we can see that in many languages it does not have the meaning "thill", but something different. We cannot be certain that the reconstructed term had the specific meaning that Anthony attributes to it (note also that Hittite, according to Anthony's model, splits off earlier from the other languages and is supposed to be isolated from them before the invention of the chariot — so the Hittite cognate must have developed the meaning "thill" subsequent to the common period). Similarly, the reconstructed term $*weg^{h'}$- does not necessitate wheeled vehicles, but it could have transferred the sense of "convey" from an earlier semantic field referring to non-wheeled transport, such as sleds or boats. Furthermore, Anthony's approach does not allow for lexical creation. As already mentioned, IE languages freely make derivatives from verbal roots. This seems to be the origin of **rot(H)o-* "wheel" from a root **ret(H)-* "run" and **k^{w}ek^{w}lo-* "wheel" from a root **k^{w}el-*"turn" (note that a common Greek word for "wheel", *trókhos*, is independently derived from a root **d^{h}reg^{h}-* "run, turn"). These lexical creations may date back to the parent language, but they may also be later creations. Also, Anthony has an over-reliance on Sanskrit vocabulary: all of Anthony's terms occur only in Sanskrit (as mentioned, the Tocharian box in *fig*. 9.2 is a mistake). The chart only shows Sanskrit cognates, rather than actual PIE "words". It is not clear that these words really were a PIE set, and we may well be making the mistake of believing that all these words belong together, when they actually have different origins (i.e. the "constellation" problem mentioned above).

Conclusion

Anthony's view of the nature of reconstructed PIE is worth quoting in full:

> Reconstructed PIE is similar, a dictionary version of a language. . . . Of course, the dictionary of reconstructed PIE is much more tattered than my copy of *Merriam-Webster's*. Many pages have been torn out, and those that survive are obscured by the passage of time. — Anthony 2007: 85-86.

This seems to me to be a major misunderstanding of what we are able to do with the comparative method: reconstructed PIE is not in fact like a dictionary. Indeed, a dictionary of this type is an unrealizable goal given the current state of reconstructed PIE (and likely to remain that way barring major discoveries of a large number of texts of earlier stages of PIE). For a proper dictionary of any language, one needs to have something approaching a comprehensive set of the words of that language, and then it is possible to establish how the meaning of words depends on and interlocks with other words in the language.

The sort of dictionary we have for PIE is very different, as comparison of one of the recently published dictionaries such as the *Lexikon der Indogermanischen Verben* (Rix et al. 2002) will show. In the format of the *Lexikon der Indogermanischen Verben* a single entry is given for a verbal root, from which various possible tense formations in different languages are listed. The words themselves, as in verbal forms meaning "he is carrying" or the like, cannot always be reconstructed with certainty. Indeed, scholars cannot always be wholly sure which of alternative ways given of forming the present tense were really used by the original speakers, as is indicated by the frequent use of question marks in the text. As I have already indicated, although it appears as if the dictionary is reconstructing words, it is better to see it as reconstructing the abstract entities known as roots and possible derivations from these which lie behind forms in the daughter languages. Furthermore, the meaning of the original term may also be uncertain. For example, the entry for the root **wegʰ'-*, discussed above, is first glossed (Rix et al. 2002: 661) as *schweben*, "float" or "hover", and only then as *fahren*, "travel in a vehicle". This is because the cognate words in Sanskrit means "blow, flow" as well as "drive", and so one scholar has tried to group these meanings into a single meaning: originally a word meaning "hover" was then transferred to motion in wheeled transport. The reconstructed meaning itself, therefore, spans both the original and later meanings. The meaning ascribed to PIE is, therefore, uncertain — it is an abstraction and a hypothesis, not a fixed meaning like the words in the daughter languages.

Accordingly, any attempt to fix the PIE lexicon to real objects in time and space is extremely hazardous. As a further example, we can look in more detail at the words for wagon. As can be seen, the words which mean "wagon" or "cart" derived from the same root *weg^{h}'-:

Greek _ókhos_ (dialectal _wókhos_) < *wog^{h}'- + *-e/os-

Sanskrit _vāhana-_ < *wēg^{h}'- + *-eno-

Latin _uehiculum_ < *weg^{h}'- + *-(e)tro-

Germanic (English _wagon_ etc.) < *wog^{h}'- + *-ono-

Old Irish _fén_ < *weg^{h}'- + *-no-

Lithuanian _vežimas_ < *weg^{h}'- + *-mo-

Now each one of these words can be derived in a different way from the root, which can also take varied forms, with an internal vowel change, short or long _e_ or _o_, and the suffix can also appear in different forms. As is clear, sometimes the suffixes are different, sometimes they seem to be related: Sanskrit, Germanic and Old Irish all have suffixes which include *n. According to my reading of Marcantonio's (2009) analysis, this is a clear case where she would accuse Indo-Europeanists of picking and choosing from a range of different options in order to produce an artefact unsupported by the actual facts. But this seems to me simplistic. These are not obscure words in the languages concerned, but usually the default term for a wagon or cart, and their similarity with each other across six different languages seems too great to explain by chance. Nor does it seem likely that this is a loan-word, since the differences from language to language would then be difficult to explain (why would the Greek, Latin and Lithuanian words then not also contain *n, why would the same root be found in the languages with the meaning "ride" or "drive"?).

However, it also seems unlikely to me that all these words are derived from the same original single word, since the differences between them appear too great to be explained. Rather, the most likely hypothesis, seems to me, is that the daughter languages have created these words independently (although using similar means, sharing the same root, and similar inherited processes of derivation) at various stages during the period following the fragmentation of the parent language into various dialects. To put it briefly, none of these formations occurs in more than one language branch. They are *all* probably new lexical creations made later than the common speech period, although using inherited patterns of formation. There was, thus, potentially a word for "wagon" formed from this root in PIE, but not necessarily so.

The word for wagon is perhaps an extreme example, but it does show the potential pitfalls for any attempt to relate the IE languages to prehistoric objects and events, and to locate prehistoric movements or migrations of peoples. The reconstructed proto-language is far too removed from actual spoken languages of the type we are familiar with to make that possible. This extremely abstract nature of the reconstructed parent language is also the reason that the results of the comparative method may appear confusing and inadequate even to linguists. The inadequacy of the results of reconstruction does not, however, mean that the whole enterprise of comparative linguistics is flawed. In the absence of any better explanation for the evident similarities between IE languages, the genetic relationship hypothesis is the only remaining scientific explanation.

What does this mean for the origin of the Indic languages, and by extension, the origin of the Indic civilization? My answer is, I am afraid, inconclusive. From the linguistic data alone, without taking into account the evidence of archaeology or early texts, it is not possible to draw definite conclusions about the homeland of the speakers of PIE, or even the age of the language family. The IE model, as a model of language relationships and of linguistic descent, tells us nothing certain about the origin of the Indic civilization.

References

Allen, W.S., 1953, "Relationship in Comparative Linguistics", *Transactions of the Philological Society* 53, 52-108.

———, "Structure and System in the Abaza Verbal Complex", *Transactions of the Philological Society* 55, 127-76.

Anthony, D.W., 2007, *The Horse, the Wheel, and Language: How Bronze-Age Riders from the Eurasian Steppes Shaped the Modern World*, Princeton: Princeton University Press.

Berlinerblau, J., 1999, *Heresy in the University: The Black Athena Controversy and the Responsibilities of American Intellectuals*, New Brunswick: Rutgers University Press.

Bernal, M., 1987, *Black Athena: The Afroasiatic Roots of Classical Civilization*, New Brunswick: Rutgers University Press.

———, 1991, *Black Athena: Afro-Asiatic Roots of Classical Civilization, Volume II: The Archaeological and Documentary Evidence*, New Brunswick: Rutgers University Press.

———, 2001, *Black Athena Writes Back. Martin Bernal Responds to His Critics* (ed. D. Chioni Moore), Durham: Duke University Press.

———, 2006, *Black Athena Volume III, The Linguistic Evidence*, New Brunswick: Rutgers University Press.

Bryant, E.F., 2001, *The Quest for the Origins of Vedic Culture: The Indo-Aryan Migration Debate*, Oxford: Oxford University Press.

Bryant, E.F. and L.L. Patton (eds.), 2005, *The Indo-Aryan Controversy: Evidence and Interference in Indian History*, Oxford: Routledge.

Clackson, J., 2007, *Indo-European Linguistics*, Cambridge: Cambridge University Press.

Croft, W., 2000, *Explaining Language Change: An Evolutionary Approach*, Harlow, Essex: Longmans.

Darwin, C., 1869, *On the Origin of Species by Means of Natural Selection*, 5th ed. London: John Murray.

Eichner, H., 1988, "Sprachwandel und Rekonstruktion", in C. Zinko, (ed.), *Akten der 13. Österreichischen Linguistientagung*, Graz: Leykam, 10-40.

Gray R.D. and Q.D. Atkinson, 2003, Language-tree Divergence Times Support the Anatolian Theory of Indo-European Origin, *Nature* 426, 435-39.

Jasanoff, J.H. and A. Nussbaum, 1996, "Word Games: the Linguistic Evidence in Black Athena, In M. Lefkowitz and G. Rogers, (eds.),

Black Athena Revisited, Chapel Hill: University of North Carolina Press. 177-205.

Marcantonio, A. (ed.), 2009, *The Indo-European Language Family: Questions About Its Status*, Washington D.C.: Institute for the Study of Man.

———, 2009, "Evidence that most Indo-European Lexical Reconstructions are Artefacts of the Linguistic Methods of Analysis, in A. Marcantonio (ed.), *The Indo-European Language Family: Questions about its Status*, Washington D.C.: Institute for the Study of Man, 10.1-10.46.

Ostler, N., 2007, *Ad Infinitum: A Biography of Latin*, London: Harper Collins.

Renfrew, C., 1987, *Archaeology and Language*, London: Jonathan Cape.

Ritt, N., 2004, *Selfish Sounds and Linguistic Evolution: A Darwinian Approach to Language Change*, Cambridge: Cambridge University Press.

Rix, H., M. Kümmel, T. Zehnder, R. Lipp and B. Schirmer (eds.). 2002, *Lexikon der Indogermanischen Verben*, 2nd edn., Wiesbaden: Reichert.

Schlerath, B., 1987, "On the Reality and Status of a Reconstructed Language", *Journal of Indo-European Studies* 15, 41-46.

Thapar, R., 2008, *The Aryan: Recasting Constructs*, Gurgaon: Three Essays Publications.

Trubetzkoy, N.S., 1939, "Gedanken über das Indogermanenproblem", *Acta Linguistica* I, 81-89.

Wallace, R., 2008, *Zikh Rasna: A Manual of the Etruscan Language and Inscriptions*, Ann Arbor/New York: Beech Stave Press.

Wodtko, D.S., B. Irslinger and C. Schneider, 2008, *Nomina im Indogermanischen Lexikon*, Heidelberg: Winter.

10

An Analysis of the Concept of Sacredness in Indus Valley Art

Retracing the Roots of the Goddess

Nalini Rao

Abstract

The art of the Indus Valley Civilization, with its tangible visual objects, substantiates the concept of sacredness in various kinds and degrees. Forming the roots of development for some of India's religious traditions, beliefs and forms, it offers valuable insights into the characteristics of the revered. The "sacred" may be said to include fire altars, architectural spaces, particular animals, figures and symbolic representations. This paper examines female figurines, focusing on elements of form, meaning and context that classify them as "sacred" by reconsidering their iconography, function and symbolic value in relation to R̥gvedic and later Indian culture. It reconsiders their representation as Mother Goddess in the light of recent researches, and articulates their social role as earth and village goddesses, that played an important religious and social role. The method of analysis — using elements of continuity in terms of iconography, modelling and contextual meaning — can provide a valuable tool in understanding the concept, nature and function of "sacredness" in Indian art.

Introduction

The word "sacred" stems from Latin *sacer* "holy, sacred" or "that which is set apart from the profane or ordinary world". Other definitions generate a variety of meanings, ranging from divine power to a sense of mystery, from faith to ritual, transcendence to devotion, objects to sacred ground — everything that has a religious meaning. Such a broad definition presupposes that there is no universal concept of sacredness and that it largely depends on the culture within which it originates. In addition, the two terms "civilization" and "sacred", when juxtaposed, appear incongruous: the former implies specialization of activity such as writing, town-planning and architecture, while sacredness is more conceptual, pertaining to beliefs, ideas. The concept poses numerous challenges in Hinduism, where the sacred includes a large number of objects and forms (ranging from gods to animals, from the natural phenomena of sun, dawn, wind, to trees and stones), referring to the entire world and the cosmos as sacred. Often the construction of the concept of sacredness flows from Vedic and Purāṇic religious texts, since these have been incorporated into Hinduism, although they do not reflect popular practice.

The nature of sacredness in the Vedic literature appears to be substantial, but its exploration in relation to the material culture of the Indus Valley poses immense challenges, particularly because of the fragmentary nature of the evidence and the great extension of the relevant area. However, the roots of sacredness can be found in the archaeological artefacts of the Indus Valley, due to the occurrence of similar forms in later Indian art as well as supporting concepts found in the *R̥gveda*. Some of the important forms and symbols that had their origins in the Indus Valley include: the *yoga*, *svastika*, fire altar, animals and female figurines. The criterion for naming them as "sacred" lies in the preservation and continuation of these objects in the religious art of later historical periods (this art remaining central throughout the religious history of India), as well as the numerous reference to them in the Vedic literature. The speculative insight into the cultural, regional and religious meanings of sacredness can be supported by evidence from the *Ṛgveda*, as we now know that the Vedic culture was contemporary and interactive with that of the Indus Valley (Rao 2013). The Indus Valley art displays a high degree of sophistication and artistry, as seen in terracotta seals that display a high level of achievement with regard to the crude female figurines. The two types of female figurines are often divided into fine and folk art, such as the dichotomy between the sacred and profane, both definition being questionable. Thus, I use a more flexible approach in defining the sacred as "revered" and as a key concept in the sociology of religion, whereby degrees of sacredness and regional variation can be found. The enigmatic female figurines are a conundrum and fall in between categories and are overlapping in meaning.

The role of the feminine has been that of a creative figure with the strong, dynamic character of a mother, warrior and fertility symbol, as well as that of village goddesses. In the Indus Valley great many female statuettes have been found and interpreted as representation of a goddess by Marshall (1931), Vats (1940), Kenoyer (1998) and others. The three-dimensional terracotta figurines (or female statuettes) from Haṛappā, Mohenjo-Dāṛo, Lothal, Kālibaṅgan and other sites exhibit some common characteristics: the area about 30 cm (1 ft) in height with a curvaceous flat body, conical breasts pinched of medium size in relation to body size, wide hips and a flat abdomen (Clark 2003: 309, fig. 1). They are generally nude, except for a very short skirt round the waist secured by a girdle (or belt), and wear a variety of jewellery, consisting of elaborate neck collars, long chains, armlets, bangles, anklets, earrings visible in flattened forms. Modelled in a rough abstract manner, the eyes and breasts are like pellets. They are usually depicted standing with their legs pressed together all the way to the feet while the lower portion of the legs is tapered. Normally, all figurines wear a distinct fan-shaped head-dress which forms part of the coiffure. They could be decorated in a variety of ways, through terracotta cones, twisted roles, possibly representing hair, flowers and other applied ornaments. Some of them have their hands raised to their heads (Clark 2004: fig. 9), others hold an infant at their breasts (Clark 2004: fig. 20) and some even have a marked rounded navel (Clark 2004: fig. 17).

Regional Variations

An analysis of the female figures from Haṛappā and Moheṅjo-Dāṛo, compared to those from provincial sites, reveals interesting aspects that are unique to the Indus Valley. A unique terracotta figure from Moheṅjo-Dāṛo is a female standing figure, wearing a lower garment, necklaces, bangles, a girdle, and an elaborate fan-shaped head-dress, thick strips of clay for jewellery, called the Great Mother Goddess (Rao, S.R., 1973. Pl. XXIC, p. 88). The physical characteristics displayed by the Indus Valley figurines may be found in those from other archaeological sites in the ancient world. The flat open base in figures from Lothal recalls those in pre-Haṛappan sites of northern and southern Baluchistan and Mehri in Pakistan, from the Kulli culture. Fan-shaped head-dresses are found in Syria and the Eastern Mediterranean regions, in the prehistoric figures of Mother Goddess from Adalia in Asia Minor, as well as the Semitic Mother Goddess Astarte, the goddess of vegetation and fertility. The fan-shaped head-dress with a cup-like projection on each side is a distinct decorative feature which appears on figures in pre-Mauryan art as well. The facial features are similar, modelled in a summary form: eyes are pellet-like and the mouth is indicated by a slit. The face is abstracted and long hair hangs down the back, as found in the figure: "The Lady of Pazardzik", rom East Balkan civilization and from Ental, Bulgaria (Baring & Cashford 1991: 48, fig. 2). However, female figures from Lothal are comparatively small in scale than those from Haṛappā or Moheṅjo-Dāṛo, although they display similar vitality and power. They bear a marked resemblance with those from Chanhudāṛo, in the way they stand upon a flat, more or less open base. In terms of a simplified modelling — flat ornaments, fan-shaped head-dress and indications of gender by unexaggerated breasts — these Lothal figures bear a close resemblance to the Haṛappā figurines (Rao 1973: Plate XXII C). Another figure from Lothal has a pillar-like body, with an abstract indication of a mouth and eyes indicated by incisions, with a nose formed by pinched-up clay (Rao, 1973: 88). In Chanhudāṛo, the female figures have a swollen belly, but no legs or fan-like head-dresses, while those from Koṭ-dījī are quite different as well.

Describing the similarities in visual form between figurines from different geographical periods and sites should assist in understanding the meaning inherent in these forms. The Indus Valley figurines neither exhibit abnormal gender features, nor are they voluminous. The unexaggerated breasts represent gender features and are one of the points of focus, while everything else has been abstracted away to highlight the central theme, probably that of nourishment. Both male and female figures have the same type of body (except for gender features), making them more earthly, symbolic and functional. Again, the feeling of fecundity does not dominate, considering the female with rudimentary breasts, neither is the female body exaggerated, making it problematic for the attribution of the function of fertility (Dales 1991, Kenoyer 1998: 137). In addition, most female figurines are not nude; most Indus female figurines wear a belt or a short skirt that covers the pubic area. These non-realistic depictions where no features have been overemphasized and it is unlikely they had any sexual or gender roles (Clark 2003: 305-28).

It is interesting to examine the type of figurines (the hollow globular type) from Haṛappā with the two female suckling babies (Clark 2005: fig. 5) and a pregnant female figurine from Mohenjo-Dāṛo (Nandagopal 2006: fig. 79). Both the figures relate to the human mother and the nurturing quality of motherhood more as a source of life and growth than as aspect of fertility. This may be substantiated by the articulation of a large hole of the belly button (Clark 2003: fig. 2), which emphasizes the umbilical cord. The emphasis on the navel rather than on the reproductive organ is interesting, since it is the navel that is the link between the life of the unborn and life of the born baby, and provides a clue regarding the non-erotic, biological and social roles of contemporary women.

Other figurines discovered in Haṛappā are legless and similar to those discovered in Crete. Legless terracotta figurines unearthed from the Zhob Valley of northern Baluchistan, especially at Periano Ghundai, Mughal Ghundai and Mehrgarh, with two Zhob type female figurines from Mundigak and Nausharo, are particularly interesting. Here, the figurines, which are two to three inches long, are known for individuality of expression and archaic patterns found on garments. They are bare-bodied, not full length, end below the waist in a pedestal-like flat base, they wear a coiffure like hood on the head, with a scarf that veils a part of their face. In some figures the hair is parted in the middle, with a line of red paint, goggle like eyes with deep eye holes probably for inserting pellets, a naturalistic nose and wide open mouth. The female figurines appear crude, made of soft clay, executed in the manner of the Indus Valley, made separately and then fixed on the body. At this regard, whilst Marshall (1931: 50) thinks at the Goddess Kālī, Mackay (1935) holds that the figurines were household deities placed on a little recess in the wall. It is likely that they were local household representations, but with the ideology of emanating from the earth (or being fixed in the earth), in this resembling representations of the Earth Goddess in later Indian art, where she is portrayed as half-emerging from the ground. As a matter of fact, women played a central role in agricultural societies. They participated — perhaps even predominately — in planting and reaping crops, and, as the ones who nourish life, they were taught to symbolically assist the earth in its productivity.

Mother Goddess

An intriguing aspect of female figurines is the discrepancy in the number of these figures in the Provincial cultures in Saurashtra, as opposed to those in Moheṅjo-Dāṛo and Haṛappā, a fact which necessitates an enquiry into the interpretation of female figurines as mother goddesses from archaeological evidences. In fact, the most extensively discussed aspect of these images in terms of function has been their identification as goddesses, particularly the figure from Moheṅjo-Dāṛo, with its characteristic iconography of heavy head-dress, jewellery, long arms, large eyes — that become an attribute in later Mauryan art. Considering the long and unbroken tradition of mother worship in India, and resulting Śāktism, or adoration of female divine power, such figures may be considered representative of goddess: symbolic of earthly (human, plant and animal) regeneration and bearers of light (on their heads, providing shade), from a broader perspective. Scholars such as Marija Gimbutas, whose provocative and controversial work has found its way into popular feminist writings, propose that the abundance of female figurines in prehistoric contexts of the Mediterranean and Southeastern Europe reflects an early pan-Mediterranean belief in a great Mother Goddess (Gimbutas 1974). The evidence of goddess reverence among the Semites of Canaan, Mesopotamia and Arabia is put forward in tablets and texts written in the Semitic languages of Akkadian, Ugaritic, Phoenician (Canaanite), Amorite, Aramaic, Hebrew and Arabic, appearing in different geographical areas of the Near East.

What is of interest to us is the link of the Semites of central Mesopotamia with the Sumerians, the names of *Ishtar* and *Inanaa* (mother goddesses of light, life, fertility and love), and their links with the Haṛappan figurines. We do find that the goddess in the ancient Near East, as the creative source of life, was frequently rendered in form through representation or symbolic imagery, as well as through the inclusion of the natural vegetative world. An example of this scene also appears on an image of a sealing from Haṛappā, as a nude female figure upside down with legs drawn apart (Rao, S.R. 1973: 135, Pl. XX1VD). A plant is issuing from the womb of the female as well as a pair of animal "Genii" on the same side of the sealing. On the reverse, there is a man holding a sickle-shaped knife and a woman who is seated on the ground in an attitude of supplication. Coming to the aspect of interpretation, the figurine is a powerful representation of the aspect of nature and fertility goddess. The mystery of the female body is the mystery of birth, which is also the mystery of the unmanifest becoming manifest in the whole of nature. This far transcends the female body and woman as carrier of this image, since the body of the female of any species leads through the mystery of birth to the mystery of life itself.

The origin of Mother Goddess cult is due to the connection between the growth of agriculture and the origin of the village communities, which shows that, to a primitive mind, the female human being played a significant role. She came to be endowed with magical power and the plant would still be the primal image of the mystery of birth, growth and regeneration. The sacred source of life is still invisible. The mother with her child illustrates the dual image of the Mother Goddess as the source and as what comes from the source: the child as the constantly renewed cycle of life — it is the issue of a human Goddess as a mother with her child celebrating the mystery of birth. However, it is difficult to know when or how the mother and her child assumed the form of Mother Goddess, but aspects such as their placement in graves as fertility objects for the protection and nourishment of the dead or women's rituals can throw light on this aspect. Unique forms of female figurines, which were made in vertical halves and then joined together, are found in Haṛappā. According to Dales (1991), in Haṛappā the female representations are five times more plentiful than the male ones; most of these are found at the cemetery area, and were probably used as votive offerings. This method of manufacturing was not followed either in Kālibaṅgan or Lothal, where female figurines are not abundant near the cemeteries. Instead, pieces of the figurines have been found near drains, being used for ritual purposes and discarded.

While the female figurines may be interpreted as fertility and Mother Goddesses in Haṛappā and Moheṅjo-Dāṛo, those in Lothal do not imply similar connotation. It is, therefore, essential to examine the flaws in the interpretation of female figures from the Provincial regions in the Indus Valley. Here, there is smaller number of female figurines, there are hardly any of them holding infants, and there is a marked absence of these types with ornament or head-dresses especially at Lothal, Deslapar, Rupaṛ, Kālibaṅgan and Lamagirpur — thereby suggesting the unpopularity of the goddess cult. In addition, the relationship in a society between its religious symbolism and everyday social behaviour is complex. Religious symbolism is rarely epi-phenomenal. Even if one could prove that some of the figurines reflect the worship of a great Mother Goddess, it is misleading to assume a direct correspondence between what appears to be the elevated status of women in the religious sphere with an elevated status in the social and political spheres. Furthermore, current arguments in support of an early Mother Goddess worship tend to cast women and matriarchies as nurturing, sensitive and pacific, as opposed to patriarchies which are viewed as aggressive, brutal and violent. Such uni-dimensional portrayals are most likely incorrect.

Finally, the myth of an early Mother Goddess and a primordial matriarchy forces feminists into a conundrum by assuming that their elevated status and power were primarily based on their reproductive capacities. These conclusions overlook the complex nature of gender structures in the past, and seriously limit the definitions of female power. The Mother Goddess notion relegates women to a static and conventional role, where power is ultimately embedded in biological capabilities. It is, therefore, essential to analyse female imagery in relation to the societies that had produced these female cults, before one can clarify the meaning of the Haṛappan Mother Goddess. What was the economic role of women, along with the ample resources and the level of technology of the society, with a focus on the evidence of a female cult in the urban area? What was this culture like? To begin to answer this question, one must first picture a town built on a high raised platform, with grid streets. On the higher area, the homes were one storey abodes entered from the side streets, with little variation in wealth or possessions. Inside each mud-brick house, there was a bath, the houses were kept immaculately clean, and refuse and sewage were disposed of. In these tightly constructed mass of housing, there is no evidence of invasion or violent destruction. The textiles and pottery indicate a remarkably high level of specialization.

Weaving wool or cotton, chipping and polishing stone tools and weapons, manufacture of beads, copper, gold jewellery, simple pottery performed with artistry, etc. tell a story of sophisticated, organized production system. Trade was carried out far and wide in order to bring the raw materials to the cities, there was plenty of food — barley, peas, wheat and milk. Impressive as the economic production was, some scholars claim that women were the primary discoverers of agriculture and assume, therefore, that women controlled this activity. As agriculture was replacing hunting as the pre-eminent source of food and wealth, the women controlled the new forms of wealth and even had a status and introduced the new female religious images.

When we look at the burial customs, we find that the woman was sometimes buried with the man, thereby suggesting that leadership roles might not have existed for her. There is no evidence of a central political organization, no major role for the military. Therefore, the positions of power that men usually held did not exist. In contrast to our lack of knowledge about male authority, we might conjecture that women exercised certain kinds of power, because the chief source of wealth was agricultural in type, but we do not know whether women were in charge of its development. They probably controlled the home and shaped the economy, and eventually moulded the religion, by incorporating into it their concerns about the fertility of crops and humans.

Some scholars have agreed that women have never held dominant positions in any society and thus never been able to shape institutions to their own needs and yield power in society. However, this might not apply to all societies. Another argument is that the society was based on agriculture, domestication of animals, weaving and pottery-making. All activities in question in some degree were women's invention and under women's control; they might not have had power over urban societies, but might have had power over other social groups, perhaps more for the purpose of co-operation than of dominance and control. In reflecting on the dependence on nature that the early Haṛappans had to contend with, it is possible that a co-operative use of power may have been necessary, indeed crucial for them. We simply do not know enough about the political organization of Indus Valley culture to say for sure what was the role and status of women and the balance of power between the two genders.

I am not making a case for an impressive female status in this society, a status that enabled women to express their own values and exist in it, if not necessarily gaining control. The sexual symbol is not to be found in female figurines, the female representations convey a sense of strength, more like objects of awe than sex objects. Evidences from early Vedic writings do not include images of goddess figures as powerful, or even as important. Only certain aspects of nature are perceived as female spirits, or, as personification, they are relatively insignificant in comparison to the descriptions of the male deities. The most dynamic female image included in the Vedas is that of Aditi, the mother of the Āryan gods. The names of Uṣā as as dawn, Sarasvatī as a river, and Pr̥thvī, the Earth Goddess, all appear in the *R̥gveda*.

The concept of the Earth Goddess both as a source of fertility and power imbues the figurines with a sense of dignity. It is probable that the form remained, while its meaning changed, hence the variation in the names of the goddesses in later Indian art. In addition, on some of the head-dresses, there is a black residue, and some historians and archaeologists suggest that oils or other similar chemicals may have been burned into them. Black stains on the side projections of the head-dress were produced from smoke, caused by burning bone and its action on clay; this combination of the two ingredients imbued the figurines with a life force (Clark 2009:

249). This is rather a celebration of fecundity and of the social role of a mother, symbol of fertility, a source of power, faceless, important at least in the major metropolis in Moheṅjo-Dāṛo and Haṛappā. In order to relate these terms to the Indus culture, the language might provide a clue, although there are no goddesses that have been portrayed on Indus seals along with script. Female figurines significantly outnumber three-dimensional terracotta male figurines at Haṛappā and other sites, and are not mirrored in the iconography of those on seals and tablets or statuary at Haṛappā or other Indus sites. Perhaps the folk or household representations were dominated by the female, while seals, tablets and statuary belonged to a more official or elite iconography and ideology (Brumfiel 1996, Joyce 1996, Pollock 1991, Kenoyer 1998: 134).

The concept of women as deity, as culture heroine, was probably not still present in the provincial culture during the period in question, although the woman as supreme, omnipotent deity has long existed in later written literature. At the other end of the spectrum stand the village deities, the local goddesses linked to particular villages and bound up with their welfare, such as the Vanavatī Mātā, that is still worshipped in Gujarat. These *grāma devīs* or village goddesses have a myriad of forms and names, uses and functions, and have played a crucial role in the maintenance and growth of the sacred female energy, that is both mysterious and inspiring. If we were to connect the oral tradition, at Lothal, of the local Sea goddess, Vanavatī Mātā, to the Canaanite Asherah, as the latter is also the "progenitress of the gods", the analogy is far-fetched. An examination of present-day women's rituals, where clay goddesses are fashioned as legless with conical breasts, signify that these were ritualistic figures with the concept of fertility and sacredness embedded within the phenomenon. The fact that ritual images are represented as part of the male clay figures leads us to rethink the idea of an overall Mother Goddess theory and the social role of women through the phenomenon of the goddess. However, the uniformity of sizes and their features attest the idea of a religious interpretation. The figurines were of local manufacture and, as suggested by Shaffer, "the religious phenomenon was indigenous to the provenience of location and religion provided a distinctive avenue of inter-societal interaction" (Shaffer 1978: 149).

Conclusion

If we acknowledge the religious significance of these figures, we cannot then dismiss them using the term "idols of fertility", since the word "idol" invariably trivializes the religious experience and overlooks the fact that many people in our time pray to the goddess to grant them children. Similarly, to call them "female figures" is to reduce the universality of a vital concept: the "mother". In order to try to restore to the figures their own original dignity, we prefer to ascribe them the simple name of "Goddess" or "Earth Goddess", Pṛthvī, in the sense of sacred images of life-giving, nourishing and regenerating powers of the universe. This could be a village goddess in a cosmic role (that may be also adopted by a smaller group), or, instead, specialized deities, such as those that presided over agricultural fertility, with regional emphases and wide local variations. The female figure was a multi-dimensional symbol, and its miraculous survival as goddess image in later Indian art and culture substantiates the fact that the goddess tradition in Indian culture had its roots in the Indus Valley Civilization. This does not preclude the fact that this tradition had connections with the Ṛgvedic or Sarasvatī Civilization, since these civilizations overlapped in geographical territory, date and other sacred forms, such as the fire altar.

Considering the wide distribution of these figures, from

the Indus Valley to Baluchistan, to eastern Iran, it is important to base our analysis and understanding of the phenomenon on the material remains found in the sites where these are numerous and display variety, such as the Indus Valley sites. The ancient figurine was expression of female power, but it is difficult to assess how meaningful a symbol it was in the life of the people: the gathering groups and the early agricultural settlements or towns that had produced the cult of the goddess. The question of women's roles in Haṛappan and other ancient cultures is a topic which, given the lack of textual evidence, is controversial among scholars. How much power did women wield in societies, in the agricultural and urban settlements? Although artefacts and myths may suggest that the females held important roles in early societies, the actual power of women cannot be known, and this remains an open question. Whether the woman is depicted as a mother, local or Earth Goddess, the symbol served as the projection of the needs of society, and as an expression of sacred values and beliefs.

Images are always open to a variety of interpretations; however, they should be analysed within the culture in which they were produced; questions of significance and signification would have been framed in wholly different ways. We might focus upon imagery as a manifestation of social structures and processes of signification. The phenomenon is not a self-conscious product, but a discursive relic, one which undergoes the same problems of interpretation as any other historical discourse. While we shall not attempt to define what is sacred, since it is a term that points to an ultimate reality that is unique for each person, its shared meaning appears over the millennia to change imperceptibly from age to age. What is important is that an experience of a sacred dimension is found in the entire Indus culture, independently of whether the images are numerous or scanty. This suggests that the sacred is not a stage in the history of consciousness, but an element in the structure of consciousness. The existence of such a sacred dimension in the Indus Valley is crucial to our understanding of its culture. In this context, female images have an equally valid claim to be sacred, and they are the testimonies of a surprisingly unified culture in ancient India.

References

Baring, A. & J. Cashford, 1991, *The Myth of the Goddess: Evolution of an Image*, London: Viking.

Brumfiel, E.M., 1996, "Figurines and the Aztec State: Testing the Effectiveness of Ideological Domination", in R.P. Wright (ed.), *Gender and Archaeology*, Philadelphia: University of Pennsylvania Press, 143-66.

Clark, Sharri R., 2003, "Representing the Indus Body: Sex, Gender, Sexuality and the Anthropomorphic Terracotta Figurines from Harappa", *Asian Perspectives*, 42/2: 305-28.

———, 2004, *Embodying Indus Life: Terracotta Figurines from Harappa*, www.hrappa.com/figurines/index.html.

———, 2009, "Material Matters: Representation and Materiality of the Harappan Body", *Journal of Archaeological Method Theory*, 16: 231-61.

Dales, G.F., 1991, "Some Specialized Ceramic Studies at Haṛappā, in R.H. Meadow (ed.), *Harappa Excavations*, 1986-1990, Madison: Prehistory Press. 61-84.

Dales, G.F. & J. M. Kenoyer, 1991, Summary of the Five Seasons of Research at Harappa (District of Sahiwal, Punjab, Pakistan). In R.H. Meadow (ed.), *Harappa Excavations*, 1986-1990, Madison: Prehistory Press, 185-262.

Gimbutas, Marija, 1974, *Goddesses and Gods of Old Europe:* 6500-3500 BCE, Berkeley: University of California Press.

Herbert, Jane, 1994, "Sacred Beliefs and Beliefs of Sacredness" in D. L. Carmichael, J. Hubert, B. Reeves & A. Schanche (eds.), *Sacred Sites, Sacred Places*, London: Routledge, 9-19.

Joyce, R.A., 1996, "The Construction of Gender in Classic Maya Monuments", in R.P. Wright (ed.), *Gender and Archaeology*, Philadelphia: University of Pennsylvania Press, 167-95.

Kenoyer, J.M., 1998, *Ancient Cities of the Indus Civilization*, Karachi:

Oxford University Press.

Mackay, E.J.H., 1935, *Chahnudaro Excavations*. American Oriental Series, 20, New Haven: American Oriental Society.

Marshall, J.H. (ed.), 1931, *Mohenjo-Daro and the Indus Civilization*, vol. 1, London: Arthur Probstnain

Nakamura, C. & L. Meskell, 2009, "Articulate Bodies: Forms and Figures at Catalhuyuk", *Journal of Archaeological Method Theory*, 16: 205-30.

Nandagopal, Choodamani, 2006, *The Arts and Crafts of the Indus Civilization*, Bangalore: International Centre for Indian Art and Cultural Studies.

Pollock, S., 1991, Women in a Men's World: Images of Sumerian Women", in J.M. Gero & M.W. Conkey (eds.), *Engendering Archaeology: Women in Prehistory*, Oxford: Blackwell, 366-87.

Rao, Nalini, 2013, *Sindhu-Sarasvati Civilization: New Perspectives*, LA: Nalanda International/New Delhi: D.K. Printworld (forthcoming).

Rao, S.R., 1973, *Lothal and the Indus Civilization*, NY: Asia Publishing House.

Shaffer, J.G., 1978, "The Later Prehistoric Periods", In F.R. Allchin (ed.), *The Archaeology of Afghanistan (From Earliest Times to the Timurid Period*), London: Hammond, 91-149.

Singh, Varun, 2010, "South Asia Perennial Backwater or Object of Biased Assessment: A Discussion based on Current Archaeological, Anthropological and Genetic Evidence, *Asian Perspectives*, 49/1: 110-47.

Vats, M.S., 1940, *Excavations at Harappa*, I-II, New Delhi: Government of India.

Contributors

B.N. Narahari Achar is retired as Professor of Physics at the University of Memphis. He got his PhD degree from the Pennsylvania State University. He has taught both at the Pennsylvania State University and Bucknell University, before joining the University of Memphis. He held positions at the Argonne National Laboratory and at the NASA Glen Research Center. He has authored more than a hundred research papers in his specialty. He pioneered in the use of 'Planetarium software' in the study of astronomy of ancient India [*address*: Dept. of Physics, The University of Memphis, 216 Manning Hall, MEMPHIS, Tennessee 38152 (USA); *e-mail* - <nachar@memphis.edu>}.

James Clackson is Reader in Comparative Philology at the University of Cambridge (United Kingdom), and Fellow and Director of Studies in Classics at Jesus College, Cambridge. His previous publications include *The Linguistic Relationship between Armenian and Greek* (1994), *Indo-European Linguistics* (2007), *The Blackwell History of the Latin Language* (with Geoffrey Horrocks) (2007) and *A Companion to the Latin Language* (2011) [*address*: Jesus College, Jesus Lane, CAMBRIDGE, CB5 8BL (UK); *e-mail*: <jptc1@cam.ac.uk>].

Koenraad Elst studied Sinology, Indology and Philosophy in his hometown, where he obtained his doctoral degree (*magna cum laude*) with a dissertation on Hindu revivalism. He served as a political journalist and as a researcher on Indian and Chinese world views. He courted controversy with his writing on Islam and the Ayodhya conflict, as well as on the origins of Indo-European. Currently he works as a research assistant in the Belgian Senate [*address*: Singel 35, 2640 MORTSEL (Belgium); *e-mail*: <koenraad.elst@telenet.be> <koenraadelst@hotmail.com>].

Girish Nath Jha is Associate Professor at the Special Centre for Sanskrit Studies, Jawaharlal Nehru University, specialising in computational linguistics. He has an honorary appointment at the Center for Indic Studies, University of Massachusetts (Dartmouth, USA), as Mukesh and Priti Chatter distinguished Professor of History of Science. He has studied computational linguistics at the University of Illinois (Urbana), and worked as software engineer in the USA. He has publications from Springer Verlag, Cambridge Scholar Publishing, Lambert Academic Publishing, and is on the editorial board of a leading journal from Springer [*address*: Associate Professor, Computational Linguistics, Special Centre for Sanskrit Studies, Jawaharlal Nehru University, NEW DELHI - 110 067; *e-mail*: <girishjha@gmail.com>].

Nicholas Kazanas is the Director of the 'Omilos Meleton, Cultural Institute' in Athen. He has produced a three year course of Sanskrit for Greeks and translated the ten principal Upanishads into Greek. He has many publications in Western and Indian Journals including: *Indoaryan Origins and other Issues* (Delhi 2009), *Economic Principles in the Vedic Tradition* (Delhi 2010). He has participated in numerous international conferences, is on the Editorial Board of *Adyar Library Bulletin* (Chennai), and is now chief editor of *Vedic Venues : Journal of the Continuity of Vedic Culture*. [*address* : 52 Aetideon Str., Holargos, 15561 ATHENS (Greece); *e-mail*: <nkazanas@omilosmeleton.gr>].

Diane A. Lichtenstein is Adjunct Professor of Anthropology at 'Baldwin-Wallace College' and the Cleveland Institute of Art, Cleveland, Ohio. Her dissertation research, conducted among the Langi of northern Uganda in 1970-72, focused on village social dynamics in the context of the advent of national military rule. She has participated in archaeological fieldwork in Egypt, Pakistan, and India and has maintained a long-term research interest in South Asian prehistory. She has coauthored several articles with Jim G. Shaffer, on archaeological details of the Indus Valley (Harappan) civilization [*address*: Liberal Arts Department, Cleveland Institute of Art, 11141 East Boulevard, CLEVELAND, Ohio 44106 (USA); *e-mail*: <dlichtenstein@cia.edu>].

Angela Marcantonio is associate professor of linguistics at the

University of Rome 'La Sapienza'. Her principle area of research and teaching is 'historical linguistics' with particular reference to the Indo-European and Uralic languages, as testified by numerous articles and several volumes including: Marcantonio (ed.), *The Indo-European Language Family: Questions about its Status* (*Journal of Indo-European Studies* n.55; Wahshington DC, 2009) and *The Uralic Language Family: Facts, Myths and Statistics* (Oxford/Boston 2002). She is in the editorial board of several international journals dealing with Indo-European and Uralic studies [*address*: Dipartimento di Scienze documentarie, Linguistico-filologiche e Geografiche, Università Degli Studi di Roma, "Sapienza" piazzale aldo moro, 5 00185 Rome (Italy); *e-mail*: <angela.marcantonio@gmail.com>].

M.G. Prasad is professor of mechanical engineering at the Stevens Institute of Technology, Hoboken, New Jersey. He is a Fellow of the American Society of Mechanical Engineers, a Fellow of the Acoustical Society of America and a Fellow of the Acoustical Society of India. He has more than 100 publications in the area of acoustics and vibrations to his credit and has written four books on Hinduism [*address*: Professor, Department of Mechanical Engineering, Stevens Institute of Technology, Castle Point on the Hudson, HOBOKEN, New Jersey 07030 (USA); *e-mail*: <mprasad@stevens.edu>].

Nalini N. Rao is professor of World Art in Soka University of America, CA. She has a Ph.D. in Art History from UCLA and a doctorate in Ancient History and Archaeology from the University of Mysore, India. She has organized Indian art exhibitions and confernces: ASPAC (2009), "Sindhu–Sarasvati Civilization: A Reappraisal" (2009) etc. Her latest publication include: *Royal Imagery and Networks of Power at Vijayanagara: A Study of Kingship in South India Originals* (Delhi: 2010), and an edited volume on *The Sindhu-Sarasvati Civilization: New Perspectives* (DKPW and Nalanda International; 2013; forthcoming) [*address*: Prof. of World Art, Soka University of America, 1 University Drive, ALISO VIEJO, CA 92656 (USA); *e-mail*: <nrao@soka.edu>].

Jim G. Shaffer is associate professor of anthropology at Case Western Reserve University, Cleveland, Ohio. His research focus on South Asian prehistory began with his dissertation on Bronze Age

10. Delegates and attendees of the symposium

Afghanistan, detailed in *Prehistoric Baluchistan: A Systematic Approach*. He has conducted archaeological fieldwork at Bronze Age and Neolithic sites in Pakistan and in India. He is author of numerous articles on the Indus Valley (Harappan) civilization and other cultures of South / Southwest Asia, with emphasis on the processes of domestication, metallurgy, urbanization, state formation, and archaeological application of "paleoethnicity" and "paleogroup migration" [*address*: Department of Anthropology, Case Western Reserve University, CLEVELAND, Ohio 44106 (USA); *e-mail*: <jim.shaffer@ case.edu>].

Bal Ram Singh is the Director of the Center for Indic Studies at UMass Dartmouth, where he teaches a course on Science of Kriyayoga. Dr Singh as a Professor of Biophysical Chemistry and Henry DreyfusTeacher-Scholar, and Director of the Botulinum Research Center, has published about 180 research articles; three dozen scholarly articles on issues related to Indian tradition, culture, and philosophy; has edited eight books; and has obtained 7 patents [*address*: Director, Center for Indic Studies, University of Massachusetts, Dartmouth, 285 Old Westport Road, DARTMOUTH, MA 02747 (USA); *e-mail*: <bsingh@umassd.edu>].

R.P. Singh is chairperson of the Centre for Philosophy, at the 'School of Social Sciences', Jawaharlal Nehru University, New Delhi. His areas of specialization include Modern Western Philosophy, Postmodern Philosophy, Indian Philosophy, specially Upanishads, Buddhism and Advaita Vedanta. He has to his credit 16 books and 152 articles published in India and abroad. He has participated in seminars at the Centre for Indic Studies, UMass, Dartmouth, USA, University of West Indies, Trinidad and Tobago and many other universities in Europe [*address*: Centre for Philosophy, School of Social Sciences, Jawaharlal Nehru University, NEW DELHI - 110 067; *e-mail:* <rpsinghjnu@yahoo.com> <rpsingh@mail.jnu.ac.in>].

Index